PHILIP ROTH

Reading Myself and Others

In 1997 Philip Roth won the Pulitzer Prize for *American Pastoral*. In 1998 he received the National Medal of Arts at the White House and in 2002 the highest award of the American Academy of Arts and Letters, the Gold Medal in Fiction, previously awarded to John Dos Passos, William Faulkner, and Saul Bellow, among others. He has twice won the National Book Award and the National Books Critics Circle Award. He has won the PEN/Faulkner Award three times. In 2005 *The Plot Against America* received the Society of American Historians' prize for "outstanding historical novel on an American theme" for 2003–2004. In 2006 Roth received PEN's most prestigious prize, the PEN/Nabokov Award for a "body of work . . . of enduring originality and consummate craftsmanship." Roth is the only living American writer to have his work published in a comprehensive, definitive edition by the Library of America.

VINTAGE

INTERNATIONAL

BOOKS BY PHILIP ROTH

Reading Myself and Others

PHILIP ROTH

Reading Myself and Others

Vintage International
Vintage Books
A Division of Random House, Inc.
New York

FIRST VINTAGE INTERNATIONAL EDITION, MAY 2001

Copyright © 1961, 1963, 1969, 1970, 1971, 1972, 1973,
1974, 1975, 1985 by Philip Roth

Library of Congress Cataloging-in-Publication Data
Roth, Philip.
Reading myself and others / Philip Roth.
p.   cm.
ISBN: 0679749071 (pbk.)
PS3568.O855 Z47 2001
00-067411

Book design by Cathryn S. Aison

www.vintagebooks.com

Printed in the United States of America
10 9 8 7 6 5 4 3 2

To Saul Bellow,
the "other" I have read from the beginning
with the deepest pleasure and admiration

ACKNOWLEDGMENTS

All but one of the pieces in this book originally appeared in the publications cited below; some were published under other titles and in slightly different form.

"Writing and the Powers That Be," *La Trappola e la Nudità: Lo Scrittore e il Potere,* edited by Walter Mauro and Elena Clementelli (Rizzoli, 1974); in English, in *The American Poetry Review,* July/August 1974.

"On *Portnoy's Complaint,*" *The New York Times Book Review,* February 23, 1969.

"How Did You Come to Write That Book, Anyway?" *The American Poetry Review,* July/August 1974.

"On *Our Gang,*" *The Atlantic Monthly,* December 1971; reprinted as an afterword to the "Watergate Edition" of *Our Gang* (Bantam Books, 1973).

"The President Addresses the Nation," *The New York Review of Books,* June 14, 1973; also included, somewhat abridged, as a skit in *Watergate Capers,* a satirical review performed in repertory at the Yale Drama School in November and December 1973.

"On *The Breast,*" *The New York Review of Books,* October 19, 1972.

"On *The Great American Novel,*" *Partisan Review,* No. 3, 1973.

"On *My Life as a Man,*" *The Literary Guild,* June 1974.

"After Eight Books," *The Ontario Review,* No. 1, Fall 1974.

"Interview with *Le Nouvel Observateur*," *Le Nouvel Observateur*, May 1981; *Esquire*, September 1981.

"Interview with *The London Sunday Times*," *London Sunday Times*, February 19, 1984; *The Nation*, June 1985.

"Interview with *The Paris Review*," *Paris Review*, No. 93, Fall 1984.

"Interview on *Zuckerman*," an interview with Philip Roth by Asher Z. Milbaner and Donald G. Watson from *Reading Philip Roth* (St. Martin's Press, 1985).

"Writing American Fiction," *Commentary*, March 1961.

"Some New Jewish Stereotypes," *American Judaism*, Winter 1961.

"Writing About Jews," *Commentary*, December 1963.

"The Story of Three Stories," *The New York Times*, October 24, 1971.

"The Newark Public Library," *The New York Times*, March 1, 1969.

"My Baseball Years," *The New York Times*, April 2, 1973.

"Cambodia: A Modest Proposal," *Look*, October 6, 1970.

"Our Castle," *The Village Voice*, September 19, 1974.

"Alan Lelchuk," *Esquire*, October 1972.

"Milan Kundera," portions in *Esquire*, March 1974, and in *The American Poetry Review*, March/April 1974; in its entirety it served as the introduction to *Laughable Loves* (Knopf, 1974).

"Fredrica Wagman," introduction to *Playing House, ou les jeux réprouvés* (Seghers, 1974).

"Imagining Jews," *The New York Review of Books*, September 29, 1974.

"'I Always Wanted You to Admire My Fasting'; or, Looking at Kafka," *American Review* 17, May 1973. Quotations from *The Castle* and *The Trial* are from the texts published by Knopf; all others from Kafka's works (and from Max Brod's biography) are from the Schocken editions.

CONTENTS

AUTHOR'S NOTE

The twenty-three pieces that appeared in the original edition of this collection were written sporadically over a period of fifteen years, between the time my first book of fiction was published in 1959 and my eighth in 1974. Most come out of the end of that period, a few are from the beginning, hardly any out of the middle—suggesting that they are largely the by-products of getting started as a novelist, and then of taking stock. (The material added for the 1985 Penguin edition—the four interviews at the end of Part One—were published between 1979 and 1984.) Because recognition—and with it, opposition—came to me almost immediately, I seem to have felt called upon both to assert a literary position and to defend my moral flank the instant after I had taken my first steps; later I tried to gain some perspective on what I'd been reading and writing since.

Together these pieces reveal to me a continuing preoccupation with the relationship between the written and the unwritten world. The simple distinction is borrowed from Paul Goodman. I find it more useful than the distinction between imagination and reality, or art and life, first, because everyone can think through readily enough to the clear-cut differences between the two, and second, because the worlds that I feel myself shuttling between every day couldn't be better described. Back and forth, back and forth, bearing fresh information, detailed instructions, garbled messages, desperate inquiries, naive expectations, baffling challenges . . . cast somewhat in the role of the courier Barnabas, whom the Land Surveyor K. enlists to traverse the steep winding road between the village and the castle in Kafka's novel about the difficulties of getting through.

Reading Myself and Others is divided into two parts, each arranged more or less chronologically. There is considerable overlap, but myself—as reader and read—is what's at the heart of Part One. This section consists mainly of interviews in which I describe what has generated my work, the means employed from book to book, and the models I associate with my efforts. The interviews reached their final form in writing, though some began in conversational exchanges that laid out the terrain and suggested the tone and focus of what appeared in print.

Part Two is made up of selected articles and essays, many of them occasioned by an invitation—to give a talk, to oppose an adversary, to introduce a writer, to mark an event. They point to difficulties, enthusiasms, and aversions that have evolved along with my work. At the bottom of the opening page of nearly every piece I have noted the occasion that prompted it; in the first section, the interviewer is identified, the date given, and where it seemed pertinent, the circumstances of the interview described. The full details of publication appear in the Acknowledgments.

ONE

Writing and the Powers That Be

Tell us first of all about your adolescence—its relationship with the type of American society you have represented in Goodbye, Columbus; *your rapport with your family; and if and how you felt the weight of paternal power.*

Far from being the classic period of explosion and tempestuous growth, my adolescence was more or less a period of suspended animation. After the victories of an exuberant and spirited childhood—lived out against the dramatic background of America's participation in World War II—I was to cool down considerably until I went off to college in 1950. There, in a respectable Christian atmosphere hardly less constraining than my own particular Jewish upbringing, but whose strictures I could ignore or oppose without feeling bedeviled by long-standing loyalties, I was able to reactivate a taste for inquiry and speculation that had been all but immobilized during my high school years. From age twelve, when I entered high school, to age sixteen, when I graduated, I was by and large a good, responsible, well-behaved boy, controlled (rather willingly) by the social regulations of the self-conscious and orderly lower-middle-class neighborhood where I had been raised, and mildly constrained

An interview conducted by the Italian critic Walter Mauro, for his collection of interviews with writers on the subject of power. (1974)

still by the taboos that had filtered down to me, in attenuated form, from the religious orthodoxy of my immigrant grandparents. I was probably a "good" adolescent partly because I understood that in our Jewish section of Newark there was nothing much else to be, unless I wanted to steal cars or flunk courses, both of which proved to be beyond me. Rather than becoming a sullen malcontent or a screaming rebel—or flowering, as I had in the prelapsarian days at elementary school—I obediently served my time in what was, after all, only a minimum-security institution, and enjoyed the latitude and privileges awarded to the inmates who make no trouble for their guards.

The best of adolescence was the intense male friendships—not only because of the cozy feelings of camaraderie they afforded boys coming unstuck from their close-knit families, but because of the opportunity they provided for uncensored talk. These marathon conversations, characterized often by raucous discussions of hoped-for sexual adventure and by all sorts of anarchic joking, were typically conducted, however, in the confines of a parked car—two, three, four, or five of us in a single steel enclosure just about the size and shape of a prison cell, and similarly set apart from ordinary human society.

Still, the greatest freedom and pleasure I knew in those years may have derived from what we said to one another for hours on end in those automobiles. And how we said it. My closest adolescent companions—clever, respectful Jewish boys like myself, all four of whom have gone on to be successful doctors—may not look back in the same way on those bull sessions, but for my part I associate that amalgam of mimicry, reporting, kibbitzing, disputation, satire, and legendizing from which we drew so much sustenance with the work I now do, and I consider what we came up with to amuse one another in those cars to have been something like the folk narrative of a tribe passing from one stage of human development to the next. Also, those millions of words were the means by which we either took vengeance on or tried to hold at bay the cultural forces that were

4

shaping us. Instead of stealing cars from strangers, we sat in the cars we had borrowed from our fathers and said the wildest things imaginable, at least in our neighborhood. Which is where we were parked.

"The weight of paternal power," in its traditional oppressive or restraining guises, was something I had hardly to contend with in adolescence. My father had little aside from peccadilloes to quarrel with me about, and if anything weighed upon me, it was not dogmatism, unswervingness, or the like, but his limitless pride in me. When I tried not to disappoint him, or my mother, it was never out of fear of the mailed fist or the punitive decree, but of the broken heart; even in post-adolescence, when I began to find reasons to oppose them, it never occurred to me that as a consequence I might lose their love.

What may have encouraged my cooling down in adolescence was the grave financial setback my father suffered at about the time I was entering high school. The struggle back to solvency was arduous, and the stubborn determination and reserves of strength that it called forth from him in his mid-forties made him all at once a figure of considerable pathos and heroism in my eyes, a cross of a kind between Captain Ahab and Willy Loman. Half-consciously I wondered if he might not collapse, carrying us under with him—instead he proved to be undiscourageable, if not something of a stone wall. But as the outcome was in doubt precisely during my early adolescence, it could be that my way in those years of being neither much more nor much less than "good" had to do with contributing what I could to family order and stability. To allow paternal power to weigh what it *should*, I would postpone until a later date the resumption of my career as classroom conquistador, and suppress for the duration all rebellious and heretical inclinations . . . This is largely a matter of psychological conjecture, of course, certainly so by this late date— but the fact remains that I did little in adolescence to upset whatever balance of power had enabled our family to come as far as it had and to work as well as it did.

Sex as an instrument of power and subjection. You develop this theme in Portnoy's Complaint *and achieve a desecration of pornography, at the same time recognizing the obsessive character of sexual concerns and their enormous conditioning power. Tell us in what real experience this dramatic fable originated or from what adventure of the mind or the imagination.*

Do I "achieve a desecration of pornography"? I never thought of it that way before, since generally pornography is itself considered a verbal desecration of the acts by which men and women are imagined to consecrate their profound attachment to one another. Actually I think of pornography more as the projection of an altogether human preoccupation with the genitalia *in and of themselves*—a preoccupation excluding all emotions other than those elemental feelings that the contemplation of genital functions arouses. Pornography is to the whole domain of sexual relations what a building manual is to hearth and home. Or so it would be, if carpentry were surrounded with the exciting aura of magic, mystery, and breachable taboo that adheres at this moment to the range of sex acts.

I don't think that I "desecrated" pornography but, rather, excised its central obsession with the body as an erotic contraption or plaything—with orifices, secretions, tumescence, friction, discharge, and all the abstruse intricacies of sex-tectonics—and then placed that obsession back into an utterly mundane family setting, where issues of power and subjection, among other things, can be seen in their broad everyday aspect rather than through the narrowing lens of pornography. Now, perhaps it is just in this sense that I could be charged with having desecrated, or profaned, what pornography, by its exclusiveness and obsessiveness, does actually elevate into a kind of sacred, all-encompassing religion, whose solemn rites it ritualistically enacts: the religion of Fuckism (or, in a movie like *Deep Throat*, Suckism). As in any religion these devotions are a matter of the utmost seriousness, and there is little more room for individual expressiveness or idiosyncrasy, for human error or mishap, than there is in the celebration of the Mass. In fact, the comedy of *Portnoy's Complaint* arises largely out of the mishaps, wholly expressive of the individual, that bedevil one would-be celebrant as he tries desperately to make his way to the altar and remove his clothes. All his attempts to enter naked into the sacred realm of pornography are repeatedly foiled because, by his own definition, Alexander Portnoy is a character in a Jewish joke—a genre which, unlike pornography, pictures a wholly *de*consecrated world: demystified, deromanticized, utterly dedeluded. Fervent religionist that he would be, Portnoy still cannot help but profane with his every word and gesture what the orthodox Fuckist most reveres.

I cannot track down for you any single experience, whether of the mind or the body, from which *Portnoy's Complaint* originated. Perhaps what you want to know is whether I have firsthand knowledge of "sex as an instrument of power and subjection." The answer is, how could I not? I too have appetite, genitals, imagination, drive, inhibition, frailties, will, and conscience. Moreover, the massive, late-sixties assault upon sexual customs came nearly twenty years after I myself hit the beach and began fighting for a foothold on the erotic homeland held in subjugation by the enemy. I sometimes think of my generation of men as the first wave of determined D-day invaders, over whose bloody, wounded carcasses the flower children subsequently stepped ashore to advance triumphantly toward that libidinous Paris we had dreamed of liberating as we inched inland on our bellies, firing into the dark. "Daddy," the youngsters ask, "what did you do in the war?" I humbly submit they could do worse than read *Portnoy's Complaint* to find out.

The relationship in your work between reality and imagination. Have the forms of power we have mentioned (family, religion, politics) influenced your style, your mode of expression? Or has writing served increasingly to free you from these forms of power?

Inasmuch as subject might be considered an aspect of "style," the answer to the first question is yes: family and religion as coercive forces have been a recurrent subject in my fiction, particularly in the work up to and including *Portnoy's Complaint;* and the coercive appetites of the Nixon Administration were very much to the point of *Our Gang.* Of course the subjects themselves "influence" their treatment and my "mode of expression," but so does much else. Certainly, aside from the Nixon satire, I have never written anything determinedly and intentionally destructive. Polemical or blasphemous assault upon the powers that be has served me more as a *theme* than as an overriding purpose in my work.

"The Conversion of the Jews," for instance, a story I wrote when I was twenty-three, reveals at its most innocent stage of development a budding concern with the oppressiveness of family feeling and with the binding ideas of religious exclusiveness which I had experienced first-hand in ordinary American-Jewish life. A good boy named Freedman brings to his knees a bad rabbi named Binder (and various other overlords) and then takes wing from the synagogue into the vastness of space. Primitive as this story seems to me now—it might better be called a daydream—it nonetheless evolved out of the same preoccupations that led me, years later, to invent Alexander Portnoy, an older incarnation of claustrophobic little Freedman, who cannot cut loose from what binds and inhibits him quite so magically as the hero I imagined humbling his mother and his rabbi in "The Conversion of the Jews." Ironically, where the boy in the early story is subjugated by figures of real stature in his world, whose power he for the moment at least is able to subvert, Portnoy is less oppressed by these people—who have little real say in his life anyway—than he is imprisoned by the rage that persists against them. That his most powerful oppressor by far is himself is what makes for the farcical pathos of the book—and also what connects it with my preceding novel, *When She Was Good,* where again the focus is on a grown child's fury against long-standing authorities believed by her to have misused their power.

The question of whether *I* can ever free myself from these forms of power assumes that I experience family and religion as power and nothing else. It is much more complicated than that. I have never really tried, through my work or directly in my life, to sever all that binds me to the world I came out of. I am probably right now as devoted to my origins as I ever was in the days when I was indeed as powerless as little Freedman and, more or less, had no other sane choice. But this has come about only after subjecting these ties and connections to considerable scrutiny. In fact, the affinities that I continue to feel toward the forces that first shaped me, having withstood to the degree that they have the assault of imagination and the test of sustained psychoanalysis (with all the cold-bloodedness *that* entails), would seem by now to be here to stay. Of course I have greatly refashioned my attachments through the effort of testing them, and over the years have developed my strongest attachment to the test itself.

Our Gang is a desecration of President Nixon and it takes its theme from a statement on abortion. In what period of your life have you most strongly felt the weight of political power as a moral coercion and how did you react to it? Do you feel that the element of the grotesque, which you often use, is the only means by which one can rebel and fight against such power?

I suppose I most strongly felt political power as moral coercion while growing up in New Jersey during World War II. Little was asked of an American schoolchild, other than his belief in the "war effort," but that I gave with all my heart. I worried over the welfare of older cousins who were off in the war zone, and wrote them long "newsy" letters to keep up their morale; I sat by the radio with my parents listening to Gabriel Heatter every Sunday, hoping upon hope that he had good news that night; I followed the battle maps and front-line reports in the evening paper; and on weekends I participated in the neighborhood collection of paper and tin cans. I was twelve when the war ended, and during the next few years my first serious political allegiances began to take shape. My entire clan—parents, aunts, uncles, cousins—were devout New Deal Democrats. In part because they identified him with Roosevelt, and also because they were by and large lower-middle-class people sympathetic to labor and the underdog, many of them voted for Henry Wallace, the Progressive Party candidate for President in 1948. I'm proud to say that Richard Nixon was known as a crook in our kitchen some twenty-odd years before this dawned on the majority of Americans as a real possibility. I was in college during Joe McCarthy's heyday—which is when I began to identify political power with *immoral* coercion. I reacted by campaigning for Adlai Stevenson and writing a long angry free-verse poem about McCarthyism for the college literary magazine.

The Vietnam War years were the most "politicized" of my life. I spent my days during this war writing fiction, none of which on the face of it would appear to connect to politics (though there was a time when I at least associated the rhetoric employed by the heroine of *When She Was Good* to disguise from herself her vengeful destructiveness with the kind of language our government used when they spoke of "saving" the Vietnamese by means of systematic annihilation). But by being "politicized" I mean something more telling than writing about politics or even taking direct political action. I mean something akin to what ordinary citizens experience in countries like Czechoslovakia or Chile: a daily awareness of government *as a coercive force,* its continuous presence in one's thoughts as far more than just an institutionalized, imperfect system of necessary controls. In sharp contrast to Chileans or Czechs, we hadn't personally to fear for our safety and could be as outspoken as we liked, but this did not diminish the sense of living in a country with a government morally out of control and wholly in business for itself. Reading the morning *New York Times* and the afternoon *New York Post,* watching the seven and then again the eleven o'clock TV news—all of which I did ritualistically—became for me like living on a steady diet of Dostoevsky. Rather than fearing for the well-being of my own kin and country, I now felt toward America's war mission as I had toward the Axis goals in World War II. One even began to use the word "America" as though it was the name, not of the place where one had been raised and to which one had a strong spiritual attachment, but of a foreign invader that had conquered the country and with whom one refused, to the best of one's strength and ability, to collaborate. Suddenly America had turned into "them"—and with this sense of dispossession and powerlessness came the virulence of feeling and rhetoric that often characterized the anti-war movement.

I don't think—to come to your last question—that *Our Gang* uses the "element of the grotesque." Rather, it tries to objectify in a style of its own that element of the grotesque that is inherent in the moral character of a Richard Nixon. He, not the satire, is what is grotesque. Of course there have been others as venal and lawless in American politics, but even a Joe McCarthy was more identifiable as human clay than this guy is. The wonder of Nixon (and contemporary America) is that a man so transparently fraudulent, if not on the edge of mental disorder, could ever have won the confidence and approval of a people who generally require at least a *little* something of the "human touch" in their leaders. It's strange that someone so unlike the types most admired by the average voter—in any Norman Rockwell drawing, Nixon would have been cast as the fuddy-duddy floorwalker or the prissy math teacher school kids love to tease; never the country judge, the bedside doctor, or the trout-fishin' dad—could have passed himself off to this *Saturday Evening Post* America as, of all things, an *American.*

Finally: "rebelling" or "fighting" against *outside* forces isn't what I take to be at the heart of my writing. *Our Gang* is only one of eight disparate works of fiction I've written in the past fifteen years, and even there what most engaged me had to do with *expressiveness,* with problems of presentation, rather than bringing about change or "making a statement." Over the years, whatever serious acts of rebelliousness I may have engaged in as a novelist have been directed far more at my own imagination's system of constraints and habits of expression than at the powers that vie for control in the world.

On *Portnoy's Complaint*

Would you say something about the genesis of Portnoy's Complaint?
How long has the idea of the book been in mind?

Some of the ideas that went into the book have been in my mind
ever since I began writing. I mean particularly ideas about style and
narration. For instance, the book proceeds by means of what I began
to think of while writing as "blocks of consciousness," chunks of
material of varying shapes and sizes piled atop one another and held
together by association rather than chronology. I tried something
vaguely like this in *Letting Go*, and have wanted to come at a narrative in this way again—or break down a narrative this way—ever since.

Then there's the matter of language and tone. Beginning with
Goodbye, Columbus, I've been attracted to prose that has the turns,
vibrations, intonations, and cadences, the spontaneity and ease, of
spoken language, at the same time that it is solidly grounded on the
page, weighted with the irony, precision, and ambiguity associated
with a more traditional literary rhetoric. I'm not the only one who
wants to write like this, obviously, nor is it a particularly new aspira-

The interviewer is George Plimpton; the interview appeared in *The New York
Times Book Review* the Sunday *Portnoy's Complaint* was reviewed there. (1969)

tion on the planet; but that's the kind of literary idea, or ideal, I was pursuing in this book.

I was thinking more in terms of the character and his predicament when I asked how long you had in mind the "idea of the book."

I know you were. That's partly why I answered as I did.

But surely you don't intend us to believe that this volatile novel of sexual confession, among other things, had its conception in purely literary motives?

No, I don't. But the conception is really nothing, you know, beside the delivery. My point is that until my "ideas"—about sex, guilt, childhood, about Jewish men and their Gentile women—were absorbed by an overall fictional strategy and goal, they were ideas not unlike anybody else's. Everybody has "ideas" for novels; the subway is jammed with people hanging from the straps, their heads full of ideas for novels they cannot begin *to write.* I am often one of them.

Given the book's openness, however, about intimate sexual matters, as well as its frank use of obscenity, do you think you would have embarked upon such a book in a climate unlike today's? Or is the book appropriate to those times?

As long ago as 1958, in *The Paris Review,* I published a story called "Epstein" that some people found very disgusting in its intimate sexual revelations; and my conversation, I have been told, has never been as refined as it should be. I think that many people in the arts have been living in a "climate like today's" for some time now; the mass media have just caught up, that's all, and with them, the general public. Obscenity as a usable and valuable vocabulary, and sexuality as a subject, have been available to us since Joyce, Henry Miller, and Lawrence, and I don't think there's a serious American writer in his thirties who has felt restricted by the times particularly, or suddenly feels liberated because these have been advertised as the "swinging sixties." In my writing lifetime the use of obscenity has, by and large, been governed by literary taste and tact and not by the mores of the audience.

What about the audience? Don't you write for an audience? Don't you write to be read?

To write to be read and to write for an "audience" are two different matters. If you mean by an audience a particular readership which can be described in terms of its education, politics, religion, or even by its literary tone, the answer is no. When I'm at work I don't really have any group of people in mind whom I want to communicate with; what I want is for the work to communicate itself as fully as it can, in accordance with its own intentions. Precisely so that it *can* be read, *but on its own terms.* If one can be said to have an audience in mind, it is not any special-interest group whose beliefs and demands one either accedes to or challenges, but those ideal readers whose *sensibilities* have been totally given over to the writer, in exchange for his seriousness.

An example which will also get us back to the issue of obscenity. My new book, *Portnoy's Complaint,* is full of dirty words and dirty scenes; my last novel, *When She Was Good,* had none. Why is that? Because I've suddenly become a "swinger"? But then apparently I was "swinging" all the way back in the fifties, with "Epstein." And what about the dirty words in *Letting Go?* No, the reason there is no obscenity, or blatant sexuality either, in *When She Was Good* is that it would have been disastrously beside the point.

When She Was Good is, above all, a story about small-town Middle Westerners who more than willingly experience themselves as conventional and upright people; and it is their own conventional and upright style of speech that I chose as my means of narration—or, rather, a slightly heightened, somewhat more flexible version of their language, but one that drew freely upon their habitual clichés, locutions, and banalities. It was not, however, to satirize them, in the manner, say, of Ring Lardner's "Haircut," that I settled eventually on this modest style, but rather to communicate, by their way of saying things, their way of seeing things and judging them. As for obscenity, I was careful, even when I had Roy Bassart, the young ex-G.I. in the novel, *reflecting*—had him safely walled-up in his own head—to show that the furthest he could go in violating a taboo was to think "f. this and f. that." Roy's inability to utter more than the initial of that famous four-letter word, even to himself, was the point I was making.

Discussing the purposes of his art, Chekhov makes a distinction between "the solution of the problem and a correct presentation of the problem"—and adds, "only the latter is obligatory for the artist." Using "f. this and f. that," instead of The Word Itself, was part of the attempt to make a correct presentation of the problem.

Are you suggesting, then, that in Portnoy's Complaint *a "correct presentation of the problem" requires a frank revelation of intimate sexual matters, as well as an extensive use of obscenity?*

Yes, I am. Obscenity is not only a kind of language that is used in *Portnoy's Complaint,* it is very nearly the issue itself. The book isn't full of dirty words because "that's the way people talk"; that's one of the *least* persuasive reasons for using the obscene in fiction. Besides, few people actually talk the way Portnoy does in this book—this is a man speaking out of an overwhelming obsession: he is obscene because he wants to be saved. An odd, maybe even mad, way to go about seeking his personal salvation; but, nonetheless, the investigation of this passion, and of the combat that it precipitates with his conscience, is what's at the center of the novel. Portnoy's pains arise out of his refusal to be bound any longer by taboos which, rightly or wrongly, *he* experiences as diminishing and unmanning. The joke on Portnoy is that for him breaking the taboo turns out to be as unmanning in the end as honoring it. Some joke.

So, I wasn't simply after verisimilitude here; I wanted to raise obscenity to the level of a subject. You may remember that, at the conclusion of the novel, the Israeli girl (whose body Portnoy has been wrestling her for on the floor of his Haifa hotel room) says to him, with loathing, "Tell me, please, *why* must you use that word all the time?" I gave her this question to ask him—and to ask at the end of this novel—altogether deliberately: Why he must is what the book is all about.

Do you think there will be Jews who will be offended by this book?

I think there will even be Gentiles who will be offended by this book.

I was thinking of the charges that were made against you by certain rabbis after the appearance of Goodbye, Columbus. *They said you were "anti-Semitic" and "self-hating," did they not?*

In "Writing About Jews,"* an essay I published in *Commentary,* in December 1963, I replied at length to those charges. Some critics also said that my work furnished "fuel" for anti-Semitism. I'm sure these charges will be made again—though the fact is (and I think there's even a clue to this in my fiction) that I have always been far more pleased by my good fortune in being born a Jew than my critics may begin to imagine. It's a complicated, interesting, morally demanding, and very singular experience, and I like that. I find myself in the

*See p. 193.

historic predicament of being Jewish, with all its implications. Who could ask for more? But as for those charges you mention—yes, they probably will be leveled at me. Because of the U.N. condemnation of Israeli "aggression," and anti-Semitic rage flaring up in the black community, many American Jews must surely be feeling more alienated than they have in a long time; consequently, I don't think it's a moment when I can expect a book as unrestrained as this one to be indulged or even tolerated, especially in those quarters where I was not exactly hailed as the Messiah to begin with. I'm afraid that the temptation to quote single lines out of the entire fictional context will be just about overwhelming on upcoming Saturday mornings. The rabbis have got their indignation to stoke, just as I do. And there are sentences in that book upon which a man could construct a pretty indignant sermon.

I have heard some people suggest that your book was influenced by the nightclub act of Lenny Bruce. Would you consider Bruce, or other stand-up comics such as Shelley Berman or Mort Sahl, or even The Second City comics, an influence upon the comic methods you employ in Portnoy's Complaint?

Not really. I would say I was more strongly influenced by a sit-down comic named Franz Kafka and a very funny bit he does called "The Metamorphosis." Interestingly, the only time Lenny Bruce and I ever met and talked was in his lawyer's office, where it occurred to me that he was just about ripe for the role of Joseph K. He looked gaunt and driven, still determined but also on the wane, and he wasn't interested in being funny—all he could talk about and think about was his "case." I never saw Bruce perform, though I've heard tapes and records, and since his death I've watched a movie of one of his performances and read a collection of his routines. I recognize and admire in him what I used to like about The Second City company at its best, that joining of precise social observation with extravagant and dreamlike fantasy.

What about the influence of Kafka that you mention?

Well, of course, I don't mean I modeled my book after any work of his, or tried to write a Kafka-*like* novel. At the time I was beginning to play with the ideas for what turned out to be *Portnoy's Complaint,* I was teaching a lot of Kafka in a course I gave once a week at the University of Pennsylvania. When I look back now on the reading I assigned that year, I realize that the course might have been called "Studies in Guilt and Persecution"—"The Metamorphosis," *The Castle,* "In the Penal Colony," *Crime and Punishment,* "Notes from Underground," *Death in Venice, Anna Karenina* . . . My own previous two novels, *Letting Go* and *When She Was Good,* were about as gloomy as the gloomiest of these blockbusters, and fascinated, obviously, as I still was by these dark books, I was actually looking for a way to get in touch with another side of my talent. Particularly after several arduous years spent on *When She Was Good,* with its unfiery prose, its puritanical, haunted heroine, its unrelenting concern with banality, I was aching to write something freewheeling and funny. It had been a long time between laughs. My students may have thought I was being strategically blasphemous or simply entertaining them when I began to describe the movie that could be made of *The Castle,* with Groucho Marx as K. and Chico and Harpo as the two "assistants." But I meant it. I thought of writing a story about Kafka writing a story. I had read somewhere that he used to giggle to himself while he worked. Of course! It was all so *funny,* this morbid preoccupation with punishment and guilt. Hideous, but funny. Hadn't I only recently sat smirking through a performance of *Othello?* And not just because it was badly done either, but because something in that bad performance revealed how *dumb* Othello is. Isn't there something ludicrous about Anna Karenina throwing herself under that train? For what? What after all had she done? I asked my students; I asked myself. I thought about Groucho walking into the village over which the Castle looms, announcing he was the

Land Surveyor; of *course* no one would believe him. Of *course* they would drive him up the wall. They had to—because of that cigar.

Now—the road from these random and even silly ideas to *Portnoy's Complaint* was more winding and eventful than I can describe here; there is certainly a personal element in the book, but not until I had got hold of guilt, you see, as a comic idea, did I begin to feel myself lifting free and clear of my last book and my old concerns.

Document Dated July 27, 1969

The two-thousand-word document that follows is an example of a flourishing subliterary genre with a long and moving history, yet one that is all but unknown to the general public. It is a letter written by a novelist to a critic, but never mailed. I am the novelist, Diana Trilling is the critic, and it was not mailed for the reasons such letters rarely are mailed, or written, for that matter, other than in the novelist's skull:

1. Writing (or imagining writing) the letter is sufficiently cathartic: by 4 or 5 A.M. the dispute has usually been settled to the novelist's satisfaction, and he can turn over and get a few hours' sleep.

2. It is unlikely that the critic is about to have his reading corrected by the novelist anyway.

3. One does not wish to appear piqued in the least—let alone to be seething—neither to the critic nor to the public that follows these duels when they are conducted out in the open for all to see.

4. Where is it engraved in stone that a novelist shall feel himself to be "understood" any better than anyone else does?

5. The advice of friends and loved ones: "For God's sake, forget it."

So novelists—for all that they are by nature usually an obsessive and responsive lot—generally do forget it, or continually remind themselves that they ought to be forgetting it during the sieges of remembering. And, given the conventions that make a person feel like something of an ass if he does "stoop" to rebutting his critics, in the long run it may even be in the writer's interest that he does forget it and goes on with his work. It is another matter as to whether it is in the interest of the literary culture that these inhibiting conventions have as much hold on us as they do, and that as a result the reviewer, critic, or book journalist generally finds himself in the comfortable position of a prosecution witness who, having given his testimony, need not face cross-examination by the defense.

July 27, 1969

Dear Mrs. Trilling:

I have just finished reading your essay-review in the August *Harper's,* in which you compare the novel *Portnoy's Complaint* to the book under review, J. R. Ackerley's *My Father and Myself.* If I may, I'd like to distinguish for you between myself and "Mr. Roth," the character in your review who is identified as the "author of *Portnoy's Complaint.*"

On the basis of your reading of his novel, you contend that "Mr. Roth" has a "position [he is] fortifying"; he is in this novel "telling us" things "by extension" about social determinism; he is, on the evidence of the novel, a "child of an indiscriminative mass society" as well as "representative . . . of post-Freudian American literary culture"; his "view of life" in the novel—as opposed to Ackerley's in his memoir—does *not* "propose . . . the virtues of courage, kindliness, responsibility"; and his "view of life [is] grimly deterministic."

Didactic, defiant, harsh, aggressively *against,* your "Mr. Roth" is a not uncommon sort of contemporary writer, and in view of the structure of your review, a perfect *ficelle,* aiding us in attaining a clearer vision of the issue you are dramatizing. Useful, however, as he may be as a rhetorical device, and clearly recognizable as a type, he is of course as much your invention as the Portnoys are mine. True, both "Mr. Roth" and I are Jews, but strong an identifying mark as that is, it is not enough, you will concede, to make us seem one and the same *writer,* especially as there is a pertinent dissimilarity to consider: the sum of our work, the accumulation of fictions from which the "positions" and "views" we hold might, with caution, be extrapolated.

Your "Mr. Roth" is a "young man from whom we can expect other books." As I understand you, he has written none previous to the one you discuss, a book whose "showy" literary manner—wherein he "achieves his effects by the broadest possible strokes"—is accounted for, if not dictated by, the fact that he is a "child of an indiscriminative mass society." You describe him as an "accomplished . . . craftsman," but so far, it would seem, strictly within the confines of his showy style.

Unlike "Mr. Roth," I have over the past thirteen years published some dozen short stories, a novella, and three novels. One of the novels, published two years before "Mr. Roth's" book, is as removed as a book could be from the spirit of *Portnoy's Complaint*. If anything proves that I am not the "Mr. Roth" of your review, it is this novel, *When She Was Good,* for where "Mr. Roth's" manner in his book is "showy," mine here is deliberately ordinary and unobtrusive; where his work is "funny"—you speak of "fiercely funny self-revelation"—mine is proper and poker-faced; and where you find "Mr. Roth" on the basis of his book "representative . . . of post-Freudian American literary culture," another critic of some prestige found me, on the basis of *When She Was Good,* to be hopelessly "retrograde."

Admittedly, an alert reader familiar with both books might find in them a similar preoccupation with the warfare between parents and children. Reading your review, I was struck in fact by the following sentence—it almost seemed that you were about to compare *Portnoy's Complaint,* not with J. R. Ackerley's memoir, but with my own *When She Was Good:* "It turns out, however, that strangely different enterprises can proceed from the same premise. Portnoy, full of complaint because of his sexual fate, is bent on tracking down the source of his grievances . . ." Well, so too with my heroine, Lucy Nelson (if "sexual" is allowed its fullest meaning). Wholly antithetic in cultural and moral orientation, she is, in her imprisoning passion and in the role she assumes of the enraged offspring, very much his soul mate. I have even thought that, at some level of consciousness, "Mr. Roth's" book might have developed as a complementary volume to my own. Though not necessarily "typical," Alexander Portnoy and Lucy Nelson seem to me, in their extreme resentment and disappointment, like the legendary unhappy children out of two familiar American family myths. In one book it is the Jewish son railing against the seductive mother, in the other the Gentile daughter railing against the alcoholic father (equally loved, hated, and feared—the most unforgettable character *she* ever met). Of course, Lucy Nelson is seen to destroy herself within an entirely different fictional matrix, but that would result, among other reasons, from the enormous difference between the two environments that inspire their rage as well as their shared sense of loss and nostalgia.

I would also like to point out that the "virtues of courage, kindliness, responsibility" that "Mr. Roth" does not seem to you to "propose" in his book, are, in my own, proposed *as a way of life* in the opening pages of the novel and continue to haunt the book thereafter (or so I intended). Here is the sentence with which the book begins—it introduces the character of Willard Carroll, the grandfather in whose home the angry heroine is raised: "Not to be rich, not to be famous, not to be mighty, not even to be happy, but to be civilized—that was the dream of his life." The chapter proceeds then to enlarge Willard's idea of "civilization," revealing through a brief family history how he has been able to practice the virtues of courage, kindliness, and responsibility, as he understands them. Only after Willard's way has been sufficiently explored does the focus of the novel turn in stages toward Lucy, and to her zeal for what *she* takes to be a civilized life, what she understands courage to be and responsibility to mean, and the place she assigns to kindliness in combat.

Now I won't claim that *I* am the one proposing those virtues here, since Daddy Will—as his family calls him—does not speak or stand for me in the novel any more than his granddaughter Lucy does. On this issue it may be that I am not so far from "Mr. Roth" after all, and that in my novel (as perhaps in his) virtues and values are "proposed" as they generally are in fiction—neither apart from the novel's predominant concern nor in perfect balance with it, but largely through the manner of presentation: through what might be called the *sensuous* aspects of fiction—tone, mood, voice, and, among other things, the juxtaposition of the narrative events themselves.

"Grimly deterministic" I am not. There again "Mr. Roth" and I part company. You might even say that the business of *choosing* is the primary occupation of any number of my characters. I am thinking of souls even so mildly troubled as Neil Klugman and Brenda Patimkin, the protagonists of the novella *Goodbye, Columbus,* which I wrote some ten years before "Mr. Roth" appeared out of nowhere with his grimly deterministic view of life. I am thinking too of the entire anguished cast of characters in my first novel, *Letting Go,* written seven years before "Mr. Roth's," where virtually a choice about his life has to be made by some character or other on every page—and there are 630 pages. Then there are the central characters in the stories published along with *Goodbye, Columbus,* "Defender of the Faith," "The Conversion of the Jews," "Epstein," "Eli, the Fanatic," and "You Can't Tell a Man by the Song He Sings," each of whom is seen making a conscious, deliberate, even willful choice *beyond* the boundary lines of his life, and just so as to give expression to what in his spirit will not be grimly determined, by others, or even by what he had himself taken to be his own nature.

It was no accident that led me to settle upon Daddy Will as the name for Lucy's modest but morally scrupulous and gently tenacious grandfather; nor was it accidental (or necessarily admirable—that isn't the point) that I came up with Liberty Center as the name for the town in which Lucy Nelson rejects every emancipating option in favor of a choice that only further subjugates her to her grievance and her rage. The issue of authority over one's life is very much at the center of this novel, as it has been in my other fiction. Though it goes without saying that the names a novelist assigns to people and places are generally no more than decoration, and do practically nothing of a book's real work, they at least signaled to me, during the writing, some broader implications to Lucy's dilemma. That a passion for freedom—chiefly from the bondage of a heart-breaking past—plunges Lucy Nelson into a bondage more gruesome and ultimately insupportable is the pathetic and ugly irony on which the novel turns. I wonder if that might not also describe what befalls the protagonist of *Portnoy's Complaint*. Now saying this may make me seem to you as "grimly deterministic" a writer as "Mr. Roth," whereas I suggest that to imagine a story that revolves upon the ironies of the struggle for personal freedom, grim as they may be—ridiculous as they may also be—is to do something more interesting, more novelistic, than what you call "fortifying a position."

As for "literary manner," I have, as I indicated, a track record more extensive than your "Mr. Roth's." The longer works particularly have been dramatically different in the kinds of "strokes" by which the author "achieves his effects"—so that a categorical statement having to do with *my* position or view might not account in full for the varieties of fiction I've written.

I am not arguing that my fiction is superior to "Mr. Roth's" work for this reason—only that they are works of an entirely different significance from those of such an ideological writer (whose book you describe as the "latest offensive in our escalating literary-political war upon society"). Obviously I am not looking to be acquitted, as a person, of having some sort of view of things, nor would I hold that my fiction aspires to be a slice of life and nothing more. I am saying only that, as with any novelist, the presentation and the "position" are inseparable, and I don't think a reader would be doing me (or even himself) justice if, for tendentious or polemical purposes, he were to divide the one into two, as you do with "Mr. Roth."

It seems to me that "Mr. Roth" might be "showy," as you call it, for a reason. His use of the "broadest possible strokes to achieve his effects" might even suggest something more basic to a successful reading of the book than that he is, as you swiftly theorize, a "child of an indiscriminative mass society." What sort of child? I wonder. And what multitudes of experience are encompassed within that dismissive phrase, "an indiscriminative mass society"? You almost seem there to be falling into a position as deterministic about literary invention as the one you believe "Mr. Roth" promulgates about human possibility. You describe the book as "farce with a thesis": yet, when you summarize in a few sentences the philosophical and social theses of the novel ("Mr. Roth's [book] blames society for the fate we suffer as human individuals and, legitimately or not, invokes Freud on the side of his own grimly deterministic view of life . . ."), not only is much of the book's material pushed over the edge of a cliff to arrive at this conclusion, but there is no indication that the reader's experience of a farce (if that is what you think it is) might work against the grain of the dreary meaning you assign the book—no indication that the farce might itself be the thesis, if not what you call the "pedagogic point."

Accounting for the wide audience that "Mr. Roth's" book has reached, you say that the "popular success of a work often depends as much on its latent as on its overt content." And as often not—but even if I am not as thoroughgoing a Freudian in such matters as you appear to be, I do agree generally. A similar explanation has even greater bearing, as I see it, upon the *authentic* power of a literary work, if "latent content" is taken to apply to something more than what is simply not expressed in so many words. I am thinking again of the presentation of the content, the broad strokes, the air of showiness, the fiercely funny self-revelation, and all that such means might be assumed to communicate about the levels of despair, self-consciousness, skepticism, vigor, and high spirits at which a work has been conceived.

You state at one conclusive point in your review, "Perhaps the unconscious . . . is . . . more hidden from us than the author of *Portnoy's Complaint* realizes." May I suggest that perhaps "Mr. Roth's" view of life is more hidden from certain readers in his wide audience than they imagine, more imbedded in parody, burlesque, slapstick, ridicule, insult, invective, lampoon, wisecrack, in nonsense, in levity, in *play*—in, that is, the methods and devices of Comedy, than their own view of life may enable them to realize.

Sincerely,

Philip Roth

In Response to Those Who Have Asked Me:

"How Did You Come to Write

That Book, Anyway?"

Portnoy's Complaint took shape out of the wreckage of four abandoned projects on which I had spent considerable effort—wasted, it seemed then—in the years 1962–7. Only now do I see how each was a kind of building block for what was to come, and was abandoned in turn because it emphasized to the exclusion of all else what eventually would become a strong element in *Portnoy's Complaint* but in itself was less than the whole story. Not that I knew then why I was so dissatisfied with the results I got at the time.

The first project, begun a few months after the publication of *Letting Go*, was a dreamy, humorous manuscript of about two hundred pages titled *The Jewboy*, which treated growing up in Newark as a species of folklore. This draft tended to cover with a patina of "charming" inventiveness whatever was genuinely troublesome to me and, as in certain types of dreams and folktales, intimated much more than I knew how to examine or confront in a fiction. Yet there were things that I liked and, when I abandoned the book, hated to lose: the graphic starkness with which the characters were presented and which accorded with my sense of what childhood had felt like; the jokey comedy and dialogues that had the air of vaudeville turns; and a few scenes I was particularly fond of, like the grand finale where

---

Written in 1974.

the Dickensian orphan-hero (first found in a shoebox by an aged *mohel* and circumcised, hair-raisingly, on the spot) runs away from his loving stepparents at age twelve and on ice skates sets off across a Newark lake after a little blond shiksa whose name, he thinks, is Thereal McCoy. "Don't!" his taxi-driver father calls after him (taxi driver because fathers I knew of invariably had cried out from behind the wheel at one exasperated moment or another, "That's all I am to this family—a taxi driver!"). "Oh, watch it, sonny"—the father calls after him—"you're skating on thin ice!" Whereupon the rebellious and adventurous son in hot pursuit of the desirable exotic calls back, "Oh, you dope, Daddy, that's only an expression," already, you see, a major in English. "It's only an expression"—even as the ice begins to groan and give beneath his eighty-odd pounds.

The second abandoned project was a play entitled *The Nice Jewish Boy*. Still more about a Jewish family, their son, and his shiksa—in its way a less comforting, more aggressive *Abie's Irish Rose*. A draft of the play was eventually read as a workshop exercise at the American Place Theatre in 1964, with Dustin Hoffman, then an off-Broadway actor, in the title role. The trouble with it was that the realistic dramatic conventions I had adopted rather unthinkingly (and strictly) didn't provide me with the room I needed to get to the character's secret life. My unfamiliarity and timidity with the form, and the collaborative effort itself, inhibited and conventionalized my own sense of things, and so rather than proceeding to a production, I decided after the reading to cut my losses. Again somewhat sadly. The comic *surface* of the play (what father said to mother, what mother said to son, what son said to shiksa) seemed to me accurate and funny; yet the whole enterprise lacked the inventive flair and emotional exuberance that had given *The Jewboy* whatever quality it had.

So: the struggle that was to be at the source of Alexander Portnoy's difficulties, and motivate his complaint, was in those early years of work still so out of focus that all I could do was recapitulate his problem *technically*, telling first the dreamy and fantastic side of the story, then the story in more conventional terms and by relatively measured means. Not until I found, in the person of a troubled analysand, the voice that could speak in behalf of both the "Jewboy" (with all that word signifies to Jew and Gentile alike about aggression, appetite, and marginality) and the "nice Jewish boy" (and what that epithet implies about repression, respectability, and social acceptance) was I able to complete a fiction that was expressive, instead of symptomatic, of the character's dilemma.

While making abortive forays into what was going to emerge years later as *Portnoy's Complaint,* I was intermittently writing equally shadowy drafts of a novel that was variously titled—as theme and emphasis shifted—*Time Away, In the Middle of America,* and *Saint Lucy,* and that was published in 1967 as *When She Was Good.* This continuous movement back and forth from one partially realized project to another is fairly typical of how my work evolves and the way I deal with literary frustration and uncertainty, and serves me as a means of both checking and indulging "inspiration." The idea, in part, is to keep alive fictions that draw their energy from different sources, so that when circumstances combine to rouse one or another of the sleeping beasts, there is a carcass around for it to feed on.

After the manuscript of *When She Was Good* was completed midway through 1966, I almost immediately began to write a longish monologue, beside which the fetid indiscretions of *Portnoy's Complaint* would appear to be the work of Louisa May Alcott. I did not have any idea where I was going, and playing (in the mud, if you like) more accurately describes my activity than does writing, or "experimenting," that much-used catchall with its flattering implications of courageous pioneering and disinterested self-abandonment.

This monologue was delivered by one of those lecturers who used to go around to schools, churches, and social groups showing slides of natural wonders. My slide show, delivered in the dark and with a pointer, and accompanied by running commentary (including humorous and illustrative anecdotes), consisted of full-color enlarge-ments of the private parts, fore and aft, of the famous. Actors and actresses, of course, but primarily—since the purpose was educational—distinguished authors, statesmen, scientists, etc. It was blasphemous, mean, bizarre, scatological, tasteless, spirited, and, largely out of timidity, I think, remained unfinished . . . except that buried somewhere in the sixty or seventy pages were several thousand words on the subject of adolescent masturbation, a personal interlude by the lecturer, that seemed to me on rereading to be funny and true, and worth saving, if only because it was the only sustained piece of writing on the subject that I could remember reading in a work of fiction.

Not that at the time I could have deliberately set out to write about masturbating and come up with anything so pointedly intimate. Rather, it would seem to have required all that wildness and roughhousing—the *merriment,* which is how I experienced it—for me just to *get* to the subject. Knowing that what I was writing about President Johnson's testicles, Jean Genet's anus, Mickey Mantle's penis, Margaret Mead's breasts, and Elizabeth Taylor's pubic bush was simply unpublishable—a writer's hijinks that might just as well not see the light of day—was precisely what allowed me to relax my guard and go on at some length about the solitary activity that is so difficult to talk about and yet so near at hand. For me writing about the act had, at the outset at least, to be as secret as the act itself.

More or less in tandem with this untitled exercise in voyeurism—which purported to enlarge and examine upon an illuminated screen the sexual parts of *others*—I began to write a strongly autobiographical piece of fiction based upon my own upbringing in New Jersey. For lack of anything more inspired, simply as a kind of genre title, it was called in its first rough draft of several hundred pages *Portrait of the Artist.* By sticking closely to the facts, and narrowing the gap between the actual and the invented, I thought I could somehow come up with a story that would go to the heart of the particular Jewish ethos I'd come out of. But the more I stuck to the actual and the strictly autobiographical, the less resonant and revealing the narrative became. Once again (as I now see it) I was oscillating between the extremes of unmanageable fable or fantasy and familiar surface realism or documentation, and thereby holding at bay what was still trying to become my subject, if only I would let it. I had already described it, unknowingly, in the antipodal titles of the two projects previously abandoned: the argument between the Abel and Cain of my own respectable middle-class background, the Jewboy and the nice Jewish boy.

Somewhere along the way in *Portrait of the Artist,* in order to broaden the scope and relieve the monotony, I invented some relatives to live upstairs from the family, loosely modeled upon my own, who were to have been at the center of the book. These upstairs relatives of "ours" I called the Portnoys. In the beginning the Portnoys were modeled, about as loosely, upon two or three families in whose apartments I used to play and snack and sometimes sleep overnight when I was a boy. In fact, an old boyhood friend of mine, who was interviewed by his local newspaper at the time of my book's publication, was quoted as saying that my family certainly did not seem to *him* to resemble the Portnoys; "but," he added, "I suppose Phil didn't see it that way." That there was a family which in certain aspects Phil did see that way, and, I suspect, which this old boyhood friend of mine sometimes saw that way as well, he did not, for reasons of filial discretion and personal modesty, let on to the reporter.

Though actually the family the Portnoys looked most like to me, as I became increasingly taken by them and began to allow them to take hold in the novel, was a family I had described in passing in an essay published in *American Judaism* some five years earlier.* The essay had grown out of a talk I had given at a B'nai B'rith Anti-Defamation League symposium in Chicago in 1961, in which I had attacked what I took to be the unreality and silliness of Jews who

*See "Some New Jewish Stereotypes," p. 183.

were being popularized around that time in books by Harry Golden and Leon Uris. The family was not called the Portnoys then, nor were they as yet the product of my own imagination. Rather, I had come upon them, in various disguises and incarnations, in my reading. Here (abridged somewhat) is what I said at the A.D.L. symposium in 1961:

> . . . There are several Jewish graduate students in a class I teach at the Writing Workshop of the State University of Iowa, and during this last semester three of them wrote stories about a Jewish childhood . . . Curiously, or perhaps not so curiously, in each story the hero is a Jewish boy, somewhere between ten and fifteen, who gets excellent grades in school and is always combed and courteous . . . [This] Jewish boy . . . is watched—he is watched at bedtime, at study time, and especially at mealtime. Who he is watched by is his mother. The father we rarely see, and between him and the boy there seems to be little more than a nodding acquaintance. The old man is either working or sleeping or across the table, silently stowing it away. Still there is a great deal of warmth in these families—especially when compared to the Gentile . . . family [in the story]—and almost all of it is generated by the mother . . . [But] the fire that warms can also burn and asphyxiate: what the hero envies the Gentile boy is his parents' *indifference,* and largely, it would seem, because of the opportunities it affords him for sexual adventure . . . I hasten to point out that in these short stories the girls to whom the Gentile friend leads the young narrator are never Jewish. The Jewish women are mothers and sisters. The sexual yearning is for the Other . . .

Here then was the folktale—transmitted to me by my students as an authentic bit of American-Jewish mythology—that began to enlarge my sense of who these Portnoys might be . . . or become. Now it even made a nice kind of sense that in that first slapdash draft of *Portrait of the Artist* I had imagined them to be "relatives" living "upstairs": here were the fallible, oversized, anthropomorphic gods who had reigned over the households of my neighborhood; here was that legendary Jewish family dwelling on high, whose squabbles over French-fried potatoes, synagogue attendance, and shiksas were, admittedly, of an Olympian magnitude and splendor, but by whose terrifying kitchen lightning storms were illuminated the values, dreams, fears, and aspirations by which we mortal Jews lived somewhat less vividly down below.

This time, rather than choosing as I had in *The Jewboy* to treat this folklore *as* folklore—emphasizing the fantastic, the charming, the quaint, the magical, the poetic—I determinedly took off in the opposite direction. Under the sway of the autobiographical impulse that had launched *Portrait of the Artist,* I began to ground the mythological in the recognizable, the verifiable, the historical. Though they might *derive* from Mt. Olympus (by way of Mt. Sinai), these Portnoys were going to live in a Newark and at a time and in a way I could vouch for by observation and experience.

(With this sleight-of-hand, if I have to say so myself, I seemed to have succeeded all too well. Among the several hundred letters I received after the book's publication, there was one from a woman in East Orange, New Jersey, who claimed to have known my sister when she and my correspondent's daughter were classmates together at Weequahic High in Newark, where the Portnoy children went to school. She remembered what a sweet, lovely, polite girl my sister was, and was shocked that I should be so thoughtless as to write as I had about her intimate life, especially to make jokes about her unfortunate tendency to gain weight. Since, unlike Alexander Portnoy, I happen never to have had a sister, I assumed it was some other Jewish Athena with a tendency to gain weight to whom my correspondent was alluding.)

However, it was to be a while yet before I began to feel so constrained by the conventions I had imposed upon myself in *Portrait of the Artist* that I abandoned that manuscript in its turn—and thus released the Portnoys from their role as supporting actors in another family's drama. They would not get star billing until sometime later, when out of the odds and ends of *Portrait of the Artist* I liked best, I began to write something I called "A Jewish Patient Begins His Analysis." This turned out to be a brief story narrated by the Portnoys' son, Alexander, purportedly his introductory remarks to his psychoanalyst. And who was this Alexander? None other than that Jewish boy who used to turn up time after time in the stories written by those Jewish graduate students back in the Iowa Writers' Workshop: the "watched-over" Jewish son with his sexual dream of The Other. Strictly speaking, the writing of *Portnoy's Complaint* began with discovering Portnoy's voice—more accurately, his mouth—and discovering, along with it, the listening ear: the silent Dr. Spielvogel. The psychoanalytic monologue—a narrative technique whose rhetorical possibilities I'd been availing myself of for years, only not on paper—was to furnish the means by which I thought I might convincingly draw together the fantastic element of *The Jewboy* and the realistic documentation of *Portrait of the Artist* and *The Nice Jewish Boy*. And a means, too, of legitimizing the obscene preoccupations of the untitled slide show on the subject of sexual parts. Instead of the projection screen (and the gaping), the couch (and the unveiling); instead of gleeful, sadistic voyeurism—brash, shameful, masochistic, euphoric, vengeful, conscience-ridden exhibitionism. Now I could perhaps to begin.

On *Our Gang*

First, is there a tradition of political satire in America to which Our Gang *belongs?*

Yes, though it probably isn't known even to most educated Americans. Political satire isn't writing that lasts. Though satire, by and large, deals with enduring social and political problems, its comic appeal lies in the use made of the situation of the moment. It's unlikely that reading even the best satiric work of another era we feel anything like the glee or the outrage experienced by a contemporary audience. Subtleties of wit and malice are wholly lost over the years, and we're left to enjoy the broadest, least time-bound aspects of the work, and to hunt through footnotes in order to make connections and draw inferences that are the teeth and claws of this

---

My remarks here grew out of a lengthy conversation I had with a Random House executive who in 1971 was uneasy about publishing *Our Gang*. He objected to the book principally on grounds of taste; also he wondered if it might not be politically counterproductive—that is, if one could imagine it having any political effect at all. Since there would doubtless be other readers who would share the publisher's point of view, I asked Alan Lelchuk (who is the interviewer here) if he would help me to reconstruct and extend my thoughts on the subjects of satire, Nixon, and *Our Gang*, so that they might appear in print in this form. (1971)

sort of writing. Except for a few students of American literature and history, no one today is going to be interested in reading James Russell Lowell's satires in doggerel verse, *The Biglow Papers,* written in the middle of the nineteenth century from an abolitionist point of view, or the dialect letters of "Petroleum V. Nasby," the work of another antislavery Northerner, David Ross Locke. Yet both are wonderful comic inventions, as virulent and funny as the political satire of Defoe and maybe even some of Swift. Lincoln admired the Nasby letter so much that he is supposed to have said he would have given up the Presidency to have been able to write them.

Another reason Americans might not realize satirical writing once flourished here is that there's hardly any around today. People would be surprised, not only by the imaginative richness, but by the ferocity of the political satire that appeared in ordinary daily newspapers throughout the country in the nineteenth century, especially during the decades leading up to and following the Civil War. I don't believe there's a daily newspaper in America today that would print the kind of sustained attack that Lowell made upon General Taylor during the campaign of 1847, or Locke made upon the Northern Democrats during Lincoln's Administration. If you look at how American Presidents were ridiculed in the daily papers in the nineteenth century, you have to conclude that editors and readers were a heartier bunch a hundred years ago, far less intimidated than they appear to be today by Emily Postish notions of respectability.

Are there any other American writers you admire who have worked along these lines?

Well, Mencken. Specifically, his attack on Harding's puerile prose style, which he called "Gamalielese." Mencken said that Harding's style was so bad that a sort of grandeur crept into it. And there is a poem by e. e. cummings, a sort of mock eulogy occasioned by Harding's death, which describes President Harding as "the only

man woman or child who wrote / a simple declarative sentence with
seven grammatical / errors . . ."

Are you suggesting a connection between Mencken's attitude toward Harding and your own toward President Nixon in Our Gang?

Yes and no. I don't feel much kinship with Mencken's *ideas*—particularly his notions as to what constitutes an aristocracy rub me the
wrong way. But as a critic of American public rhetoric, he was very
funny. I think, yes, there is in my book a concern similar to his in the
essay "Gamalielese." But we approach the problem of debased political language in different ways. Where he analyzes and evaluates
Harding's prose in a journalistic essay, *Our Gang* is an exaggerated
impersonation, a parody, of Nixon's style of discourse and thought. I
go about my work in the manner of a fantasist and *farceur;* Mencken
uses the weapons of a literary critic.

I believe he was also more amused by Mr. Harding than I am by Mr.
Nixon. The reason may be that there's been a lot of terror packed into
the short space of time that separates Mencken's "Gamalielese" from
George Orwell's "Newspeak"—related kinds of double-talk at which
President Nixon is equally adept. Mencken might never have drawn
the same conclusions from rotten political prose that Orwell did
twenty-eight years later in the novel *1984.* Mencken thought it was
inevitable that American democracy would produce as leaders clowns
and charlatans who, along with their other disabilities, couldn't speak
English. He considered what they said and the way they said it *entertainment,* rivaled only by Barnum and Bailey. It took an Orwell—and
a second world war, and savage totalitarian dictatorships in Germany and Russia—to make us realize that this seemingly comical
rhetoric could be turned into an instrument of political tyranny.

You've mentioned specifically two nineteenth-century satirical works, The
Biglow Papers *and the Nasby letters, both growing out of the Civil War*

period, and now Mencken's essays. Any other literary works of a satiric nature that seem to you relevant to our discussion of Our Gang?

It might be as much to the point to mention satiric works of a non-literary, or popular, nature. "Satiric" probably isn't the right word here—I mean broadly comic in the style of Olsen and Johnson, the Marx Brothers, the Three Stooges, Laurel and Hardy, Abbott and Costello, and the like. Recently I saw Abbott and Costello in a segment from an old movie of theirs, doing that famous baseball dialogue, "Who's on First?" It's a marvel of punning and verbal confusion, characterized by the sort of buffoonery that I was trying for in the longest section of *Our Gang,* "Tricky Has Another Crisis." Obviously, Tricky—in contrast to either the colorless straight man Abbott or the benign fool Costello—is an old-fashioned villain in the Tartuffian mold. Still, the *style* of some of Abbott and Costello's slapstick comedy seems to me suited to the monkey business that Tricky and his friends engage in in that "crisis" section.

Do you remember Charlie Chaplin and Jack Oakie as Hitler and Mussolini in *The Great Dictator?* Well, in their performances there's something, too, of the flavor I hoped to get into the more outlandish sections of *Our Gang.*

All I'm saying, of course, is that the level of comedy in *Our Gang* isn't exactly what it is in *Pride and Prejudice*—in case anybody should fail to notice. *Our Gang* is out to destroy the protective armor of "dignity" that shields anyone in an office as high and powerful as the Presidency. It was no accident, for instance, that President Nixon took it into his head a few years ago to tart up the White House police staff in the imperial garb of Junkers out of *The Student Prince.* He knows better than anybody how much he needs all the trappings of dignified authority—or authoritarian dignity. But rather than accept his "official" estimate of himself, which we see for Mr. Nixon is very regal indeed, I prefer to place him in a baggy-pants burlesque skit. It seems to me more appropriate.

Clearly, satire of this kind has no desire to be decorous. Decorum—and what hides behind it—is often just what it's attacking. To ask a satirist to be in good taste is like asking a love poet to be less personal. Is *The Satyricon* in good taste? Is *A Modest Proprosal*? Swift recommends the stewing, roasting, and fricasseeing of one-year-old children so as to unburden their impoverished parents and provide food for the meat-eating classes. How nasty and vulgar that must have seemed, even to many who shared his concern for Ireland's misery. Imagine how this went down in polite society: "A Child will make two Dishes at an Entertainment for Friends; and when the Family dines alone, the fore or hind quarter will make a reasonable Dish, and seasoned with a little Pepper or Salt will be very good Boiled on the fourth Day, especially in Winter."

Now that's considered Literature. It's called "Swiftian." Back in 1729 it probably seemed, to a lot of Swift's contemporaries, bad taste, and worse. Similarly, Rabelais is no longer an obscene writer who can't resist a joke about feces, urine, or the apertures—four hundred years in the grave and he's "Rabelaisian." The trick, apparently, is to turn yourself from a proper noun into an adjective, and the best way to accomplish that is to die.

Imagine if today you were to write a satire modeled upon Swift's *Modest Proposal* about our "involvement"—nice euphemism, that—in Southeast Asia. As it turns out, under orders from Presidents Johnson and Nixon, our armed forces have been following Swift's advice for some time now, boiling and fricasseeing the children in Vietnam and Laos, and lately roasting succulent Cambodian infants. Suppose someone were to propose in print to President Nixon that instead of killing these Asian children for no good reason, as we do now, we adopt a policy at once more practical and humane. Since statistics prove that x number of children are going to die anyway, why not slaughter them for food for the Vietnamese refugees? The proposal might be written in the style of the Pentagon Papers. This fellow named McNaughton could probably have drafted a first-rate contingency plan on how to barbecue with napalm, sprinkle with soy sauce, and serve—including a breakdown in Pentagonian percentage points of the various minimum daily vitamin requirements fulfilled by the liver, lungs, and brains of an Asian infant, when mixed with a bowl of rice.

We can safely conclude that few American newspapers would rush to publish such a piece. "Swiftian" it is, if it's about what Englishmen were doing to Irishmen in 1729; if, however, you were to employ similar means to indict our country for what it has done to the Vietnamese now—which is a thousand times more vicious than anything the British could hope to do in the eighteenth century with their limited arsenal of torture devices—you would find your satire unpublishable in most places because of bad taste.

Which it is. All the works I've mentioned, by ordinary community standards, or whatever the legal phrase is to describe the lowest common denominator of social conformism, are in execrable taste. By ordinary community standards they are shocking—just in order to dislocate the reader and get him to view a familiar subject in ways he may be unwilling or unaccustomed to. You know how people taking offense will sometimes say, "Now, stop kidding around, this is serious." But in satire it is *by* kidding around that one hopes to reveal just *how* serious. This is illustrated by the modest proposal to use Asian infants for barbecued spareribs instead of "wasting" them as cannon fodder.

A distinctive characteristic of shocking and tasteless satire is its high degree of distortion. On the whole, Americans are more familiar with distortion and exaggeration in the art of caricature than in literary works. Newspaper readers deal with distortion every day in political cartoons, and are not only untroubled by it but easily grasp the commentary implicit in the technique. Well, the same techniques of distortion apparent in the work of Herblock, Jules Feiffer, and David Levine—or, to invoke the names of giants, in the satirical drawings of Hogarth and Daumier—are operating in prose satire. Distortion is a dye dropped onto the specimen to make vivid traits and qualities otherwise only faintly visible to the naked eye.

You've begun to touch upon the impulses behind writing Our Gang. *Can you be more specific about motives? Previous to this, you have written and published four books of fiction; is it clear to you why you have chosen to write political satire just now in your career?*

Well, at Bucknell University, where I went to college and edited a literary magazine in the early fifties, I spent nearly as much time writing satire as I did trying to write fiction. Then in the middle fifties I began to publish pieces in *The New Republic,* most of them ostensibly movie reviews, but with the appeal—in that they had any—of satirical comedy. I once did a parody in *The New Republic* of President Eisenhower's religous beliefs (and prose style) inspired by a Norman Vincent Peale sermon that had revealed to Reverend Peale's parishioners that Ike was on a first-name basis with Jehovah. By the way, Oliver Jensen wrote a very funny version back then of the Gettysburg Address as Eisenhower might have composed and delivered it. The first sentence went, "I haven't checked these figures, but eighty-seven years ago, I think it was, a number of individuals organized a governmental set-up here in this country, I believe it covered certain Eastern areas, with this idea they were following up based on a sort of national independence arrangement and the program that every individual is just as good as every other individual."

My own first book of fiction, *Goodbye, Columbus,* was described by Alfred Kazin as "acidulous," suggesting a satiric intention. To a degree that's true, but in retrospect that book seems to me very mild comedy, in turn ironical and lyrical in the way of books about sensitive upstarts in summer romances. Nothing since would seem to qualify as satire, unless you call *Portnoy's Complaint* a satirical lament.

Why have I turned to political satire? In a word: Nixon.

What triggered—that's the word for it, too—what triggered *Our Gang* was his response to the Calley conviction back in April 1971. Do you remember what the army lawyer, Joseph Welch, said to Senator McCarthy at the Senate hearings after McCarthy had gratuitously insinuated that a junior member of Welch's Boston law firm had a Communist background? "Until this moment, Senator, I think I never really gauged your cruelty or your recklessness." Well, when Nixon announced that Calley, who had been convicted of murdering four times as many unarmed civilians as Charles Manson, would not have to await his appeal in the post stockade (alongside the monsters who go AWOL and the Benedict Arnolds who get caught snoozing on guard duty) but need only be restricted to quarters until such time as Nixon (with his nose to the wind) reviewed the decision of the appeals court, I thought: Tricky, I knew you were a moral ignoramus, I knew you were a scheming opportunist, I knew you were fraudulent right down to your shoelaces, but truly, I did not think that even you would sink to something like this.

I am, like so many satirists, just a naïf at heart. Why *shouldn't* he sink to that? But what that statement of his on Calley "made perfectly clear" was that if it seemed to him in the interest of his career, he would sink to anything. If 50.1 percent of the voters wanted to make a hero out of a convicted multiple murderer, then maybe there was something in it—for him.

Look at him today [Fall 1971], positively gaga over his trip to Red China, as he used to like to call it when he was debating Kennedy. Now he says the "People's Republic of China" as easily as any Weatherman. Doesn't he stand for *anything*? It turns out he isn't even anti-Communist. He never even believed in *that*. I remember joking back in 1968 that if Rockefeller got the Republican nomination, Nixon would divorce Pat, remarry, and try again in '72. But who, even in his most cynical wisecracks, could have imagined that the Nixon who gave it to Khrushchev about "freedom" in that kitchen would one day be delirious with joy about visiting a "tyrant" who had "enslaved" eight hundred million Chinese? Talk about bad taste. Doesn't his heart bleed for "enslaved peoples" any more? Or did they take everybody's shackles off over there? If so, he neglected to mention it on his two-minute spot commercial for the People's Republic of China. No more explanation from Nixon about his ideological turnabout than from the rulers in 1984, when they interrupt news broadcasts every other day to inform the people that their enemies are now their friends and their friends their enemies. You would think that the people—here, not in Orwell's Oceania—might want their Commie-chasing President to explain to them what it is about godlessness, totalitarianism, and slavery that is less repugnant to him today than it was ten years ago, or even ten months ago. And if it's suddenly okay with the United States for eight hundred million people in China not to be able "to determine their own future in free elections," why isn't it okay for a mere thirteen million more in Vietnam? By comparison, that's only a drop in the enslavement bucket. But nobody asks, and he doesn't tell. The liberal newspapers even praise him for his "flexibility."

Then you've also been inspired to write this book out of frustration with the ways in which popular spokesmen—newspaper columnists, TV commentators, even congressmen and senators—respond to Nixon?

Only to a small degree. Nixon is sufficient unto himself to make the steam rise. Of course, the high seriousness with which "responsible" critics continue to take his public statements does tend to increase frustration. There is this shibboleth, "respect for the office of the Presidency"—as though there were no distinction between the man who holds and degrades the office and the office itself. And why all the piety about the office anyway? A President happens to be in *our* employ.

The best journalists I've read on Nixon are Tom Wicker, Nicholas von Hoffman, Murray Kempton, and Garry Wills in *Nixon Agonistes*. They don't seem to consider it a setback to the species to point up how utterly bizarre this guy is. And then, in public life, there's the Arkansas Traveler, Senator William Fulbright. Cross-examining Laird, after that Terry and the Pirates raid on the POW camp in

North Vietnam, he was as beautifully droll—his timing as perfect, his assumed innocence as effective—as Mark Twain. When Fulbright retires, he ought to go around the country, the way Twain and Artemus Ward and Will Rogers used to, doing humorous monologues about his experiences as Chairman of the Foreign Relations Committee. He and Eugene McCarthy could be a very dry comic duo, on the order of Lum 'n' Abner.

Do you actually think Our Gang *will do anything to restrain or alter Nixon's conduct? Affect his conscience? Shame him? What do you expect to accomplish by publishing a satire like this one?*

Do I expect the world to change? Hardly. True, when we all first learned about satire in school, we were told that it was a humorous attack upon men or institutions for the purpose of instigating reform, or words to that effect about its ameliorative function. Now, that's a very uplifting attitude to take toward malice, but I don't think it holds water. Writing satire is a literary, not a political act, however volcanic the reformist or even revolutionary passion in the author. Satire is moral rage transformed into comic art—as an elegy is grief transformed into poetic art. Does an elegy expect to accomplish anything in the world? No, it's a means of organizing and expressing a harsh, perplexing emotion.

What begins as the desire to murder your enemy with blows, and is converted (largely out of fear of the consequences) into the attempt to murder him with invective and insult, is most thoroughly sublimated, or socialized, in the art of satire. It's the imaginative flowering of the primitive urge to knock somebody's block off.

Of course, you have the villainous President in your book murdered, don't you? The next-to-last chapter of Our Gang *begins with the announcement that Trick E. Dixon has been assassinated, and for the next thirty pages or so you give us everything exuded by the television networks in the wake of*

46

that announcement. Do you think there will be readers who will accuse you of advocating or encouraging the murder of President Nixon?

If so, it will be because they have failed to read the chapter—and the book—with even a minimal amount of comprehension. I'm not saying the chapter is in good taste. But I just can't imagine that the ludicrous manner in which Trick E. Dixon is disposed of would serve to fire the will of a would-be Presidential assassin. The President of *Our Gang* is found stuffed in a Baggie in the fetal position, so that he resembles one of those "unborn" for whose rights he speaks so eloquently throughout the book. That he meets his end in a Baggie is just satiric retribution, parodic justice.

And in the next chapter he's alive and well anyway. In Hell, admittedly, but debating the pants off Satan, whom he's running against for Devil. I subtitled that last chapter "On the Comeback Trail" to suggest that you can't hold a Trick E. Dixon down, even by stuffing him into a Baggie and turning the twister seal.

Back in 1966, Max Hayward edited and translated a chilling, depressing document that he called *On Trial*. It was the transcript of the Moscow trial of the Soviet writers Yuli Daniel and Andrei Sinyavsky, who were given five- and seven-year sentences in a forced-labor camp for "slandering" the state in their literary works. Andrei Sinyavsky's final plea to the judge, prior to the sentencing, was particularly memorable. Throughout the trial the judge had brutally chastised Sinyavsky for "lecturing the court on literature"—of all things—whenever the writer tried to explain his intentions in *The Makepeace Experiment*, a fantastic novel, or fable, in which (among other funny things) the people in a provincial Russian town eat toothpaste and think they're dining on caviar because their leader tells them it's so. The judge didn't want to hear about satire or fantasy or hyperbole or playfulness or humor or the make-believe aspect of literature; he didn't want to hear any comparison to Gogol or Pushkin or Mayakovsky—all he wanted to know was: "Why do you slander Lenin?" "Why do you slander the Russian people who suffered so in the war?" "Why do you play into the hands of our ene-mies in the West?" Yet, when the time came for Sinyavsky to speak his final words to the court—or to *anyone* in the outside world for a long, long time—he proceeded, with incredible determination, to say: "I want to repeat a few elementary arguments about the nature of literature. The most rudimentary thing about literature—it is here that one's study of it begins—is that words are not deeds . . ."

I hardly presume to compare myself to Andrei Sinyavsky, or my situation as a writer to his, or Daniel's, in Russia. I am wholly in awe of writers like Sinyavsky and Daniel, of their personal bravery and their uncompromising devotion and dedication to literature. To write in secrecy, to publish pseudonymously, to work in fear of the labor camp, to be despised, ridiculed, and insulted by the mass of writers turning out just what they're supposed to—it would be pre-sumptuous to imagine one's *art* surviving in such a hostile environ-ment, let alone coming through with the dignity and self-possession displayed by Sinyavsky and Daniel at their trial.

I use the case of Sinyavsky because it is an extreme and horrifying example of the kind of "misunderstanding" one's adversaries might wish to encourage in order to defame a work that makes fun of them. In other words, I am aware of the problem that you raise, and I don't take it lightly. I expect some readers will miss the point, clear as it seems to me. But all I can say to those who will fear for the President's life is that they would do better to lobby for a strong federal gun-control bill than to worry about the influence of *Our Gang* on potential assassins. Admittedly, it might be easier to get Attorney General Mitchell to push for a bill outlawing literature than for one making it impossible to buy a rifle through the mail for fifteen bucks, but the fact remains, more people are killed in this country every year by bullets than by satires.

What is your purpose then in writing the chapter entitled "The Assassina-tion of Tricky"?

Well, to me it seems so obvious that I feel uncomfortable having to explain it . . . What's ridiculed here is the discrepancy between official pieties and the unpleasant truth. On the one hand, I have tens of thousands of people flocking to Washington to confess to assassinating Trick E. Dixon, and on the other, the television commentators who persist in describing these self-avowed killers as though they were the mourners who thronged to Washington after President Kennedy was killed—or President Charisma, as he is called in the book. It really isn't Nixon and his friends who are being mocked in this chapter so much as the platitudinous mentality of the media. (Pardon the Agnewesque rhetoric; I assure you, there's no similarity between the Vice President's attitude toward TV and my own. That he should find this utterly conformist medium, these mammoth corporations like NBC and CBS, to be heretical and treasonous is a perfect measure of his powers of social observation.) Partly, the point is that Tricky, living or dead, in the White House or in the grave, is unworthy of such tribute, but the joke in that chapter entitled "The Assassination of Tricky" is largely at the expense of network blindness. The implication is that the mass media are purveyors of the Official Version of Reality and, for all their so-called criticism of the government, can be counted on, when the chips are down, to cloud the issue and miss the point.

Lastly, the chapter is concerned with the fine art of government lying, but then so is the entire book.

Let me press you further on "The Assassination of Tricky" with a question that some people might want to raise about it. Won't certain details about that chapter be particularly disturbing, if not repellent, to those who continue to grieve over the death by assassination of the two Kennedy brothers and Martin Luther King?

I expect that even Mrs. Martin Luther King and Senator Edward Kennedy would agree that every time we allude to an act of criminal brutality, such as the murder of a national leader, it is not necessary to draw a long face and make pious testimony to our abhorrence of violence.

I think, really, whatever there might be that is disturbing or unsettling here arises out of the imaginative exploration of a violent fantasy. To give an extreme and well-known literary example: what could be more unsettling than reading *Crime and Punishment?* I recently assigned it to a literature class and found those students who habit it is to read a novel straight through the night before the class meeting in a state of anxiety that had to do with something more than just going without their sleep. Reading *Crime and Punishment* is a disgusting, if not repellent, experience, among other things; so is watching *Othello.* Even Synge's *Playboy of the Western World,* which just toys with the theme of parricide, has been known to cause audiences in Ireland to riot.

In *Our Gang,* the farcical style seems to me to work to *becalm* whatever anxiety might be aroused in the reader by a parricidal (or, I suppose, regicidal) fantasy made "real." It doesn't dilute it as much as a Bugs Bunny cartoon—where the violence is morally inconsequential because of the utter silliness of the situation—but there is a similar kind of relief felt as a result of the comedy. However, simultaneous with the pleasure taken in the harmless, make-believe, sadistic fun, the reader probably can't help remembering that Presidents of the United States *have* been assassinated—and knowing that it is possible for President Nixon to be assassinated too. So suddenly it's not so funny after all—and I think what is then most disturbing to the reader is that he has found himself *enjoying* a fantasy that he has known in reality to be terrible.

The President Addresses the Nation

My fellow Americans:

I have an announcement to make to you tonight of the greatest national importance. As you know, the Senate has voted this afternoon to remove me from the Office of the President. That, of course, is their right under the Constitution of the United States of America, and as you know, I have not interfered in any way with their deliberations on this matter, as I did not interfere some weeks ago when the House of Representatives arrived at their decision after their own deliberations. They have a right to express their opinion, as does any American, without Presidential interference or pressure of any kind from the Executive branch. That is what is known as the separation of powers. You probably know by now that there were even members of my own political party among those in the Legislative branch who voted to remove me from the Presidency. I consider that to be a vigorous and reassuring sign of their independence of mind, and of their personal integrity. I applaud them for their actions, which can only strengthen the democratic process here at home, and enhance the image of American democracy abroad.

However, according to the doctrine of the separation of powers,

---

A Nixon parody written some twenty months after *Our Gang* was published, at the height of the Senate Watergate hearings. (1973)

the Executive branch has an equal voice in the management of government, along with the Legislative and the Judicial branches. That, after all, is only fair. It is what is meant by the "American Way." Moreover, the President has the sole responsibility for safeguarding the security of the nation. That responsibility is spelled out in the oath of Office, which, as you all know, every President takes on Inauguration Day. President Washington, whose picture you see here, took that oath. So did President Lincoln, pictured here. And so did our great President Dwight David Eisenhower, whose grandson has just completed serving his country in the United States Navy and is married to my daughter Julie, whom you see pictured here. My other daughter, Tricia, is pictured here, in her wedding dress. And of course standing beside Tricia is my wife Pat. My fellow Americans, I owe it not only to these great American Presidents who preceded me in this high Office but to my family, and to you and your families, to respect and honor that oath to which I swore on the Holy Bible on my Inauguration Day. To speak personally, I just couldn't live with myself if I went ahead and shirked my duty to safeguard the security of the nation.

And that is why I have decided tonight to remain in this Office. My fellow Americans, though I respect the sincerity and integrity of those Senators who voted earlier in the day for my removal, I find, after careful study and grave reflection, that to accept their decision would be to betray the trust placed in me by the American people, and to endanger the security and the well-being of this nation.

As you all know, there has never been an American President yet who has stepped down in the middle of his term of Office because of Congressional pressure of any kind. That is something for which there is just no precedent in American history—and let me tell you, straight from the shoulder, I don't intend to break the record my predecessors have established of standing up under fire.

You know, no one, I don't care which party he belongs to, expects this Office to be a bed of roses. If he does he shouldn't run for the

Presidency to begin with. As the late President Harry Truman put it—and you remember, Harry Truman didn't always see eye to eye on everything with us Republicans—"If you can't take the heat, you shouldn't be in the kitchen." Well, I happen to pride myself on the amount of heat I've taken over the years—some of it, as you older folks may remember, in a kitchen in the Soviet Union with Premier Khrushchev. But in the name of the American people, I stood up to Premier Khrushchev in that kitchen; and in the name of the American people, I am standing up to the Congress tonight.

Richard Nixon is not going to be the first President in American history to be removed from Office by the Legislative branch. I am sure that is not the kind of President that the American people elected me to be. Frankly, if I were to give in to this Congressional pressure to remove me from Office, if I were to come on television tonight to tell you, yes, President Nixon is quitting because he can't take the heat, well, that to my mind would constitute a direct violation of my oath of Office, and I would in fact *voluntarily* step down from the Presidency, out of a sense of having profoundly failed you, the American people, whose decision it was to place me in Office in the first place.

My fellow Americans, during my years as President I have, as you know, devoted myself to one goal above and beyond all others: the goal of world peace. As I talk to you here tonight, negotiations and discussions are being conducted around the globe by Dr. Kissinger, Secretary Rogers, and key members of the Department of State to bring peace with honor to America, and to all of mankind. These negotiations are taking place at the highest diplomatic level and necessarily in secret—but I am pleased to report to you tonight that we are pursuing them with every hope of success.

Now I am sure that no one in Congress would willingly or knowingly want to endanger the chances of world peace, for us, for our children, and for generations to come. And yet, by calling upon the President to pack up and quit just because the going is a little rough, that is precisely what they are doing. And that is precisely why I will *not* quit. I happen to care more about world peace now and for generations to come than about making myself popular with a few of my critics in the Congress. Oh, I am sure that the easier choice would be to retire to San Clemente and bask there in the honors and tributes that we Americans lavish upon our former Presidents. But I prefer to take the hard road, the high road, if that is the road that leads to the end of warfare and to world peace for our children and our children's children. My fellow Americans, I was raised to be a Quaker, not a quitter.

Now I have to say some things to you that you may not care to hear, especially those of you who try to think the best of our country, as I do myself. But tonight I must speak the truth, unpleasant as it may be; you deserve no less. My fellow Americans, I understand there are going to be those in Congress who will not respect the decision I have announced here tonight, as I respected theirs, arrived at earlier in the day. We have reason to believe that there are those who are going to try to make political capital out of what I have said to you tonight from the bottom of my heart. There are even going to be some who will use my words to attempt to create a national crisis in order to reap political gain for themselves or their party. And, most dangerous of all, there are some elements in the country, given to violence and lawlessness as a way of life, who may attempt to use force to remove me from Office.

Let me quickly reassure you that this Administration will not tolerate lawlessness of any kind. This Administration will not permit the time-honored constitutional principle of the separation of powers to be subverted by a disgruntled, ambitious, or radical minority. This Administration intends to maintain and defend that great American tradition that has come down to us unbroken from the days of the Founding Fathers—the great tradition of a President of the United States, duly elected by the people of the United States, serving out his Office without violent interference by those who disagree with his policies. Disagreement and dissent are, of course, in the great tradition of a democracy like our own; but the violent overthrow of the elected government is something that is repugnant to me, as it is to every American, and so long as I am President, I promise you that I will deal promptly and efficiently with those who advocate or engage in violence as a means of bringing about political change.

In order to discourage those who would resort to violence of any kind, and in order to maintain law and order in the nation and to safeguard the welfare and well-being of law-abiding American citizens, I have tonight, in my constitutional role as Commander-in-Chief, ordered the Joint Chiefs of Staff to place the Armed Forces on a stand-by alert around the nation. The Department of Justice and the Federal Bureau of Investigation have also been advised to take all necessary steps to ensure domestic tranquillity. The National Guard has already been notified, and throughout the fifty states units are being mobilized for duty. Furthermore, the state and local police have been encouraged to request whatever assistance they may require, in the way of personnel or equipment, in order to maintain law and order in your communities.

My fellow Americans, I swore upon taking this Office to safeguard this nation and its citizens, and I intend to stand on my word. No one—and that includes your Congressman and your Senator, just as it does the armed revolutionary—is going to tell the American people that they cannot have sitting in the White House the President they have chosen in a free and open election. And I don't care whether that President happens to be myself, President Washington, President Lincoln, or President Eisenhower. I give you every assurance tonight that the President you, the American people, elected for a second four-year term will not permit the votes you cast so overwhelmingly in his favor to have been cast in vain.

God bless each and every one of you.

Good night.

On *The Breast*

I'd like to ask about the origins of The Breast. *How do you account for the idea itself? Do you think this is a strange or unusual book for you to have written? Do you see any connection between* The Breast *and your previous work, or do you consider it a work really a little out of your line?*

Thinking back over my work, it seems to me that I've frequently written about Bruno Bettelheim calls "behavior in extreme situations." Or until *The Breast* perhaps what I've written about has been extreme behavior in ordinary situations. At any rate, I have concerned myself with men and women whose moorings have been cut, and who are swept away from their native shores and out to sea, sometimes on a tide of their own righteousness or resentment. For instance, in an early story, "The Conversion of the Jews," a little Jewish boy finds himself playing God on a synagogue roof; now he may not be in such dire straits as Kepesh in *The Breast,* but he is definitely in a new and surprising relationship with his everyday self, his family and his friends. Lucy Nelson in *When She Was Good,* Gabe Wallach and Paul Herz in *Letting Go,* Alex Portnoy in *Portnoy's Complaint*—all are living beyond their psychological and moral means; it isn't a matter of sinking or swimming—they have, as it were, to invent the crawl.

The interviewer is Alan Lelchuck. (1972)

56

Kepesh's predicament is similar—with a difference: his unmooring can't be traced (much to his dismay, too) to psychological, social, or historical causes. His longing to be at one again with his fellows and his old self is, to my mind, far more poignant and harrowing than Lucy Nelson's or Portnoy's. Those two characters, at the same time that they yearn for a more sociable and settled existence, are hell-bent on maintaining their isolation with all the rage and wildness in their arsenals. They are two very stubborn American children, locked in prototypical combat with the beloved enemy: the spirited Jewish boy pitted against his mother, the Cleopatra of the kitchen; the solemn Gentile girl pitted against her father, the Bacchus of Hometown, U.S.A. Kepesh strikes me as far more heroic than either of these two: perhaps a man who turns into a breast is the first heroic character I've ever been able to portray.

What problems did you face while writing The Breast? *Were there any special pitfalls you worried over while you were at work? Or did the story unfold more or less of a piece?*

One difficulty in writing this kind of story is deciding what sort of claim to make on the reader's credulity: whether to invite him to accept the fantastic situation as taking place in the recognizable world (and so to respond to the imagined actuality from that vantage point, with that kind of concern) or whether to ignore the matter of belief and move into other imaginative realms entirely—the worlds of dream, hallucination, allegory, nonsense, play, literary self-consciousness, sadism, and so on.

In "The Metamorphosis" Kafka asserts at the outset that the catastrophe is happening to his hero in the very real, believable, mundane world of families, jobs, bosses, money, and housekeepers. If you don't accept this, if you read "The Metamorphosis" as if it were Gogol's "The Diary of a Madman," and think of Samsa as someone trapped in an insane hallucination, then you will not be on the right wave length to receive the full impact of the story. Kafka doesn't go more than a dozen sentences before he tells you, point-blank, "It was no dream." On the other hand, Gogol, in "The Nose," is intermittently provocative and teasing about Kovalev's misfortune. There is a playful, sadistic imagination back of the story that keeps expressing itself in farcical and satiric turns and, in that way, keeps alive and unresolved the question of the story's "reality." As Gogol says in the end, maybe it's only a cock-and-bull story anyway—then again, maybe not. Clearly he can't have it both ways, but perverse trickster that he is here (Chichikov-as-writer), *that* suits him to a T.

I refer to these masters of fantasy to illustrate possibilities, not to lay claim to similarities of accomplishment or stature. In *The Breast* my approach to the outlandish seems to me to be something like a blending of the two methods that I've just described. I want the fantastic situation to be accepted as taking place in what we call the real world, at the same time that I hope to make the reality of the horror one of the issues of the story. "Is it really happening? Can I believe this?"—the questions that Kafka settles (or suppresses) on the very first page by asserting that the metamorphosis is "no dream," and that Gogol is so prankish about at the reader's expense, are absorbed into *The Breast* by Kepesh himself. Whether it is or isn't a dream, a hallucination, or a psychotic delusion, is no small matter to my hero (or to me)—consequently, I didn't choose to render the problem unproblematical by a wave of the author's magic wand.

"The Nose" and "The Metamorphosis" are both cited by Kepesh in the story, part of his desperate struggle to make some sense of what's happened to him. I thought it was fitting for a serious, dedicated literature professor to think of Gogol and Kafka when his own horrible transformation occurs; it also seemed a good idea not to leave it to the reader to speculate on his own about my indebtedness to "The Nose" and "The Metamorphosis," but instead to make that issue visible in the fiction. *The Breast* proceeds, in fact, by attempting to answer the objections and the reservations that might be raised in a skeptical reader by its own fantastic premise. It has the design of a rebuttal or a rejoinder, rather than a hallucination or a nightmare. Above all, I thought it would be in the story's best interest to try to be straightforward and direct about this bizarre circumstance, and for the protagonist to be no less intelligent than the reader about the implications of his misfortune. No crapola about Deep Meaning; instead, try to absorb that issue, the issue of meaning, into the story—along with the issues of literary antecedents and the "reality" of the horror.

You say you wanted to be straightforward and direct. Yet one critic has complained that "on the metaphorical level the fantasy remains rather opaque."

First off, that a fiction is clear and straightforward about itself on the narrative level, and opaque or difficult on the metaphorical level, is not necessarily a bad thing. To use Kafka again as an illustration— it isn't the transparency of "The Metamorphosis" that accounts for its power; Kafka's strategy (and brilliance) is to resist interpretation, even of a very high order, at the very same time that he invites it. Whatever intellectual handle you use to get a hold on a Kafka story is never really adequate to explain its appeal; and to address yourself primarily to the "meaning" has always seemed to me the way to miss much of his appeal.

I'm not arguing that impenetrability is itself some kind of virtue. It's not hard, after all, for a writer to delude himself into believing he is being deep just because he is being difficult or vague. The issue isn't opacity or transparency anyway—it's usability. What makes an image telling or even, if you prefer, meaningful, is not how much meaning we can associate to it but the quality of the overall invention that it inspires, the freedom it gives the writer to explore his obsessions and his talent. A novelist doesn't persuade by what he is "trying to say," but by a sense of fictional authenticity he communicates, the sense of an imagination so relentless and thoroughgoing that it is able to convert into its own nonconvertible currency whatever the author has absorbed through reading, thinking, and "raw experience."

To get back to your critic's complaint: what's frustrating him is very like what's killing Kepesh. I wish I had thought to give Professor *Kepesh* those words to speak: "On the metaphorical level the fantasy remains rather opaque." What a marvelous, chilling conclusion that would have made! What your critic senses as a literary problem seems to me the human problem that triggers a good deal of Kepesh's ruminations. To try to unravel the mystery of "meaning" here is really to participate to some degree in Kepesh's struggle— and to be defeated, as he is. Not all the ingenuity of all the English teachers in all the English departments in America can put David Kepesh together again. For him there is no way out of the monstrous situation, not even through literary interpretation. There is only the unrelenting education in his own misfortune. What he learns by the end is that, whatever else it is, it is the real thing: he *is* a breast, and must act accordingly.

Now what "accordingly" means is still another question, and the one Kepesh raises near the end of the story, with his daydream about becoming his own one-man, or one-breast circus. Unlike Gregor Samsa, who accepts his transformation into a beetle from the first sentence, Kepesh is continually challenging, questioning, and defying his fate, and even after he consents to believe that he has actually become a mammary gland, his mind is alive with alternative ways of being one.

I'm interested in the relationship between the sexual ecstasy that Kepesh discovers as a breast and his spiritual pain, his excruciating sense of exile and aloneness. Doesn't the connection you make here recapitulate, in a more extreme way, a psychological motif that was central to Portnoy's Complaint, where the hero feels increasingly at odds with himself and his past the more sexually adventurous he becomes?

Yes, though with a different emphasis and implications. Speaking broadly, it's the struggle to accommodate warring (or, at least, contending) impulses and desires, to negotiate some kind of inner peace or balance of power, or perhaps just to maintain hostilities at a low destructive level, between the ethical and social yearnings and the implacable, singular lusts for the flesh and its pleasures. The measured self vs. the insatiable self. The accommodating self vs. the ravenous self. In these works of fiction, of course, the sides are not this clearly drawn, nor are they in opposition right on down the line. These aren't meant to be diagrams of conflicting "selves" anyway but stories of men experiencing the complicated economics of human satisfaction, men in whom spiritual ambitions *and* sensual ambitions are inextricably bound up with the overarching desire to somehow achieve their own true purpose.

However, I don't think of the two works simply as variations on a sexual theme. The grotesqueness of Kepesh's transformation complicates the sexual struggle to a point where it's no longer really useful to view him and Portnoy as blood brothers—or to describe his trouble as only sexual. Portnoy, for all his confusion and isolation, knows the world like the back of his own hand (to make the kind of joke that book seems to inspire). Kepesh is *lost*—somewhat the way Descartes claims to be lost at the beginning of the *Meditations:* "I am certain that I am, but what am I? What is there that can be esteemed true?" Unlike Portnoy, Kepesh is not interested in making his misery entertaining, nor is he able to bridge the gap between what he looks like and what he feels like with wild humor. If Portnoy could do that, it was because he had less territory to cover.

Is there any implied criticism in The Breast *of ideas about sexual freedom that are currently enjoying a vogue? When you speak of the "economics of human satisfaction," with its implications of loss as well as gain, I wonder if perhaps you may have had a satiric intention—if there's a critique here aimed at the high value placed upon a "liberated" sexual life. Along this line, I'd like to ask you if you didn't also set out to criticize, or deromanti-cize, certain extreme but increasingly popular notions about madness and alienation—in particular, the idea that either is a desirable alternative to sanity and to a sense of harmony with ordinary life.*

I don't think you're describing my intentions so much as a point of view that may have stimulated my imagination along the way but that was consumed—I'd like to think—by the invention itself. For me, one of the strongest motives for continuing to write fiction is an increasing distrust of "positions," my own included. This is not to say that you leave your intellectual baggage at the door when you sit down to write, or that in your novel you discover that you really think just the opposite of what you've been telling people—if you do, you're probably too confused to be producing good work. I'm only saying that I often feel that I don't really know what I'm talking about until I've stopped *talking* about it and sent everything down through the blades of the fiction-making machine, to be ground into something else, something that is decidedly *not* a position but that allows me to say, when I'm done, "Well, that isn't what I mean either—but it's more like it."

So—I intended to write a critique of nobody's ideas but my own. Not that I think that madness or alienation are glamorous or envi-able conditions; being insane and feeling estranged don't accord with my conception of the good life. You correctly identify the bias, but are sniffing after a polemical objective that isn't there. I see what you mean about "deromanticizing" these "voguish" ideas, but if that happens, it happens by the way. And had I intended to write a satire, even of the most muted kind, I would have flashed a different set of signals from the coach's box to the reader.

Do you anticipate hostile reactions to The Breast *from voices within the women's movement? I know that there has already been discussion of the book which characterizes the hero, disapprovingly, as a man who thinks of women as existing solely for his sexual pleasure. What do you think of this sort of reading of your story?*

I think it's inaccurate and misses the point. Whatever Kepesh thinks, whether about women, art, reality, or his father, hasn't to do with his being a man but with the fact that he *isn't* one any longer, that he's all but lost touch, to quote him, with the "professor of literature, the lover, the son, the friend, the neighbor, the customer, the client, and the citizen" that he was before his transformation. What he's become has narrowed his life down to a single issue: his anatomy.

I would think that there might even be women, particularly those who have been sensitized by the women's movement, who will feel a certain *kinship* with my hero and his predicament. Surely if anybody has ever been turned totally into a "sexual object," both to himself and to others, it is David Alan Kepesh. Isn't this all-encompassing sexualization exactly what he struggles with from the moment he discovers he's an enormous female breast with a supersensitive five-inch nipple? The battle to be, not simply that shape and those dimensions, but simultaneously to be something *other*, constitutes the entire action of the book.

Of course it's an ambiguous struggle, shot through with contradiction and bewilderment, and waged with varying degrees of wisdom and success—but then it's the *confused* nature of Kepesh's battle with his own soft adipose tissue that might well strike a chord familiar to women who are thoughtful about the relationships possible between their physical and their psychic selves.

One of the surprising aspects of the book is its elegiac tone—David Kepesh mourning his predicament the way, say, Tommy Wilhelm mourns his in Bellow's Seize the Day. *Given that the book begins with such a bizarre, freakish catastrophe, one might have expected either comedy or grotesquerie, not elegy. Can you explain why you took the approach you did?*

I'm not sure I'd call the tone elegiac. It's a sad story and Kepesh is mournful sometimes, but it's more to the point to say that there is an elegiac note *trying* to make itself heard but held in check by the overriding (and, I think, in the circumstances, ironic) tone of reasonableness. The mood is less plaintive than reflective—horror recollected in a kind of stunned tranquillity. The mood of the convalescent.

The story could have been more comic, or more grotesque, or both. Certainly there are wonderful models for the kind of humor that manages to be wildly funny and perfectly gruesome all at once. "The Nose" treats mutilation as a marvelous joke, and then in *Molloy* and *Malone Dies,* Samuel Beckett does for bodily decomposition what Jack Benny used to do on Sunday nights for stinginess. I like that kind of comedy, and it goes without saying that at the outset I recognized the gruesomely comic possibilities in the idea of a man turning into a breast.

But I resisted comedy or farce in large part because the possibility was so immediately apparent. Since the joke was there before I even began, perhaps the best thing was to stand it on its head by *refusing* to take it as a joke . . . Then a certain contrariness probably figured in my decision, a reluctance, such as I imagine any writer might feel, to do what is supposed to be his "number."

In all, it seemed to me that if I was going to come up with anything new (in terms of my own work), it might best be done by taking this potentially hilarious situation and treating it perfectly *seriously.* I think there are still funny moments in the story, but that's okay with me too. I didn't feel I had necessarily to make myself over into William Ernest Henley just for the sake of going against the expectations aroused by the material or by my own track record.

On *The Great American Novel*

To begin with, how extreme a departure from your previous fiction is The Great American Novel?

   If *The Great American Novel* is an extreme departure, it's because the tendency to comedy that's been present even in my most somber books and stories was allowed to take charge of my imagination and lead it where it would. I was no less farcical, blatant, and coarse-grained in *Our Gang*, but that book, aimed at a precise target, had a punitive purpose that restricted the range of humorous possibilities. And in *Portnoy's Complaint*, though the comedy may have been what was most obvious about the novel, strains of pathos, nostalgia, and (as I see it) evocative lyricism worked to qualify the humor and to place the monologue in a reasonably familiar setting, literary and psychological; comedy was the means by which the character synthesized and articulated his sense of himself and his predicament.

   In *The Great American Novel* the satiric bull's-eye has been replaced by a good-sized imaginary world more loosely connected to the actual than in *Our Gang*. And except for the Prologue and Epilogue, the comedy is not turned on and off, or on and on, by a self-conscious narrator using humor to shape your (and his) idea of him-

---

I conducted this interview with myself. (1973)

self, as in *Portnoy's Complaint*. Widening the focus, and by and large removing the comedian himself from the stage, allowed for a less constrained kind of comic invention. The comedy here is not softened or mitigated by the familiar human presence it flows through and defines, nor does the book try to justify whatever is reckless about it by claiming some redeeming social or political value. It follows its own comic logic—if one can speak of the "logic" of farce, burlesque, and slapstick—rather than the logic of a political satire or a personal monologue.

But there is certainly satire in this novel, directed, however playfully, at aspects of American popular mythology. The comedy may not be so free of polemical intent, or even of redeeming social or moral value as you might like to think. And why would you want to think that anyway?

The comedy in *The Great American Novel* exists for the sake of no higher value than comedy itself; the redeeming value is not social or cultural reform, or moral instruction, but *comic inventiveness.* Destructive, or lawless, playfulness—and for the fun of it.

Now, there is an art to this sort of thing that distinguishes it from sadism, nonsense, or even nihilism for the fun of it; however, a *feel* for the sadistic, the nonsensical, and the nihilistic certainly goes into making such comedy (and into enjoying it). I don't like using the word "satiric" for describing this book because the suggestion of cruel means employed for a higher purpose doesn't square with what I felt myself to be doing. "Satyric," suggesting the sheer pleasure of exploring the anarchic and the unsocialized, is more like it.

The direction my work has taken since *Portnoy's Complaint* can in part be accounted for by my increased responsiveness to, and respect for, what is unsocialized in me. I don't mean that I am interested in propagandizing for the anarcho-libidinists in our midst; rather, *Portnoy's Complaint*, which was concerned with the comic side of the struggle between a hectoring superego and an ambitious id, seems now, in retrospect, to have realigned those forces as they act upon my imagination.

Can you explain why you are trying to come on like a bad boy—although in the manner of a very good boy indeed? Why quarrel, in decorous tones, no less, with decorum? Why insist, in balanced sentences, on libido? Why "reckless" and "anarchic" to describe one's work, rather than "responsible" and "serious" and "humane"? In "Writing About Jews,"* the essay you published in Commentary *in 1963, answering charges of "self-hatred" and "anti-Semitism," your argument consisted almost entirely of an attempt to demonstrate your righteousness through the evidence of your work. Does that now seem to you so much defensive obfuscation?*

No, it expressed concerns central to the stories under attack; and my rhetoric then, far from being borrowed to obfuscate the issue, was all too close at hand, the language of a preoccupation with conscience, responsibility, and rectitude rather grindingly at the center of *Letting Go*, the novel I was writing in those years.

At that time, still in my twenties, I imagined fiction to be something like a religious calling, and literature a kind of sacrament, a sense of things I have had reason to modify since. Such elevated notions aren't (or weren't, back then) that uncommon in vain young writers; they dovetailed nicely in my case with a penchant for ethical striving that I had absorbed as a Jewish child, and with the salvationist literary ethos in which I had been introduced to high art in the fifties, a decade when cultural, rather than political, loyalties divided the young into the armies of the damned and the cadre of the blessed. I might turn out to be a bad artist, or no artist at all, but having declared myself *for* art—the art of Tolstoy, James, Flaubert, and

*See p. 193.

Mann, whose appeal was as much in their heroic literary integrity as in their work—I imagined I had sealed myself off from being a morally unacceptable person, in others' eyes as well as my own.

The last thing I expected, having chosen this vocation—*the* vocation—was to be charged with heartlessness, vengeance, malice, and treachery. Yet that was to be one of the first experiences of importance to befall me out in the world. Ambitious and meticulous (if not wholly enlightened) in conscience, I had gravitated to the genre that constituted the most thoroughgoing investigation of conscience that I knew of—only to be told by more than a few Jews that I was a conscienceless young man holding attitudes uncomfortably close to those promulgated by the Nazis. As I saw it then, I had to argue in public and in print that I was not what they said I was. The characterization was ill-founded, I explained, and untrue, and yes, I maintained that Conscience and Righteousness were the very words emblazoned upon the banner I believed myself to be marching under, as a writer *and* as a Jew.

I think now—I didn't then—that this conflict with my Jewish critics was as valuable a struggle as I could have had at the outset of my career. For one thing, it yanked me, screaming, out of the classroom; all one's readers, it turned out, weren't New Critics sitting on their cans at Kenyon. Some people out there took what one wrote to *heart*—and wasn't that as it should be? I resented *how* they read me, but I was never able to complain afterward that they didn't read me; I never felt neglected.

Also, the attack from Jewish critics and readers, along with personal difficulties I was having during those years, made me begin to understand that admiration for me and my mission on earth was, somewhat to my surprise, going to be less than unanimous, and probably hardest to win closest to home. Above all, I eventually came to realize that my way of taking myself seriously was more at odds than I ever could have imagined with what others believed seriousness to be. In time (more, probably, than it should have taken) I became aware of enormous differences of *sensibility* between my Jewish adversaries and myself—a good deal of the disagreement, I realized, had to do with somewhat antithetical systems of aversion and tolerance, particularly with respect to subjects that are conventionally described as "distasteful."

In brief, the opposition was instructive—partly because opposition wasn't all that my early work aroused. However, one shouldn't conclude that a friendly, or enthusiastic, readership functions as a kind of countervailing soporific, or "ego trip," for the writer. The greatest value of an appreciative audience may even be the irritant that it provides, specifically by its collective (therefore simplistic) sense of the writer, the place it chooses for him to occupy on the cultural pecking order, and the uses it wants to make of selective, disconnected elements of his work and of his own (imagined) persona. Like antagonistic opposition, the amiable irritant is useful insomuch as it arouses whatever is stubborn, elusive, or even defiant in the writer's nature, whatever resents being easily digested. Almost invariably one's reaction *against* will exceed the necessities of one's work (certainly as they might narrowly be defined), and the relationship with an attentive audience may even come, as in the case of J. D. Salinger on the one idiosyncratic extreme, and Norman Mailer on the other, to shape one's conduct, not only as a writer, but as a friend, a husband, a citizen, a colleague, etc.

"Fame," Rilke wrote, "is no more than the quintessence of all the misunderstandings collecting around a new name." Mailerism and Salingerism are vigorous, highly conscious responses to that kind of misunderstanding: the first assaults the misunderstanding at the source, challenging its timidity and conventionality ("You think I'm bad? You don't know how bad! You think I'm a brute? Well, I'm a courtly gentleman! You think I'm a gentleman? I'm a brute!" and so on), deliberately, as it were, *exceeding* the misunderstanding in an indefatigable act of public self-realization; the second, Salingerism, refuses to be vexed by misunderstanding (and misappropriation) in any way, even, if need be, by not being published. I suspect that serious American novelists with a sense of an audience swing on a pendulum from Mailerism to Salingerism, each coming to rest at a point on the arc that appears (and needless to say, a man can be wrong) to be congruent with his temperament and nourishing to the work.

To get back to the defense I made of my own work in *Commentary* in 1963—in that essay I evoked the name of Flaubert and the example of Emma Bovary, a memorable character, I said, because of the vividness and depth with which she was presented, and not because she was necessarily representative of French middle-class women of her day; likewise, I went on, *my* characters were not intended to provide a representative sampling of Jews, though they were well within the range of Jewish possibilities.

I wish now that instead of describing my intentions—or validating them—by referring to a revered artist out of the World Literature Pantheon, I had mentioned the name of Henny Youngman, a Jewish nightclub and vaudeville comic, whose wisecracks, delivered in an offhand whine while he played atrociously on the violin from the stage of the Roxy, had impressed me beyond measure at the age of ten. But because it was precisely my seriousness, my sense of proportion and consequence, that was under attack, I did not have the nerve to appear frivolous in any way. So much the worse for me. Had I had it in me to admit, in just those circumstances, that it was to the low-minded and their vulgarity that I owed no less allegiance than I did to the high-minded with whom I truly did associate my intentions, I might at least have provided *myself* with a fuller description and explanation of the work I was doing, if a still more repugnant one to those who disapproved of me.

Really, do you think of yourself as a disciple of Henny Youngman?

I do now. Also of Jake the Snake H., a middle-aged master of invective and insult, and a repository of lascivious neighborhood gossip (and, amazingly, the father of a friend of mine), who owned the corner candy store in the years when I much preferred the pinball machine to the company of my parents. I am also a disciple of my older brother's friend and navy buddy, Arnold G., an unconstrained Jewish living-room clown whose indecent stories of failure and confusion in sex did a little to demythologize the world of the sensual for me in early adolescence. As Jake the Snake demythologized the world of the respectable. As Henny Youngman, whining about family and friends while eliciting laughable squeaks from the violin (the very violin that was to make of every little Jewish boy, myself included, a world-famous, urbane, poetic, dignified, and revered Yehudi), demythologized our yearnings for cultural superiority—or for superiority through culture—and argued by his shlemieldom that it was in the world of domestic squabble and unending social compromise, rather than on the concert stage, that the Jews of his audience might expect to spend their lives.

Later I also became a disciple of certain literature professors and their favorite texts. For instance, reading *The Wings of the Dove* all afternoon long in the graduate-school library at the University of Chicago, I would find myself as transfixed by James's linguistic tact and moral scrupulosity as I had ever been by the coarseness, recklessness, and vulgar, aggressive clowning with which I was so taken during those afternoons and evenings in "my" booth at the corner candy store. As I now see it, one of my continuing problems as a writer has been to find the means to be true to these seemingly inimical realms of experience that I am strongly attached to by temperament and training—the aggressive, the crude, and the obscene, at one extreme, and something a good deal more subtle and, in every sense, refined, at the other. But that problem is not unique to any single American writer, certainly not in this day and age.

Back in 1939, Philip Rahv wrote a brief, incisive essay wherein he noted the opposition in American literature between "the thin, solemn, semiclerical culture of Boston and Concord" and "the lowlife world of the frontier and the big cities," and accordingly grouped American writers around two polar types he called the "paleface" and the "redskin." According to Rahv's scheme, James was a paleface, as was T. S. Eliot: "The paleface continually hankers after religious norms, tending toward a refined estrangement from reality. . . . At his highest level the paleface moves in an exquisite moral atmosphere, at his lowest he is genteel, snobbish, and pedantic." Whitman and Twain—and after them Anderson, Wolfe, Farrell, etc.—Rahv identified as redskins: their "reactions are primarily emotional, spontaneous, and lacking in personal culture. . . . In giving expression to the vitality and to the aspirations of the people, the redskin is at his best; but at his worst he is a vulgar anti-intellectual, combining aggression with conformity, reverting to the crudest forms of frontier psychology."

What happened in postwar America is that a lot of redskins—if not to the wigwam, then to the candy store and the borscht belt born—went off to universities and infiltrated the departments of English, till then almost exclusively the domain of the palefaces. All manner of cultural defection, conversion, confusion, enlightenment, miscegenation, parasitism, transformation, and combat ensued. This is not the place to go into all that studies in English and American literature meant, in personal and social terms, to that tribe of redskins like myself, from the semiliterate and semiassimilated reaches of urban Jewish society, or all that the presence of such Jews signified to those directing their studies (what a novel that would make!). The point here is that the weakening of social and class constraints accelerated by World War II, and the cultural exchanges thus encouraged, has produced a number of writers, many now in their forties, who have to some degree reconciled what Rahv described as this "disunity of the American creative mind," though not in any way necessarily congenial to Philip Rahv, or even to the writers themselves. For what this "reconciliation" often comes down to is a feeling of being *fundamentally ill at ease in, and at odds with, both worlds*, although, one hopes, ill at ease with style, alert to the inexhaustible number of intriguing postures that the awkward may assume in public, and the strange means that the uneasy come upon to express themselves. In short: neither the redskin one was in the days of innocence, nor the paleface one could never be in a million (or, to be precise, 5,733) years, but rather, at least in my own case, what I would describe as a "redface."

To my mind, being a redface accounts as much as anything for the self-conscious and deliberate zigzag that my own career has taken, each book veering sharply away from the one before, as though the author were mortified at having written it as he did and preferred to put as much light as possible between that *kind* of book and himself. Rahv, in his essay, reminds us that the contemporaries Paleface James and Redskin Whitman "felt little more than contempt for each other." The redface sympathizes equally with both parties in their disdain for the other, and, as it were, reenacts the argument within the body of his own work. He can never in good conscience opt for either of the disputants; indeed, bad conscience is the medium in which his literary sensibility moves. Thus the continuing need for self-analysis and self-justification.

Let's go back to Jake the Snake. In The Great American Novel, *your allegiance to him is obviously stronger than it is to Henry James, wouldn't you say?*

Yes, there is more of Jake the Snake in there than in *Letting Go* or in *When She Was Good*. Not that I regret now that I wasn't writing books like *The Great American Novel* all along. I don't know if I would ever have found my way to this "recklessness" if I hadn't first tried to dramatize, in a series of fictions—*When She Was Good* is one—the problematical nature of moral authority and of social restraint and regulation. Though I was not deliberate about this at all, it seems to me now that the question of who or what shall have influence and jurisdiction over one's life has been a concern in much of my work. From whom shall one receive the Commandments? The Patimkins? Lucy Nelson? Trick E. Dixon? These characters, as I imagined them, are hardly identical in the particulars of their lives, nor do they inhabit similar fictional worlds, but invariably the claim each makes to being the legitimate moral conscience of the community is very much what is at issue in the book. The degree to which irony, pathos, ridicule, humor, or solemnity permeate *Goodbye, Columbus, When She Was Good,* and *Our Gang* seems to me now to have been determined by what I took to be the dubiousness (and relative danger) of that claim.

The question of moral sovereignty, as it is examined in *Letting Go, Portnoy's Complaint,* and *The Breast,* is really a question of the kind of commandment the hero of each book will issue to himself; here the skepticism is directed inward, upon the hero's ambiguous sense of personal imperatives and taboos. I can even think of these characters—Gabe Wallach, Alexander Portnoy, and David Kepesh—as three stages of a single explosive projectile that is fired into the barrier that forms one boundary of the individual's identity and experience: that barrier of personal inhibition, ethical conviction and plain, old monumental fear beyond which lies the moral and psychological unknown. Gabe Wallach crashes up against the wall and collapses; Portnoy proceeds on through the fractured mortar, only to become lodged there, half in, half out. It remains for Kepesh to pass right on through the bloodied hole, and out the other end, into no-man's-land.

To sum up: the comic recklessness that I've identified with my old mentor, Jake the Snake, the indecent candy-store owner, apparently could not develop to its fullest until the *subject* of restraints and taboos had been dramatized in a series of increasingly pointed fictions that revealed the possible consequences of banging your head against your own wall.

*Did it help and encourage the anarchic spirit to be writing about baseball,
morally a "neutral" subject, rather than about Jews, say, or sexual relations?*

Maybe; though before beginning this novel I wrote a long story,
"On the Air," in which a small-time Jewish theatrical agent is put
through a series of grotesque adventures, some violently sexual, that
were as extreme in their comedy as anything in *The Great American
Novel*. But it was only a story, and perhaps I couldn't go further with
it because the dreadful comic fantasies of persecution and humiliation depicted there were, to my mind, decidedly "Jewish."

I think one reason I finally have finished a novel about baseball is
that it happens to be one of the few subjects that I know much
about. If I were as familiar with forestry, music, ironmongering,
or the city of Rotterdam, I am sure I would have written fiction
grounded in that knowledge long ago. I have not gotten around
sooner to a subject as close to me as this one because I had thought
that it could not be made to yield very much, the old bugaboo once
again of seriousness, or profundity. Over the last fifty years some
gifted writers had done pretty well by it, of course—Ring Lardner,
Mark Harris, and Bernard Malamud particularly—but despite my
admiration for their ingenuity (and the pleasure I took in baseball
stories by writers as good, and as serious, as Isaac Rosenfeld and J. F.
Powers), a certain snobbishness about the material held my own
imagination in check.

What changed your mind?

The point I had reached in my own career: the confidence I had
developed in my literary impulses, combined with the experience of
the sixties, the demythologizing decade.

This confidence expressed itself partly in a greater willingness to
be deliberately, programmatically perverse—subversive not merely

of the "serious" values of official literary culture (such subversion, after all, is the standard stuff of our era, if not the new convention), but subversive of my own considerable investment (witness this interview)* in seriousness.

I had been at something like this for a while—in the chapter of *Portnoy's Complaint* called "Whacking Off," in much of *Our Gang*, in "On the Air"—but I still had not come anywhere near being as thoroughgoingly *playful* as I now aspired to be. In an odd way—maybe not so odd at that—I set myself the goal of becoming the writer some Jewish critics had been telling me I was all along: irresponsible, conscienceless, *unserious*. Ah, if only they knew what that entailed! And the personal triumph that such an achievement would represent! A quotation from Melville began to intrigue me, from a letter he had sent to Hawthorne upon completing *Moby Dick*. I pinned it up along with the other inspirational matter on my bulletin board. "I have written a wicked book, and feel spotless as the lamb." Now I knew that no matter how hard I tried I could never really hope to be wicked; but perhaps, if I worked long and hard and diligently, I could be frivolous. And what could be more frivolous, *in my own estimation*, than writing a novel about sports?

If perversity, contrariness, my pursuit of the unserious helped to relax my snobbishness about baseball as a subject for my fiction, the decade we had just been through furnished me with the handle with which to take hold of it. Not that I knew that at the outset, or even, in so many words, at the conclusion; but I know it now. I'll try to explain.

Earlier I described the sixties as the demythologizing decade. I mean by this that much that had previously been considered in my own brief lifetime to be disgraceful and disgusting forced itself upon the national consciousness, loathsome or not; what was assumed to be beyond reproach became the target of blasphemous assault; what

*Witness this book.

was imagined to be indestructible, impermeable, in the very nature of American things, yielded and collapsed overnight. The shock to the system was enormous—not least for those like myself who belong to what may have been the most propagandized generation of young people in American history, our childhoods dominated by World War II, our high school and college years colored by the worst of the Cold War years—Berlin, Korea, Joe McCarthy; also the first American generation to bear the full brunt of the mass media and advertising. Mine was of course no *more* gullible than any other generation of youngsters—it's only that we had *so* much to swallow, and that it was stuffed into us by the most ingenious methods of force-feeding yet devised to replace outright physical torture. The generation known in its college years as "silent" was in actuality straitjacketed, at its most dismal bound by the sort of pieties, fantasies, and values that one might expect to hear articulated today only by a genuine oddball like Tricia Nixon.

Even to have been a dissident, highly skeptical member of that generation did not make one any better prepared than the straitjacketed to absorb the shocks and upheavals of post-Oswald America—for in retrospect the first act of demythologizing committed in the decade seems to me to have been the "demythologizing" of John F. Kennedy by Lee Harvey Oswald. The remythologizing of Kennedy began the instant the last shot had been fired, but once the President of Camelot, as they called it, was pronounced dead, the point about the vulnerability and mortality of the charismatic and indestructible had been made. It remained for Sirhan Sirhan to demythologize Bobby Kennedy, and for the lesser characters like Jackie and Teddy Kennedy to demythologize themselves, the one with Aristotle Onassis and the other with Mary Jo Kopechne, for the decade to turn completely inside out that legend of glamour, power, and righteousness.

Disorienting, shocking, all this may have been, but it did not begin to work deeply to test or alter one's ties to America; Vietnam did that. To have been trained to be a patriotic schoolchild on the rhetoric of World War II, to have developed an attachment to this country in good part on the basis of the myth (*and* reality) of that wartime America made my own spiritual entanglement with *this* wartime America probably more like Lyndon Johnson's than Jerry Rubin's. That I came eventually to despise Johnson did not mean that I was impervious, ever, to his sense, which I took to be genuine, that the America whose leader he was simply could not be on the wrong side, even if for some reason everything seemed to look that way. No, no, cried the America of World War II—"Say it ain't so, Lyndon." Instead, he went on television and said it was, in the only real way he was ever able to admit it publicly, by washing his hands of the whole hideous mess. L.B.J., the last of the decade's great demythologizers. *Après lui,* the bullshit artists once again.

All that by way of background. Here's what I'm getting at: the fierce, oftentimes wild and pathological assault launched in the sixties against venerable American institutions and beliefs and, more to the point, the emergence of a counterhistory, or *countermythology,* to challenge the mythic sense of itself the country had when the decade opened with General Eisenhower, our greatest World War II hero, still presiding—it was these social phenomena that furnished me with a handle by which to take hold of baseball, of all things, and place it at the center of a novel. It was not a matter of demythologizing baseball—there was nothing in that to get fired up about—but of discovering in baseball a means to dramatize the *struggle* between the benign national myth of itself that a great power prefers to perpetuate, and the relentlessly insidious, very nearly demonic reality (like the kind we had known in the sixties) that will not give an inch in behalf of that idealized mythology.

Now, to admit to the discovery of thematic reverberations, of depth, of overtone, finally of meaning, would seem to contradict what I have said about wanting fundamentally to be unserious; and it does. Yet out of this opposition, or rather out of the attempt to maintain these contradictory impulses in a state of contentious equi-librium, the book evolved. Sustaining this sort of opposition is not simply a mechanical means of creating literary energy, either; rather, it is itself an attempt to be simultaneously as loyal to one's doubts and uncertainties as to one's convictions, of being as skepti-cal of the "truth" turned up by imagination as of the actuality that may have served as inspiration or model. A full-scale farce is rarely directed outward only, but takes its own measure as well; much of its inventiveness goes into calling itself into question as a statement, satiric, humane, or what have you. In this sense, the genre is the mes-sage, and the message is agnostic: "I tell you (and I tell you and I tell you), I don't know."

An early reader of my book, meaning to offer praise, told me, "This is what America is really like." I would have been happier had he said, "This is what a farce written in America is really like." Now *that* is praise. I don't claim to know what America is "really like." *Not* knowing, or no longer knowing for sure, is just what perplexes many of the people who live and work here and consider this country home. That, if I may say so, is why I invented that paranoid fantasist Word Smith—the narrator who calls himself Smitty—to be (pur-portedly) the author of *The Great American Novel*. What he describes is what America is really like to one like *him*.

I do not mean by this to disown the novel, or to pretend, defen-sively, that it is what is called a put-on. Whom would I be trying to put on? And why? By attributing the book to Smitty, I intended, among other things, to call into question the novel's "truthful-ness"—to mock any claim the book might appear to make to be delivering up *the* answer—though in no way is this meant to discredit the book itself. The idea is simply to move off the question "What is America really like?" and on to the kind of fantasy (or rewriting of history) that a question so troublesome and difficult has tended of late to inspire. I would not want to have to argue that Smitty's is the true dream of our lives, his paranoia a wedge into the enigmatic

American reality. I would claim, however, that his are not so unlike the sort of fantasies with which the national imagination began to be plagued during this last demythologizing decade of disorder, upheaval, assassination, and war.

I finally anchored this book in the investigations into Communist activities conducted by the House Committee on Un-American Activities in order to give Smitty a break, too. As far off in an American never-never land as he may sound with his story of the destruction of the imaginary Ruppert Mundys of the imaginary Patriot League, his version of history has its origins in something that we all recognize as *having taken place,* and moreover, at a level of bizarre, clownish inventiveness similar to much of the "real" American history that Smitty has obviously invented out of whole cloth. I was trying, then, at the conclusion of the book, to establish a kind of passageway from the imaginary that comes to seem real to the real that comes to seem imaginary, a continuum between the credible incredible and the incredible credible. This strikes me as an activity something like what many of our deranged countrymen must engage in every morning, reading the newspaper on the one hand and swooning over the prophetic ingenuity of their paranoia on the other. Truly, America *is* the Land of Opportunity—now even the nuts are getting an even break.

So, to conclude: Smitty is to my mind correct in aligning himself with Melville and Hawthorne, whom he calls "my precursors, my kinsmen." They too were in search of some encapsulating fiction, or legend, that would, in its own oblique, charged, and cryptic way, constitute the "truth" about the national disease. Smitty's book, like those of his illustrious forebears, attempts to imagine a myth of an ailing America; my own is to some extent an attempt to imagine a book about imagining that American myth.

On *My Life as a Man*

In My Life as a Man, *as in other books of yours, there is an important relationship between a character and his psychoanalyst. Why is that a recurring situation in your work? Of what particular interest is it to you and what uses do you put it to?*

I take it you're referring to four books: *Letting Go,* where Libby Herz, a frantic young woman in despair over her husband's increasing remoteness and gloom, spends a hapless hour with an analyst in Chicago; *Portnoy's Complaint,* a novel cast in the form of an analytic monologue by a lust-ridden, mother-addicted young Jewish bachelor; *The Breast,* in which David Kepesh, an intelligent professor of imaginative literature who has turned overnight into an enormous female breast, engages in a daily dialectic with his former analyst about his new condition; and *My Life as a Man,* in which Peter Tarnopol, a baffled writer and humiliated husband, suffers a breakdown following the collapse of a disastrous marriage and, during the long effort to make sense of what happened, struggles with his doctor over fundamental differences of opinion (and values and language), a struggle that eventually destroys their genuine, therapeutic friendship.

The interviewer is Martha Saxton. (1974)

All of these characters, in pain and in trouble, turn to doctors because they believe psychoanalysis may help them from going under completely. *Why* they believe this is a subject I haven't the space to go into here, nor is it what I've given most thought to in these books. I've mainly been interested in the extent to which unhappy people *do* define themselves as "ill" or agree to view themselves as "patients," and in what each then makes of the treatment prescribed. The connection between patient and analyst varies considerably from one book to the next, as do the relationships, say, between the lay Catholics and their priests in the stories of J. F. Powers.

Until *My Life as a Man,* the psychoanalyst in my fiction hasn't been much of a character, in the conventional novelistic sense. In *Portnoy's Complaint,* Dr. Spielvogel was nothing more than he for whom Portnoy re-enacted the drama, or vaudeville skit, of his life. Much like the priest discreetly hidden away in the confessional (or the audience beyond the footlights), Spielvogel is silent until the last mortifying detail (or routine) has been extracted from the babbling sinner/ showman seeking absolution/applause. Moreover, it is a highly stylized confession that this imaginary Spielvogel gets to hear, and I would guess that it bears about as much resemblance to the drift and tone of what a real psychopathologist hears in his everyday life as a love sonnet does to the iambs and dactyls that lovers whisper into one another's ears in motel rooms and over the phone.

What I was looking for when I wrote *Portnoy's Complaint* was a stratagem that would permit me to bring into my fiction the sort of intimate, shameful sexual detail, and coarse, abusive sexual language, that had largely been beside the point of my first three books. One would just as soon not—if one has a sense of propriety, that is— serve vodka out of a milk carton: what I wanted was the appropriate vessel for the unpalatable stuff that I was ready to dispense. And I found it, I thought, in the *idea* of the psychoanalytic session, wherein pile driving right on through the barriers of good taste and discretion is considered central to the task at hand. In *Portnoy's Complaint* I did not set out to write a book "about" an analysis, but utilized the permissive conventions of the patient-analyst situation to get at material that had previously been inaccessible to me, and that in another fictional environment would have struck me as pornographic, exhibitionistic, and nothing *but* obscene.

In *The Breast,* another analyst appears, this time one who speaks, and does so more or less in the voice of enlightened common sense. Dr. Klinger favors the cadences and vocabulary of psychotherapeutic demystification. The difficulty is that the affliction confronting him—Kepesh's transformation into a human-size mammary gland—is bottomlessly mysterious and horrifying. But to the suffering patient, what affliction isn't? Then too, in the course of a day, a doctor in Klinger's line of work dutifully hears out half a dozen patients who, if they do not consider themselves to be breasts, imagine with some degree of conviction that they are testicles, or vaginas, or bellies, or brains, or buttocks, or noses, or two left feet, or all thumbs, or all heart, or all eyes, or what-have-you. "I'm a prick! She's a cunt! My partner is an asshole!" Granted, say the doctors Klinger, but nonetheless what shall you do out in the great world where you are obliged to call yourself (and may even wish others to refer to you) by another name?

Dr. Klinger prevails. By attending to the doctor's homely, anti-apocalyptic, demystifying view of things ("Come off it, Mr. Kepesh," he has the nerve to say to the surreal sexual object), David Kepesh manages to maintain a tenuous hold, not only on his sanity—which is just the half of it for this former literature professor—but on his moral dignity.

The Dr. Spielvogel who turns up as the analyst in *My Life as a Man* has no such luck with his patient—nor does the patient (in this case Peter Tarnopol) with his doctor. In the end there is no meeting of minds or capitulation on either side to the other's sense of reality. And not because Spielvogel is a fool and a tyrant—he is neither the All-Knowing Analyst out of patient fairy tales, nor is he the Big Bad

Idiot Analyst out of anti-Freudian folklore—or because Tarnopol lacks sympathy for the man or the method. If Tarnopol cannot agree to see himself as Spielvogel sees him, it is partly because Tarnopol cannot for any length of time see himself as Tarnopol sees Tarnopol either. Tarnopol the patient finally rejects Spielvogel's version of him and his world as so much fiction; but as a novelist who takes himself and his personal life as his subject, so too does he reject his *own* fictions as so much fiction.

Now, how Portnoy conceives of Portnoy is not much of an issue in that book (at least not until the doctor delivers, at the conclusion, his one and only line). Portnoy knows precisely how to present himself—a good part of his complaint is that his sense of himself, his past, and his ridiculous destiny is so *fixed*. In *The Breast*, Kepesh must be educated to understand what he is, and very much against the grain of his own defiant hopefulness. Only by the end of the book does he capitulate and take the doctor's word for what has seemed so utterly impossible all along, accepting finally both the preposterous description of what he's become and the equally preposterous prescription as to what now to do about it ("Tolerate it"). But for Tarnopol the presentation or description of himself is what is most problematical—and what remains unresolved. To my mind, Tarnopol's attempt to realize himself with the right words—as earlier in life he attempted realizing himself through the right deeds—is what's at the heart of the book, and accounts for my joining his fictions about his life with his autobiography. When the novel is considered in its entirety, I hope it will be understood as Tarnopol's struggle to achieve a description.

After Eight Books

Your first book, Goodbye, Columbus, *won the most distinguished American literary honor—the National Book Award—in 1960; you were twenty-seven years old at that time. A few years later, your fourth book,* Portnoy's Complaint, *achieved a critical and popular success—and notoriety—that must have altered your personal life, and your awareness of yourself as a writer with a great deal of public "influence." Do you believe that your sense of having experienced life, its ironies and depths, has been at all intensified by your public reputation? Have you come to know more because of your fame? Or has the experience of enduring the bizarre projections of others been at times more than you can reasonably handle?*

My public reputation—as distinguished from the reputation of my work—is something I try to have as little to do with as I can. I know it's out there, of course—a concoction spawned by *Portnoy's Complaint* and compounded largely out of the fantasies that book gave rise to because of its "confessional" strategy, and also because of its financial success. There isn't much else it can be based on, since outside of print I lead virtually no *public* life at all. I don't consider this a sacrifice, because I never much wanted one. Nor have I the temperament for it—in part this accounts for why I went into fiction

The interviewer here is Joyce Carol Oates. (1974)

writing (and not acting, which interested me for a while in college) and why writing in a room by myself is practically my whole life. I enjoy solitude the way some people I know enjoy parties. It gives me an enormous sense of personal freedom and an exquisitely sharp sense of being alive—and of course it provides me with the quiet and the breathing space I need to get my imagination going and my work done. I take no pleasure at all in being a creature of fantasy in the minds of those who don't know me—which is largely what the fame you're talking about consists of.

For the solitude (and the birds and the trees), I have lived mostly in the country for the last five years, right now more than half of each year in a wooded rural region a hundred miles from New York. I have some six or eight friends scattered within a twenty-mile radius of my house, and I see them a few evenings a month for dinner. Otherwise I write during the day, walk at the end of the afternoon, and read at night. Almost the whole of my life in public takes place in a classroom—I teach one semester of each year. I began to earn my living teaching full-time in 1956, and though I can now live on my writing income, I have stayed with teaching more or less ever since. In recent years my public reputation has sometimes accompanied me into the classroom, but usually after the first few weeks, when the students observe that I have neither exposed myself nor set up a stall and attempted to interest them in purchasing my latest book, whatever anxieties or illusions about me they may have had begin to recede and I am largely allowed to be a literature teacher instead of Famous.

"Enduring the bizarre projections of others" isn't just something that famous novelists have to contend with, of course. Defying a multitude of bizarre projections, or submitting to them, would seem to me at the heart of everyday living in America, with its ongoing demand to be something palpable and identifiable. Everyone is invited to imitate in conduct and appearance the grossest simplifications of self that are mercilessly projected upon them by the mass media and

advertising, while they must, of course, also contend with the myriad expectations that they arouse in those with whom they have personal and intimate associations. In fact, these "bizarre projections"
arising out of ordinary human relations were a concern of mine in
My Life as a Man—a novel that might have been called *"Don't Do with
Me What You Will."*

*Since you have become fairly well established (I hesitate to use that unpleas-
ant word "successful"), have less-established writers tried to use you, to
manipulate you into endorsing their work? Do you feel you have received
any especially unfair or inaccurate critical treatment? I am also interested
in whether you have come to feel more communal now than you did when
you were beginning as a writer.*

No, I haven't felt, nor have I been, "manipulated" into endorsing
the work of less-established writers. I don't like to give "endorse-
ments" for advertising or promotion purposes—not because I'm shy
about my enthusiasms, but because I can't say in fifteen or twenty
words what I find special or noteworthy about a book. If I particularly like something I've read, I write the writer directly. At times when
I've been especially taken by an aspect of some writer's work which I
think is likely to be overlooked or neglected, I've tried to help by
writing longish paragraphs for the writer's hardcover publishers,
who always promise to use the endorsement in its entirety. However,
eventually—since it's a fallen world we live in—what started out as
seventy-five words of critical appreciation seems to wind up on the
paperback-edition cover as a two-word cry of marquee ecstasy.

Since becoming "fairly well established" I've written paragraphs
on behalf of books by five writers: Edward Hoagland (*Notes from the
Century Before*), Sandra Hochman (*Walking Papers*), Alison Lurie (*The
War Between the Tates*), Thomas Rogers (*Pursuit of Happiness* and *The
Confession of a Child of the Century*), and Richard Stern (*1968* and
Other Men's Daughters). In 1972, *Esquire*, for a feature they were plan-

ning, asked four "older writers" (as they called them), Isaac Bashevis Singer, Leslie Fiedler, Mark Schorer, and me, each to write a brief essay about a writer under thirty-five he admired. Singer wrote about Barton Midwood, Fiedler about Bill Hutton, Schorer about Judith Rascoe, and I chose to write about Alan Lelchuk.* I'd met him when we were both guests over a long stretch at Yaddo, and afterwards had read in manuscript his novel *American Mischief,* which I admired considerably. I restricted myself to a description and a somewhat close analysis of the book, which, though it hardly consisted of unqualified praise, nonetheless caused some consternation among the Secret Police. One prominent newspaper reviewer wrote in his column that "one would have to go into the Byzantine feuds and piques of the New York literary scene" to be able to figure out why I had written my fifteen-hundred-word essay, which led the reviewer to describe me as a "blurb writer." That I might simply have enjoyed a new writer's novel, and like Singer, Schorer, and Fiedler, taken *Esquire*'s invitation as an occasion to talk about his work, never occurred to him. Too unconspiratorial.

In recent years I've run into somewhat more of this kind of "manipulation"—malicious hallucination mixed with childish naïveté and disguised as Inside Dope—from marginal "literary" journalists (the "lice of literature," Dickens called them) than from working writers, young *or* established. In fact, I don't think there's been a time since graduate school when genuine literary fellowship has been such a valuable and necessary part of my life. Contact with writers I admire or toward whom I feel a kinship is precisely my way *out* of isolation and furnishes me with whatever sense of community I have. I seem almost always to have had at least one writer I could talk to turn up wherever I happened to be teaching or living. These novelists I've met along the way—in Chicago, Rome, London, Iowa City, at Yaddo, in New York, in Philadelphia—are by and large people I

* See p. 232.

continue to correspond with, exchange finished manuscripts with, try out ideas on, listen to, and visit, if I can, once or twice a year. By now, some of us whose friendships go back a ways have fallen out of sympathy with the direction the other's work has taken, but since we seem not to have lost faith in one another's integrity or good will, the opposition tends to be without the mandarin superiority, or academic condescension (or theoretical hobbyhorsing, or competitive preening, or merciless gravity), that sometimes tends to characterize criticism written by professionals for *their* public. Novelists are, as a group, the most *interesting* readers of novels that I have yet come across.

In a sharp and elegantly angry little essay called "Reviewing," Virginia Woolf once suggested that book journalism ought to be abolished (because 95 percent of it was worthless) and that the serious critics who do reviewing should put themselves out to hire to the novelists, who have a strong interest in knowing what an honest and intelligent reader thinks about their work. For a fee the critic—to be called a "consultant, expositor or expounder"—would meet privately and with some formality with the writer, and "for an hour," writes Virginia Woolf, "they would consult upon the book in question. . . . The consultant would speak honestly and openly, because the fear of affecting sales and of hurting feelings would be removed. Privacy would lessen the shop-window temptation to cut a figure, to pay off scores. . . . He could thus concentrate upon the book itself, and upon telling the author why he likes or dislikes it. The author would profit equally. . . . He could state his case. He could point to his difficulties. He would no longer feel, as so often at present, that the critic is talking about something that he has not written. . . . An hour's private talk with a critic of his own choosing would be incalculably more valuable than the five hundred words of criticism mixed with extraneous matter that is now allotted him."

A very good idea. It surely would have seemed to me worth a hundred dollars to sit for an hour with Edmund Wilson and hear everything he had to say about a book of mine—nor would I have objected to paying to hear whatever Virginia Woolf might have had to say to me about *Portnoy's Complaint,* if she had been willing to accept less than all the tea in China to undertake that task. Nobody minds swallowing his medicine, if it is prescribed by a real doctor. One of the nicer side effects of this system is that since nobody wants to throw away his hard-earned money, most of the quacks and the incompetents would be driven out of business.

As for "especially unfair critical treatment"—of course my blood has been drawn, my anger aroused, my feelings hurt, my patience tried, etc., and in the end, I have wound up enraged most of all with myself, for allowing blood to be drawn, anger aroused, feelings hurt, patience tried. When the "unfair critical treatment" has been associated with charges too serious to ignore—accusations against me, say, of "anti-Semitism"—then, rather than fuming to myself, I have answered the criticism at length and in public. Otherwise I fume and forget it; and keep forgetting it, until actually—miracle of miracles— I *do* forget it.

Lastly: who gets "critical treatment" anyway? Why dignify with such a phrase most of what is written about fiction? What one gets, as far as I can see, is what Edmund Wilson describes as a "collection of opinions by persons of various degrees of intelligence who have happened to have some contact with [the writer's] book."

What Edmund Wilson says is true, ideally, yet many writers are influenced by the "critical treatment" they receive. The fact that Goodbye, Columbus *was singled out for extraordinarily high praise must have encouraged you, to some extent; and the critics, certainly, guided a large number of readers in your direction. I began reading your work in 1959 and was impressed from the start by your effortless (effortless-seeming, perhaps) synthesis of the colloquial, the comic, the near-tragic, the intensely moral . . . within wonderfully readable structures that had the feel of being traditional stories, while being at the same time rather revolutionary. I am thinking of*

"The Conversion of the Jews," "Eli, the Fanatic," and the novella, "Good-bye, Columbus," among others.

One of the prominent themes in your writing seems to be the hero's recognition of a certain loss in his life, along with a regret for the loss, and finally an ironic "acceptance" of this regret (as if the hero had to go this way, fulfill this aspect of his destiny, no matter how painful it might be). Consider the young girl in Goodbye, Columbus *and her twin in* My Life as a Man, *both of whom are eventually rejected. But the loss might have broader emotional and psychological implications as well—that is, the beautiful too-young girl must have represented qualities that were also transpersonal.*

1. You correctly spot the return of an old character in a new incarnation. The *Goodbye, Columbus* heroine, inasmuch as she existed as a character at all or "represented" an alternative of consequence to the hero, is reconstituted (reappraised?) in *My Life as a Man* as Tarnopol's Dina Dornbusch, the "rich, pretty, protected, smart, sexy, adoring, young, vibrant, clever, confident, ambitious" Sarah Lawrence girl he gives up because she's not what the young literary fellow, in his romantic ambitiousness, recognizes as a "woman"—by which he means a knocked-around, on-her-own, volatile, combative, handful like Maureen.

Furthermore, Dina Dornbusch (incidental character that she is) is herself reconstituted and reappraised by Tarnopol, in the two short stories preceding his own autobiographical narrative (the "useful fictions"). First in "Salad Days," she appears as the licentious, childish, slavish, nice suburban Jewish girl whom he buggers under her family ping-pong table, and then, in "Courting Disaster," as the altogether attractive, astute, academically ambitious college senior who tells Professor Zuckerman, after he has severed relations with her—to take up with his own brand of "damaged" woman—that under all his flamboyant "maturity" he is "just a crazy little boy."

Both these characters are called Sharon Shatzky, and together stand in relation to Dina Dornbusch as fictional distillations do to their models in the unwritten world. These Sharons are what can happen to a Dina when a Tarnopol sets her free from his life to play the role such a woman does in his personal mythology. This mythology, this legend of the self (the useful fiction frequently mistaken by readers for veiled autobiography), is a kind of idealized architect's drawing for what one may have constructed—or is yet to construct—out of the materials actuality makes available. In this way, a Tarnopol's fiction is his *idea* of his fate.

Or, for all I know, the process works the other way around and the personal myth meant to *reveal* the secret workings of an individual destiny actually makes even *less* readable the text of one's own history. Thereby increasing bewilderment—causing one to tell the story once again, meticulously reconstructing the erasures on what may never have been a palimpsest to begin with.

Sometimes it seems to me that only the novelists and the nuts carry on in quite this way about living what is, after all, only a life—making the transparent opaque, the opaque transparent, the obscure obvious, the obvious obscure, etc. Delmore Schwartz, from "Genesis": "'Why must I tell, hysterical, this story/ And must, compelled, speak of such secrecies?/ . . . Where is my freedom, if I cannot resist/So much speech blurted out . . . ?/How long must I endure this show and sight/Of all I lived through, all I lived in: Why?'"

2. ". . . . loss, along with a regret for the loss, and finally an ironic 'acceptance' of this regret." You point to a theme I hadn't thought of as such before—and that I'd prefer to qualify some. Of course Tarnopol is relentlessly kicking himself for his mistake, but it is just those kicks (and the accompanying screams) that reveal to him how strongly determined by character, how characteristically Tarnopolian, that mistake was. He is his mistake and his mistake is him. "This me who is me being me and none other!" The last line of *My Life as*

a Man is meant to point up a harsher attitude toward the self, and the history it has necessarily compiled, than "ironic 'acceptance'" suggests.

To my mind it is Bellow, in his last two pain-filled novels, who has sounded the theme of "loss . . . regret for the loss, and . . . ironic 'acceptance' of the regret"—as he did early on (and less convincingly, I thought) at the conclusion to *Seize the Day,* whose final event I always found a little forced, and then further schmaltzed-up with its sudden swell of *Urn-Burial* prose to elevate Tommy Wilhelm's misery. I prefer the conclusion of "Leaving the Yellow House," with its moving, ironic *rejection* of loss—no "sea-like music" necessary there to make the elemental human feeling felt. If there is an ironic acceptance of anything at the conclusion of *My Life as a Man* (or even along the way), it is of *the determined self.* And angry frustration, a deeply vexing sense of characterological enslavement, is strongly infused in that ironic acceptance. Thus the exclamation mark.

I have always been drawn to a passage that comes near the end of *The Trial,* the chapter where K., in the cathedral, looks up toward the priest with a sudden infusion of hope—that passage is pertinent to what I'm trying to say here, particularly by the word "determined," which I mean in both senses: driven, resolute and purposive—yet utterly fixed in position. "If the man would only quit his pulpit, it was not impossible that K. could obtain decisive and acceptable counsel from him which might, for instance, point the way, not toward some influential manipulation of the case, but toward a circumvention of it, a breaking away from it altogether, a mode of living completely outside the jurisdiction of the Court. This possibility must exist, K. had of late given much thought to it."

As who hasn't of late? Enter Irony when the man in the pulpit turns out to be oneself. If only one *could* quit one's pulpit, one might well obtain decisive and acceptable counsel. How to devise a mode of living completely outside the jurisdiction of the Court when the

Court is of one's own devising? It is the ironic acceptance of the loss that follows *that* struggle that I would point to as a theme of *My Life as a Man.*

Was it you, or someone more or less imitating you, who wrote about a boy who turned into a girl . . . ? How would that strike you, as a nightmare possibility? (I don't mean The Breast: *that seems to me a literary work, rather than a real psychological excursion, like other writings of yours.) Could you—can you—comprehend, by any extension of your imagination or your unconscious, a life as a woman?—a writing life as a woman? I know this is speculative but had you the choice, would you have wanted to live your life as a man, or as a woman (you could also check "other").*

Answer: Both. Like the hero-heroine of *Orlando.* That is, sequentially (if you can arrange it) rather than simultaneously. It wouldn't be much different from what it's like now, if I weren't able to measure the one life against the other. It would also be interesting not to be Jewish, after having spent a lifetime as a Jew. Arthur Miller imagines the reverse of this as a "nightmare possibility" in *Focus,* where an anti-Semite is taken by the world for the very thing he hates. However, I'm not talking about mistaken identity or skin-deep conversions, but magically becoming *totally* the other, all the while retaining knowledge of what it was to have been one's original self, wearing one's original badges of identity. In the early sixties I wrote (and shelved) a one-act play called *Buried Again,* about a dead Jewish man who, when given the chance to be reincarnated as a goy, refuses and is consigned forthwith to oblivion. I understand perfectly how he felt, though, if in the netherworld I am myself presented with this particular choice, I doubt that I will act similarly. I know this will produce a great outcry in *Commentary,* but alas, I shall have to learn to live with that the second time around as I did the first.

Sherwood Anderson wrote "The Man Who Turned Into a Woman," one of the most beautifully sensuous stories I've ever read, where the boy at one point sees himself in a barroom mirror as a girl, but I doubt if that's the piece of fiction you're referring to. Anyway, it wasn't I who wrote about such a sexual transformation, unless you're thinking of *My Life as a Man,* where the hero puts on his wife's undergarments one day, but just to take a sex *break.*

Of course I have written *about* women, some of whom I identified with strongly and, as it were, imagined myself into, while I was working. In *Letting Go,* Martha Reganhart and Libby Herz; in *When She Was Good,* Lucy Nelson and her mother; and in *My Life as a Man,* Maureen Tarnopol and Susan McCall (and Lydia Ketterer and the Sharon Shatzkys). However much or little I am able to extend my imagination to "comprehend . . . life as a woman" is demonstrated in those books.

I never did much with the girl in *Goodbye, Columbus,* which seems to me apprentice work and weak on character invention all around. Maybe I didn't get very far with her because she was cast as a pretty imperturbable type, a girl who knew how to get what she wanted and how to take care of herself, and as it happened, that didn't arouse my imagination much. Besides, the more I saw of young women who had flown the family nest—just what Brenda Patimkin decides *not* to do—the less imperturbable they seemed. Beginning with *Letting Go,* where I began to write about female vulnerability, and to see this vulnerability not only as it determined the lives of the women—who felt it frequently at the center of their being—but the men to whom they looked for love and support, the women became characters my imagination could take hold of and enlarge upon. How this vulnerability shapes their relations with men (each vulnerable in the style of *his* gender) is really at the heart of whatever story I've told about these eight woman characters.

In parts of Portnoy's Complaint, Our Gang, The Breast, *and most recently in your baseball extravaganza,* The Great American Novel, *you seem to be celebrating the sheer playfulness of the artist, an almost egoless condition in which, to use Thomas Mann's phrase, irony glances on all sides. There is a Sufi saying to the effect that the universe is "endless play and endless illusion"; at the same time, most of us experience it as deadly serious—and so we feel the need, indeed we cannot not feel the need, to be "moral" in our writing. Having been intensely "moral" in* Letting Go *and* When She Was Good, *and in much of* My Life as a Man, *and even in such a marvelously demonic work as the novella "On the Air," do you think your fascination with comedy is only a reaction against this other aspect of your personality, or is it something permanent? Do you anticipate (but no: you could not) some violent pendulum-swing back to what you were years ago, in terms of your commitment to "serious" and even Jamesian writing?*

Sheer Playfulness and Deadly Seriousness are my closest friends; it is with them that I take those walks in the country at the end of the day. I am also on friendly terms with Deadly Playfulness, Playful Playfulness, Serious Playfulness, Serious Seriousness, and Sheer Sheerness. From the last, however, I get nothing; he just wrings my heart and leaves me speechless.

I don't know whether the works you call comedies are so egoless. Isn't there really more *self* in the ostentatious display and assertiveness of *The Great American Novel* than in a book like *Letting Go*, say, where a devoted effort at self-removal and self-obliteration is necessary for the kind of investigation of self that goes on there? I think that the comedies may be the most ego-ridden of the lot; at least they aren't exercises in self-abasement. What made writing *The Great American Novel* such a pleasure for me was precisely the self-assertion that it entailed—or, if there is such a thing, self-pageantry. (Or will "showing off" do?) All sorts of impulses that I might once have put down as excessive, frivolous, or exhibitionistic I allowed to surface and proceed to their destination. When the censor in me rose responsibly in his robes to say, "Now look here, don't you think that's just a little too—" I would reply, from beneath the baseball cap I often wore when writing that book, "Precisely why it stays! Down in front!" The idea was to see what would emerge if everything that was "a little too" at first glance was permitted to go all the way. I understood that a disaster might ensue (I have been informed by some that it did), but I tried to put my faith in the fun that I was having. *Writing as pleasure.* Enough to make Flaubert spin in his grave.

I don't know what to expect or anticipate next. *My Life as a Man,* which I finished a few months ago, is a book I'd been writing, abandoning, and returning to ever since I published *Portnoy's Complaint.* Whenever I gave up on it I went to work on one of the "playful" books—maybe my despair over the difficulties with the one book accounted for why I wanted to be so playful in the others. At any rate, all the while that *My Life as a Man* was simmering away on the "moral" back burner, I wrote *Our Gang, The Breast,* and *The Great American Novel.* Right now nothing is cooking; at least none of the aromas have as yet reached me. *For the moment* this isn't distressing; I feel (again, for the moment) as though I've reached a natural break of sorts in my work, nothing nagging to be finished, nothing as yet pressing to be begun—only bits and pieces, fragmentary obsessions, bobbing into view, then sinking, for now, out of sight. Book ideas usually have come at me with all the appearance of pure accident or chance, though by the time I am done I can generally see how what has taken shape was spawned by the interplay between my previous fiction, recent undigested personal history, the circumstances of my immediate, everyday life, and the books I've been reading and teaching. The shifting relationship of these elements of experience brings the subject into focus, and then, by brooding, I find out how to take hold of it. I use "brooding" only to describe what this activity apparently looks like; inside I am actually feeling very Sufisticated indeed.

Interview with *Le Nouvel Observateur*

Before Portnoy's Complaint, *you had become a well-known writer. Portnoy made you famous all over the world, and in America you became a star. I even read that, while living in seclusion in the countryside, you were reported in the press to be going around Manhattan with Barbra Streisand. What does it mean to be a celebrity in a media-dominated country like the United States?*

For one thing, it's likely to mean that your income is going to go up, at least for a while. You may have become a celebrity just because your income has gone up. What distinguishes the merely famous from a celebrity or a star has usually to do with money, sex, or, as in my case, with both. I was said to have made a million dollars, and I was said to be none other than Portnoy himself. To become a celebrity is to become a brand name. There is Ivory soap, Rice Krispies, and Philip Roth. Ivory is the soap that floats; Rice Krispies the breakfast cereal that goes snap-crackle-pop; Philip Roth the Jew who masturbates with a piece of liver. And makes a million out of it. It isn't much more interesting, useful, or entertaining than that, not after the first half hour. The elevation to celebrity that's thought to bring

The interviewer is Alain Finkielkraut, a French journalist and author. (1981)

a writer a wider readership is just another obstacle that most readers have to overcome to achieve a direct perception of his work.

In the late sixties, sex was being touted as the *thing: the heart of life, the redeemer, et cetera.* Portnoy's Complaint, *with its obscene language and erotomaniacal candor, appeared to many to be in sympathy with that viewpoint. But then, in subsequent works, you have seemed to withdraw from this "advanced" position. Instead of Sade or Bataille you refer in essays and interviews to such sexually restrained authors as James, Chekhov, Gogol, Babel, Kafka. Do you mean to disappoint sex worshipers or to regain credibility in respectable society?*

I haven't withdrawn from any position because I never held any position. I would never have written a book as farcical as *Portnoy's Complaint* if I had any devotion to the cause of sex; causes don't thrive on self-satire. Causes expel you for self-satire. Nor was I a soldier in the cause of obscenity. Portnoy's obscenity is intrinsic to his situation, not to my style. I have no case to make for dirty words, in or out of fiction—only for the right of access to them when they seem to the point.

Three years after *Portnoy's Complaint,* I published a novella about a man who turns into a female breast. I imagined scenes more lurid and less lighthearted than anything in *Portnoy's Complaint* but not necessarily to the satisfaction of "sex worshipers." *The Breast* has even been read as a critique of sexual salvationism.

Several of your novels are written in the first person. And their heroes have a lot in common with·you. Portnoy is brought up in Newark, much as you were; David Kepesh in The Professor of Desire *is a professor and teaches the same literature courses that you have taught at the University of Pennsylvania. Your recent book* The Ghost Writer *begins some twenty years ago with a young writer's search for a spiritual father who will validate his art. This young writer, Nathan Zuckerman, has just published a group of stories that remind us necessarily of your first work,* Goodbye, Columbus. *Does all this mean that we should read your books as confession, as autobiography barely disguised?*

You should read my books as fiction, demanding the pleasures that fiction can yield. I have nothing to confess and no one I want to confess to. Nor has anyone asked me to make a confession or promised forgiveness if I do so. As for my autobiography, I can't begin to tell you how dull it would be. My autobiography would consist almost entirely of chapters about me sitting alone in a room looking at a typewriter. The uneventfulness of my autobiography would make Beckett's *The Unnamable* read like Dickens.

This is not to say that I haven't drawn heavily from my general experience to feed my imagination. But this isn't because I care to reveal myself, exhibit myself, or even express myself. It's so that I can invent myself. Invent my selves. Invent my worlds. To label books like mine "autobiographical" or "confessional" is not only to falsify their suppositional nature but, if I may say so, to slight whatever artfulness leads some readers to think that they must be autobiographical. You don't create the aura of intimacy by dropping your pants in public; do that and most people will instinctively look away.

These words *confessional* and *autobiographical* constitute yet another obstacle between the reader and the work—in this case, by strengthening the temptation, all too strong in a distracted audience anyway, to trivialize fiction by turning it into gossip.

Not that this is anything new. Rereading Virginia Woolf these last few months, I came across this passage of dialogue in *The Voyage Out,* her 1915 novel. The words are spoken by a character who wants to write books. "Nobody cares. All you read a novel for is to see what sort of person the writer is, and, if you know him, which of his friends he's put in. As for the novel itself, the whole conception, the way one's seen the thing, felt about it, made it stand in relation to other things, not one in a million cares for that."

"L'art, c'est une idée qu'on exagère," said Gide. One exaggeration gave birth to Portnoy, and we know his destiny: this character has become an archetype. Another exaggeration produced Maureen, the majestically deranged woman, the Fury of jealousy and paranoia in My Life as a Man. *But it is as if* Portnoy *had exhausted the curiosity of the reader in France.* My Life as a Man, *a book of yours that I much admire, is virtually unknown here. How was it received in America—for instance, by women's lib?*

I can only tell you that a few years after the appearance of *My Life as a Man,* a front-page article by a woman activist appeared in the influential Manhattan weekly *The Village Voice,* bearing this two-fisted headline: WHY DO THESE MEN HATE WOMEN? Beneath were photographs of Saul Bellow, Norman Mailer, Henry Miller, and me. *My Life as a Man* was the most damaging evidence brought against me by the prosecution.

Why? Because in 1974 the world had just recently discovered that women were good and only good, persecuted and only persecuted, exploited and only exploited, and I had depicted a woman who was not good, who persecuted others and who exploited others—and that spoiled everything. A woman without conscience, a woman who misused every power, a vindictive woman with limitless cunning and wild, unfocused hatred and rage—and to depict such a woman was contrary to the new ethics and to the revolution that espoused them. It was antirevolutionary. It was on the wrong side of the cause. It was taboo.

Of course, My Life as a Man *is more than a challenge to feminist piety. In one scene Maureen buys a sample of urine from a pregnant black woman in order to pass the rabbit test and trick Peter Tarnopol into marriage. In*

*another scene—their last brutal fight—when beaten by him, Maureen defe-
cates in her pants, thus depriving them both of tragedy at the most painful
moment of their marriage. Surely this novel is intended as a challenge to the
pieties of American culture in general, to the moralizing and corny sentimentality so pervasive there. Do you agree with this interpretation?*

That it was intended, conceived, realized, as a challenge? No. I am
more ambitious than that. You may be further describing the way it
was received, however. The book was reviewed harshly, sold poorly,
and went out of print in a mass paperback edition shortly after it was
published, the first book of mine ever to disappear like that. It isn't
for me to speculate in public on why that should have happened. I
leave that to Tocquevilles like you. If it's any comfort to you as a
Frenchman, the book is almost as unknown in my country as in yours.

*You seem deeply concerned with the obstacles that our society places
between a work of art and its readers. We have talked about fame and the
media's distortion of the writer's purpose. We have talked about gossip, the
middlebrow distortion that reduces reading to voyeurism. We have talked
about piety, the activist distortion that would exploit literature as propaganda. But there is yet another obstacle, is there not? The structuralist
cliché, which is criticized in his introductory lecture by David Kepesh, your
professor of desire: "You will discover (and not all will approve) that I do
not hold with certain of my colleagues who tell us that literature, in its most
valuable and intriguing moments, is fundamentally non-referential. I may
come before you in my jacket and tie, I may address you as madam and sir,
but I am going to request nonetheless that you restrain yourself from talking
about 'structure,' 'form,' and 'symbols' in my presence." What makes the
principles of the literary avant-garde so pernicious?*

I don't think of the words *structure, form,* and *symbol* as the property of the avant-garde. In America they are usually the stock-in-
trade of the most naive high school literature teachers. When I teach,

I am not so gentle as my professor of desire, Mr. Kepesh: I *forbid* my students to use those words, on pain of expulsion. This results in a charming improvement in their English and even, sometimes, in their thinking.

As for structuralism: It really hasn't played any part in my life. I'm afraid I can't satisfy you with a vituperative denunciation.

I was not expecting a vituperative denunciation. I was just interested in what your idea of reading is.

I read fiction to be freed from my own suffocatingly narrow perspective on life and to be lured into imaginative sympathy with a fully developed narrative point of view not my own. It's the same reason that I write.

How would you assess the sixties now? Was it a decade of liberation that gave permission to write as one felt and to live the life one wanted, or an era of arrogance, of narrow new dogmas to which you had better pay tribute if you didn't want to get into trouble?

I have no judgment to make of something so colossal as ten years of world history. As an American citizen I was appalled and mortified by the war in Vietnam, frightened by the urban violence, sickened by the assassinations, confused by the student uprisings, sympathetic to the libertarian pressure groups, delighted by the pervasive theatricality, disheartened by the rhetoric of the causes, excited by the sexual display, and enlivened by the general air of confrontation and change. During the last years of the decade, I was writing *Portnoy's Complaint*, a raucous, aggressive, abrasive book whose conception and composition were undoubtedly influenced by the mood of the times. I don't think I would or could have written that book in that way a decade earlier, not only because of the social, moral, and cultural patterns that prevailed in the fifties but because, as a younger writer still strongly involved with literary studies, I had pledged my loyalty to a more morally earnest line of fiction.

But by the mid-sixties, I had already written two indisputably earnest books—*Letting Go* and *When She Was Good*—and was dying to turn my attention to something else, something that would call into play a more playful side of my talent. I now had the confidence to reveal that side in my fiction, in part because I was into my thirties and no longer had to work quite so hard as I did in my twenties at establishing my maturity credentials, and in part because of the infectious volatility of a moment that was inspiring feats of self-transformation and self-experimentation in virtually everyone.

You are know to us here in France as an American-Jewish writer—even as a member (along with Bellow and Malamud) of a so-called New York–Jewish school. Do you accept this label?

It's a journalistic cliché almost wholly devoid of content and inaccurate in the bargain. To begin with, only Malamud, of the three of us, comes from New York and spent his childhood there, in a poor neighborhood in Brooklyn. Virtually all of Malamud's adult life has been spent far away from New York, teaching at colleges in Oregon and Vermont. Bellow was born in Montreal and has lived almost all of his life in Chicago, eight hundred miles west of New York, a city as different from New York as Marseilles is from Paris or Manchester is from London. The book that brought him his first popular recognition, *Adventures of Augie March,* doesn't begin "I am a Jew, New York–born" but "I am an American, Chicago-born."

I was born in Newark, New Jersey, in my childhood an industrial port city of 150,000, mostly white and working class and, during the thirties and forties, still very much the provinces. The Hudson River, separating New York from New Jersey, could as easily have been the channel separating England from France—the anthropological divide was nearly that great, at least for people in our social position.

I lived in a lower-middle-class Jewish neighborhood in Newark until I was seventeen and went off to a small college in rural Pennsylvania that had been founded by Baptists in the mid-nineteenth century and still required of its students weekly attendance at chapel services. You couldn't have gotten further from the spirit of New York or of my Newark neighborhood. I wanted to find out what the rest of "America" was like. America in quotes—because it was still almost as much of an idea in my mind as it had been in Franz Kafka's. I was, at sixteen and seventeen, strongly under the sway of Thomas Wolfe and his lyrical sense of ordinary American life. I was still under the sway of the populist rhetoric that had risen out of the Depression and had been transformed by the patriotic fervor of World War II into the popular national myth about the "vastness" of the "land," the "rich diversity" of the "people." I'd read Sinclair Lewis and Sherwood Anderson and Mark Twain, and none of them led me to think that I would find "America" in New York City or even at Harvard. I could get a good education at Harvard, but secretly that wasn't what I was looking for.

So I chose an ordinary college in a pretty little town in a beautiful farming valley in central Pennsylvania, where I went to chapel once a week with the Christian boys and girls who were my classmates, youngsters from conventional backgrounds with predominantly philistine interests. My attempt to throw myself wholeheartedly into the traditional college life of that era lasted about six months, though chapel I could never stomach and I made it a habit conspicuously to be reading Schopenhauer in my pew during the sermon. I quickly took on the role of a Houhynhnm who had strayed onto the campus from *Gulliver's Travels*.

I spent the year after college in graduate school at the University of Chicago, then went to Washington, D.C., where I served my stint in the Army. In 1956 I returned to Chicago to teach at the university for two years. I began to write the stories that were collected in my first book, *Goodbye, Columbus*. When the book was accepted for publication in the summer of 1958, I resigned my job at the university to move to Manhattan to live the life of a young writer instead of a young professor. I lived on the Lower East Side for about six months, quite unhappily: I didn't like the "literary" scene; I wasn't interested in the publishing world; I couldn't master the styles of sexual combat in vogue there in the late fifties; and as I wasn't employed in merchandising, manufacturing, or finance, I didn't see much reason to stay. In the years that followed I lived in Rome, London, Iowa City, and Princeton. When I returned to New York in 1963, it was to get away from a marriage fifty miles south in Princeton, where I was teaching at the University, and then, later, to be psychoanalyzed. When the analysis was over—and the sixties were over—I left for the countryside, where I've lived ever since.

So New York is wrong. But the Jewish background is a major source of inspiration in your work. And what strikes me, from Goodbye, Columbus *to* The Ghost Writer, *is that as a novelist you are drawn to the Jewish world for all the comic possibilities it offers you, but not for the tragic ones, as might be expected. How do you explain that?*

By my biography.

Like Bellow and Malamud, I was born to Jewish parents and raised self-consciously as a Jew. I don't mean that I was raised according to Jewish traditions or raised to be an observant Jew but that I was born into the situation of being a Jew, and it did not take me long to be aware of its ramifications.

I lived in a predominantly Jewish neighborhood and attended public schools where about 90 percent of the pupils and the teachers were Jewish. To live in an ethnic or cultural enclave like this wasn't unusual for an urban American child of my generation. Newark is now a predominantly black city in a nightmarish state of decay, but until the late fifties it was demographically divided up like any number of American industrial cities that had been heavily settled in the late nineteenth and early twentieth centuries by waves of immigration from Germany, Ireland, Italy, Eastern Europe, and Russia. As soon as they could climb out of the slums where most of them began in America, more or less penniless, the immigrants formed neighborhoods within the cities where they could have the comfort and security of the familiar while undergoing the arduous transformations of a new way of life. These neighborhoods became rivalrous, competing, somewhat xenophobic subcultures within the city; each came to have an Americanized style of its own, and rather than dissolving when immigration virtually ceased, with the onset of World War I, they were transformed by their own growing affluence and stability into a permanent feature of American life.

My point is that my America in no way resembled the France or the England I would have grown up in as a Jewish child. It was not a matter of a few of us and all of them. What I saw was a few of *everyone*. Rather than growing up intimidated by the monolithic majority—or in defiance of it or in awe of it—I grew up feeling a part of the majority composed of the competing minorities, no one of which impressed me as being in a more enviable social or cultural position than our own. By the time I was ready for college, it was no wonder that I chose as I did: I had never really known at first hand any of these so-called Americans who were also said to be living in our country.

However, I had simultaneously been surrounded from birth with a *definition* of the Jew of such stunning emotional and historical proportions that I couldn't but be enveloped by it, contrary though it was to my own experience. This was the definition of the Jew as sufferer, the Jew as an object of ridicule, disgust, scorn, contempt, derision, of every heinous form of persecution and brutality, including murder. If the definition was not supported by my own experience, it surely was by the experience of my grandparents and their forebears, and by the experience of our European contemporaries. The disparity between this tragic dimension of Jewish life in Europe and the actualities of our daily lives as Jews in New Jersey was something that I had to puzzle over myself, and indeed, it was in the vast discrepancy between the two Jewish conditions that I found the terrain for my first stories and later for *Portnoy's Complaint*. Being a Jew in New Jersey was comical just because it was somehow bound up with these ghastly events.

And let me say something about "school," the last word in that useless label. One more nail in the coffin, then we'll be done with it.

Obviously, Bellow, Malamud, and I do not constitute a New York school of anything. If we constitute a Jewish school, it is only in the odd sense of having each found his own means of transcending the immediate parochialism of his Jewish background and transforming what once had been the imaginative property of anecdotal local colorists—and of apologists, nostalgists, publicists, and propagandists—into a fiction having entirely different intentions, but which nonetheless remains grounded in the colorful specificity of the locale. And even this similarity amounts to little when you think about all that must follow from our differences in age, upbringing, regional origin, class, temperament, education, intellectual interests, moral ideologies, literary antecedents, and artistic aims and ambitions.

Of course, The Ghost Writer *is not only about Jews. One of its subjects is what you have called "writing about Jews": young Nathan is accused, at the very outset of his career, of informing, of collaborating with the enemy, the anti-Semite. What makes writing about Jews so problematical?*

What makes it problematical is that Jews who register strong objections to what they see as damaging fictional portrayals of Jews are not necessarily philistine or paranoid. If their nerve endings are frayed, it is not without cause or justification. They don't want books that will give comfort to anti-Semites or confirm anti-Semitic stereotypes. They don't want books that will wound the feelings of Jews already victimized, if not by anti-Semitic persecution in one form or another, by the distaste for Jews still endemic in pockets of our society. They don't want books that offend Jewish self-esteem and that do little, if anything, to increase the prestige of Jews in the non-Jewish world. In the aftermath of the horrors that have befallen millions of Jews in this century, it isn't difficult to understand their concern. In fact, it's the *ease* with which one understands it that presents a problem of conflicting loyalties that's difficult to solve. For however much I may loathe anti-Semitism, however enraged I may be when faced with the slightest real manifestation of it, however much I might wish to console its victims, my job in a work of fiction is not to offer consolation to Jewish sufferers or to mount an attack upon their persecutors or to make the Jewish case to the undecided. My Jewish critics, and in America there are many, would tell you that I bend over backward not to make the Jewish case. After more than twenty years of disagreement with them on this subject, I can only say that that is the way they see it and not the way I see it. It's a fruitless discussion—which is exactly what makes it so problematical to write about Jews.

Having read The Ghost Writer *before our talk, I took it for granted that you were the young writer Nathan Zuckerman and that Lonoff—the austere, ascetic older writer Zuckerman so much admires—was an imaginary amalgam of Malamud and Singer. But I see now that, not unlike Lonoff, you live like a semi-recluse in New England; you seem to write and read most of the time—in other words, to spend most of your life, in Lonoff's self-descriptive phrase, "turning sentences around." Are you Lonoff? Or, to put it less bluntly: Do you share the ideal of the writer as hermit, a self-ordained monk who must remain secluded from life for the sake of art?*

Art is life too, you know. Solitude is life, meditation is life, pretending is life, supposition is life, contemplation is life, language is life. Is there less life in turning sentences around than in manufacturing automobiles? Is there less life in reading *To the Lighthouse* than in milking a cow or throwing a hand grenade? The isolation of a literary vocation—the isolation that involves far more than sitting alone in a room for most of one's waking existence—has as much to do with life as accumulating sensations, or multinational corporations, out in the great hurly-burly. It seems to me that it's largely through art that I have a chance of being taken to the heart at least of my *own* life.

Am I Lonoff? Am I Zuckerman? Am I Portnoy? I could be, I suppose. I may be yet. But as of now I am nothing like so sharply delineated as a character in a book. I am still amorphous Roth.

You seem to me to be made particularly rebellious by the strain of sentimental moralizing in American culture. At the same time, you strenuously claim your American heritage. My last question is very simple, if not simplistic: What does America mean to you?

America allows me the greatest possible freedom to practice my vocation. America has the only literary audience that I can ever imagine taking any sustained pleasure in my fiction. America is the place I know best in the world. It's the *only* place I know in the world. My consciousness and my language were shaped by America. I'm an American writer in ways that a plumber isn't an American plumber or a miner an American miner or a cardiologist an American cardiologist. Rather, what the heart is to the cardiologist, the coal to the miner, the kitchen sink to the plumber, America is to me.

Interview with *The London Sunday Times*

I imagine you get annoyed when critics read this trilogy as straight confession. Zuckerman as Philip Roth. Yet sometimes it's hard not to read it this way.

It's very easy to read it this way. This is the easiest possible way to read. It makes it just like reading the evening paper. I only get annoyed because it isn't the evening paper that I've written. Shaw wrote to Henry James, "People don't want works of art from you, they want help." They also want confirmation of their beliefs, including their beliefs about you.

But surely the journalistic approach is inescapable—unless the reader forgets everything he knows or has read about you, Philip Roth.

If my books are so persuasive that they are utterly convinced, these readers, that I give them life red hot, untransformed, as it's lived, well, I suppose that's not the worst cross any novelist has had to bear. Better than their not believing me at all. The fashion now is to praise books you don't believe in. "This is really a great book—I don't believe in it at all." But I *want* belief, and I work to try to get it.

The interviewer is the English poet, critic, and biographer, Ian Hamilton. (1984)

If all these subtle readers can see in my work is my biography, then they are simply numb to fiction—numb to impersonation, to ventriloquism, to irony, numb to the thousand observations of human life on which a book is built, numb to all the delicate devices by which novels create the illusion of a reality more like the real than our own. End of lecture. Or shall we pursue this further?

Since you're enjoying it so, why not a little further? In The Anatomy Lesson *there is the character Milton Appel, a distinguished and powerful literary critic. Reviewers have confidently identified him as Irving Howe. I won't ask you to confirm or deny this. I do think, though, that once the identification is made, it becomes hard for the reader not to pursue the biographical interest (i.e., Roth versus Howe) at the expense, sometimes, of the fictional clash between Zuckerman and Appel.*

I wouldn't write a book to win a fight. I'd rather go 15 rounds with Sonny Liston. At least it would be over in an hour and I could go to bed. But a book takes me two years, if I'm lucky. Eight hours a day, seven days a week, 365 days a year, that's the only way I know how to do it. You have to sit alone in a room with only a tree out the window to talk to. You have to sit there churning out draft after draft of crap, waiting like a neglected baby for just one drop of mother's milk.

Anybody who did this to win a fight would have to be even more obsessive than I am. And angrier too. Milton Appel is not in this book because I was once demolished in print by Irving Howe. Appel is in this book because half of being a writer is being indignant. And being *right*. If you only knew how *right* we are. Show me a writer who isn't furious about being misrepresented, misread, or unread, and who isn't sure he's right.

You can't. My trilogy is about the vocation of an American writer, who is a Jew, to boot. If I left out the feuds and the paranoia and the brooding indignation, if I left out the fact that *they are wrong and we are right,* I would not be telling the whole unpretty truth about what goes on inside the heads of even Nobel Prize winners. I happen to know a couple of Nobel Prize winners. Move in very lofty circles, I do, and let me assure you, despite Their Great Contribution to Humanity, they are not so sweet and forgiving as you might expect. They too might not object if their critics were pelted with offal while being drawn down Fifth Avenue in cages.

Appel does come out of their argument rather well—better than Zucker-man, in fact. In their showdown telephone conversation one rather squirms for Zuckerman.

Of course you give the other guy the best lines. Otherwise it's a mug's game.

That old magnanimity.

Yes, my strong suit. Known for it. But it happens also to be a structural necessity. Tilting at yourself is *interesting,* a lot more interesting than winning. Let the vituperation flow and the mouth froth, but underestimate the opposition and you weaken the book. For me the work, the writing work, is transforming the I-madness into he-madness. Last point about Appel. Zuckerman's rage against Appel has less to do with Appel than with Z.'s physical condition. As if the willed self-absorption of the writer isn't imprisoning enough, there is the forced self-absorption in his chronic pain.

If it weren't for Zuckerman's physical pain, there'd be no Appel in this book. Zuckerman wouldn't have his harem of Florence Nightingales. Wouldn't decide at forty to become a doctor and bolt for Chicago, oozing Percodan at every pore. Forget Appel. This book is about physical pain and the havoc it wreaks on one's human credentials. If Zuckerman were in good fighting shape, why would he fight with his literary enemies on the Jewish magazine he calls *Foreskin?* He wouldn't bother.

But because the pain isn't diagnosed, because it's a mystery pain, we might tend to view it as symbolic pain, as pain visited upon him by the Appels, by the less than first-rate women, by the state of Zuckerman's career, and so on.

Symbolic pain? Could be for all I know. But in a real shoulder. What hurts is a real neck and shoulder. The trouble with pains is they don't feel symbolic, except maybe to critics.

What is your diagnosis?

I'm a writer, not a doctor. My diagnosis is that these things happen. When I was writing this book, I said to myself, "I want someone who has known chronic pain to be able to read this book and say, "That's it, that's what it's like." I wanted to be as realistic and *un*symbolic as possible. Not knowing the source of one's pain doesn't make it symbolic: it just makes it hurt more. Not that it would be a comfort to Zuckerman if he knew, say, that he had cancer. Sometimes knowing is worse, sometimes not knowing is worse. My book is about not knowing. Look, diagnoses abound in this book. Everybody *else* knows. They've all got him pegged, just like Appel. All his women know what's wrong with him. Even the trichologist who treats his baldness knows why he's losing his hair: "undue pressure." This book is *crammed* with people who know what's wrong with Zuckerman. I leave the diagnosing to his comforters. I try to stay out of it.

Of course Zuckerman ends the book in an advanced state of metaphor, with his mouth wired shut by surgery.

He breaks his jaw falling on a tombstone in a Jewish cemetery, after overdosing on painkillers and booze. What's so metaphorical about that? Happens all the time.

But he's silenced, completely. He can't write because of his agonising shoulder, and he can't speak because of his broken mouth.

Let me tell you a story. Back in 1957 I published, in *The New Yorker*, a short story called "Defender of the Faith." I was twenty-four and I was pretty excited about it. Then the story came out and it enraged a lot of Jewish readers of *The New Yorker*. Among the enraged was an eminent New York rabbi who wrote a letter of protest to the Anti-Defamation League of the B'nai Brith—a very worthy organisation, by the way, that's fought anti-Semitic discrimination in the U.S. courts for decades, and keeps an eye on the anti-Semites so they don't get out of hand. They've been known to do that. Anyway, one line of the rabbi's letter I never forgot. "What is being done to silence this man?" Well, to their credit, they never tried it. Free country, the U.S.A., and nobody appreciates that better than the Jews. But I remembered that line. What is being done to silence this man? It came to me when I was writing this book, and that's why I broke Zuckerman's jaw. I did it for the rabbi.

So the charge of defamation started early on?

It started when I started. It has somewhat distinguished my career from most of my American colleagues. I was taken to be an inflammatory fellow when I was still in my swaddling clothes. In its own strange way, the furor coming right at the start probably has given my writing a direction and emphasis that it might not have had otherwise. It's difficult to ignore such an assault, particularly at twenty-four. Back then I did two things: began to explain myself and began to defend myself.

How did you make your case?

I was invited to speak at synagogues and temples and Jewish community centres, and I went out and spoke. People stood up and shouted at me during the question periods. It was a good thing. I owe a lot to the opposition. They dragged me screaming out of the Department of English. There were real people out there who got inflamed. They didn't write papers about what they read—they got mad. What a surprise.

So by the time you wrote Portnoy's Complaint, *you already had an inflamed Jewish readership, so to speak?*

I also had an appreciative Jewish readership. Even a few Gentiles reading me, too. But as for my Jewish detractors, no, they wouldn't stop. They wouldn't let up, no matter what I wrote. So I thought finally, "Well, you want it, I'll give it to you." And out came Portnoy, apertures spurting.

What about your own family? How did they respond?

To the attacks on me? They were stunned. They were hurt. They heard a lot about my inadequacies from their hoity-toity neighbours. They would go to a lecture about me at their temple, expecting a star to be pinned on their boy just like back in grade school. Instead they'd hear from the platform that sleeping in my bedroom all those years, and eating with them at their table, was a self-hating anti-Semitic Jew. My mother had to hold my father down in his seat, he'd get so angry. No, they were all right. They recognised too many folks they knew to think such people as I'd described had never walked around New Jersey.

Your own father then isn't like Zuckerman's father, who on his deathbed curses his son for the books he writes?

I never said he was. You're confusing me with all those astute book reviewers who are sure that I am the only novelist in the history of literature who has never made anything up.

In each of these last two books, Zuckerman suffers a bereavement. In the second book, Zuckerman Unbound, *his father dies calling him "Bastard." In* The Anatomy Lesson, *Zuckerman's mother dies, and Zuckerman is left with a piece of paper on which his mother has written the word "Holocaust."*

Yes. She's dying of a brain tumor. Her neurologist comes to her hospital room to ascertain just how far gone she is and asks her to write her name for him on a piece of paper. This is in Miami Beach in 1970. She's a woman whose writings otherwise consist of recipes on index cards, knitting instructions, and thank-you notes. When the doctor puts the pen in her hand and asks her to write her name, instead of writing "Selma" she writes "Holocaust," perfectly spelled. The doctor can't throw it away and after her death he gives it to Zuckerman. Zuckerman can't throw it away either and carries it around in his wallet.

Why can't he throw it away?

Who can? Who has? Zuckerman isn't the only one who can't throw this word away and is carrying it with him all the time, whether he knows it or not. Without this word there would be no Nathan Zuckerman, not in Zuckerman's fix. No chiropodist father and his deathbed curse, no dentist brother with his ferocious chastisement. There'd of course be no Amy Bellette, the young woman in *The Ghost Writer* who he likes to think could have been Anne Frank. There'd be no Milton Appel with his moral ordinances and literary imperatives. And Zuckerman wouldn't be in his cage. If you take away that word—and with it the fact—none of these Zuckerman books would exist.

But you're not saying that your subject in these books has been the Holocaust?

No, no, of course not—certainly not in the way it's the subject at the center of Styron's novel *Sophie's Choice.* I think for a Jewish American writer there's not the same impetus, or, oddly, even the necessity, that there is for a Christian American, like Styron, to take the Holocaust up so nakedly as a subject, to unleash upon it so much moral and philosophical speculation, so much harrowing, furious invention. It works through Jewish lives less visibly and in less spectacular ways. And that's the way I prefer to deal with it in fiction. For most reflective American Jews, I would think, it is simply there, hidden, submerged, emerging, disappearing, unforgotten. You don't make use of it—it makes use of you. It certainly makes use of Zuckerman. There is a certain thematic architecture to these three books that I hope will make itself felt when they're published in one volume. I don't mean that everyone is going to be knocked off his feet then by my conceptual grandeur. I just mean that the little piece of paper in Zuckerman's wallet might not seem quite so small.

Interview with *The Paris Review*

How do you get started on a new book?

Beginning a book is unpleasant. I'm entirely uncertain about the character and the predicament, and a character in his predicament is what I have to begin with. Worse than not knowing your subject is not knowing how to treat it, because that's finally everything. I type out beginnings and they're awful, more of an unconscious parody of my previous book than the breakaway from it that I want. I need something driving down the center of a book, a magnet to draw everything to it—that's what I look for during the first months of writing something new. I often have to write a hundred pages or more before there's a paragraph that's alive. Okay, I say to myself, that's your beginning, start there; that's the first paragraph of the book. I'll go over the first six months of work and underline in red a paragraph, a sentence, sometimes no more than a phrase, that has some life in it, and then I'll type all these out on one page. Usually it doesn't come to more than one page, but if I'm lucky, that's the start of page one. I look for the liveliness to set the tone. After the awful

The interviewer is Hermione Lee, a lecturer in English at the University of York. She has published books on Virginia Woolf, Elizabeth Bowen, and Philip Roth. (1984)

beginning come the months of freewheeling play, and after the play come the crises, turning against your material and hating the book.

How much of a book is in your mind before you start?

What matters most isn't there at all. I don't mean the solutions to problems, I mean the problems themselves. You're looking, as you begin, for what's going to resist you. You're looking for trouble. Sometimes in the beginning uncertainty arises not because the writing is difficult, but because it isn't difficult enough. Fluency can be a sign that nothing is happening; fluency can actually be my signal to stop, while being in the dark from sentence to sentence is what convinces me to go on.

Must you have a beginning? Would you ever begin with an ending?

For all I know I *am* beginning with the ending. My page one can wind up a year later as page two hundred, if it's still even around.

What happens to those hundred or so pages that you have left over? Do you save them up?

I generally prefer never to see them again.

Do you work best at any particular time of the day?

I work all day, morning and afternoon, just about every day. If I sit there like that for two or three years, at the end I have a book.

Do you think other writers work such long hours?

I don't ask writers about their work habits. I really don't care. Joyce Carol Oates says somewhere that when writers ask each other what time they start working and when they finish and how much time they take for lunch, they're actually trying to find out "Is he as crazy as I am?" I don't need that question answered.

Does your reading affect what you write?

I read all the time when I'm working, usually at night. It's a way of keeping the circuits open. It's a way of thinking about my *line* of work while getting a little rest from the work at hand. It helps inasmuch as it fuels the overall obsession.

Do you show your work-in-progress to anyone?

It's more useful for my mistakes to ripen and burst in their own good time. I give myself all the opposition I need while I'm writing, and praise is meaningless to me when I know something isn't even half finished. Nobody sees what I'm doing until I absolutely can't go any further and might even like to believe that I'm done.

Do you have a Roth reader in mind when you write?

No. I occasionally have an anti-Roth reader in mind. I think, "How he is going to hate this!" That can be just the encouragement I need.

You spoke of the last phase of writing a novel being a "crisis" in which you turn against the material and hate the work. Is there always this crisis, with every book?

Always. Months of looking at the manuscript and saying, "This is wrong—but what's wrong?" I ask myself, "If this book were a dream, it would be a dream of what?" But when I'm asking this I'm also trying to *believe* in what I've written, to forget that it's writing and to say,

"This *has* taken place," even if it hasn't. The idea is to perceive your invention as a reality that can be understood as a dream. The idea is to turn flesh and blood into literary characters and literary characters into flesh and blood.

Can you say more about these crises?

In *The Ghost Writer* the crisis—one among many—had to do with Zuckerman, Amy Bellette, and Anne Frank. It wasn't easy to see that Amy Bellette *as* Anne Frank was Zuckerman's own creation. Only by working through numerous alternatives did I decide that not only was she his creation, but that she might possibly be her own creation too, a young woman inventing herself *within* Zuckerman's invention. To enrich his fantasy without obfuscation or muddle, to be ambiguous *and* clear—well, that was my writing problem through one whole summer and fall. In *Zuckerman Unbound* the crisis was a result of failing to see that Zuckerman's father shouldn't already be dead when the book begins. I eventually realized that the death should come at the conclusion of the book, allegedly as a consequence of the son's blasphemous best-seller. But, starting off, I'd got the thing back to front, and then I stared at it dumbly for months, seeing nothing. I knew that I wanted the book to veer away from Alvin Pepler— I like to be steamrolling along in one direction and then to spring my surprise—but I couldn't give up the premise of my earliest drafts until I saw that the novel's obsessive concern with assassinations, death threats, funerals, and funeral homes, was leading up to, rather than away from, the death of Zuckerman's father. How you juxtapose the events can tie you in knots and rearranging the sequence can free you suddenly to streak for the finish line. In *The Anatomy Lesson* the discovery I made—having banged the typewriter with my head far too long—was that Zuckerman, in the moment that he takes flight for Chicago to try to become a doctor, should begin to impersonate a pornographer. There had to be willed extremism at either end of the moral spectrum, each of his escape-dreams of self-transformation subverting the meaning and mocking the intention of the other. If he had gone off solely to become a doctor, driven only by that high moral ardor, or, if he had just gone around impersonating a pornographer, spewing only that anarchic and alienating rage, he wouldn't have been my man. He has two dominant modes: his mode of self-abnegation, and his fuck-'em mode. You want a bad Jewish boy, that's what you're going to get. He rests from one by taking up the other, though, as we see, it's not much of a rest. The thing about Zuckerman that interests me is that everybody's split, but few so openly as this. Everybody is full of cracks and fissures, but usually we see people trying very hard to hide the places where they're split. Most people desperately want to heal their lesions, and keep trying to. Hiding them is sometimes taken for healing them (or for not having them). But Zuckerman can't successfully do either, and by the end of the trilogy has proved it even to himself. What's determined his life and his work are the lines of fracture in what is by no means a clean break. I was interested in following those lines.

What happens to Philip Roth when he turns into Nathan Zuckerman?

Nathan Zuckerman is an act. It's all the art of impersonation, isn't it? That's the fundamental novelistic gift. Zuckerman is a writer who wants to be a doctor impersonating a pornographer. I am a writer writing a book impersonating a writer who wants to be a doctor impersonating a pornographer—who then, to compound the impersonation, to barb the edge, pretends he's a well-known literary critic. Making fake biography, false history, concocting a half-imaginary existence out of the actual drama of my life *is* my life. There has to be some pleasure in this job, and that's it. To go around in disguise. To act a character. To pass oneself off as what one is not. To *pretend*. The sly and cunning masquerade. Think of the ventriloquist. He speaks so that his voice appears to proceed from someone at a distance from himself. But if he weren't in your line of vision you'd get no pleasure from his art at all. His art consists of being present *and* absent; he's most himself by simultaneously being someone else, neither of whom he "is" once the curtain is down. You don't necessarily, as a writer, have to abandon your biography completely to engage in an act of impersonation. It may be more intriguing when you don't. You distort it, caricature it, parody it, you torture and subvert it, you exploit it—all to give the biography that dimension that will excite your verbal life. Millions of people do this all the time, of course, and not with the justification of making literature. They *mean* it. It's amazing what lies people can sustain behind the mask of their real faces. Think of the art of the adulterer: under tremendous pressure and against enormous odds, ordinary husbands and wives, who would freeze with self-consciousness up on a stage, yet in the theater of the home, alone before the audience of the betrayed spouse, they act out roles of innocence and fidelity with flawless dramatic skill. Great, great performances, conceived with genius down to the smallest particulars, impeccably meticulous naturalistic acting, and all done by rank amateurs. People beautifully pretending to be "themselves." Make-believe can take the subtlest forms, you know. Why should a novelist, a pretender by profession, be any less deft or more reliable than a stolid unimaginative suburban accountant cheating on his wife? Jack Benny used to pretend to be a miser, remember? Called himself by his own good name and claimed that he was stingy and mean. It excited his comic imagination to do this. He probably wasn't all that funny as just another nice fellow writing checks to the U.J.A. and taking his friends out to dinner. Céline pretended to be a rather indifferent, even irresponsible physician when he seems in fact to have worked hard at his practice and to have been conscientious about his patients. But that wasn't interesting.

But it is. Being a good doctor is interesting.

For William Carlos Williams maybe, but not for Céline. Being a devoted husband, an intelligent father, and a dedicated family physician in Rutherford, New Jersey, might have seemed as admirable to Céline as it does to you, or to me for that matter, but *his* writing drew its vigor from the demotic voice and the dramatization of his outlaw side (which was considerable), and so he created the Céline of the great novels in somewhat the way Jack Benny, also flirting with the taboo, created himself as a miser. You have to be awfully naïve not to understand that a writer is a performer who puts on the act he does best—not least when he dons the mask of the first-person singular. That may be the best mask of all for a second self. Some (many) pretend to be more lovable than they are and some pretend to be less. Beside the point. Literature isn't a moral beauty contest. Its power arises from the authority and audacity with which the impersonation is pulled off; the belief it inspires is what counts. The question to ask about the writer isn't "Why does he behave so badly?" but "What does he gain by wearing this mask?" I don't admire the Genet that Genet presents as himself any more than I admire the unsavory Molloy impersonated by Beckett. I admire Genet because he writes books that won't let me forget who that Genet is. When Rebecca West was writing about Augustine, she said that his *Confessions* was too subjectively true to be objectively true. I think this is so in the first-person novels of Genet and Céline, as it is in Colette, books like *The Shackle* and *The Vagabond*. Gombrowicz has a novel called *Pornografia* in which he introduces himself as a character, using his own name—the better to implicate himself in certain highly dubious proceedings and bring the moral terror to life. Konwicki, another Pole, in his last two novels, *The Polish Complex* and *A Minor Apocalypse,* works to close the gap between the reader and the narrative by introducing "Konwicki" as the central character. He strengthens the illusion that the novel is true—and not to be discounted as "fiction"—by impersonating himself. It all goes back to Jack Benny. Need I add, however, that it's hardly a disinterested undertaking? Writing for me isn't a natural thing that I just keep doing, the way fish swim and birds fly. It's something that's done under a certain kind of provocation, a particular urgency. It's the transformation, through an elaborate impersonation, of a personal emergency into a public act (in both senses of that word). It can be a very trying spiritual exercise to siphon through your being qualities that are alien to your moral makeup—as trying for the writer as for the reader. You can wind up feeling more like a sword-swallower than a ventriloquist or impersonator. You sometimes use yourself very harshly in order to reach what is, literally speaking, beyond you. The impersonator can't afford to indulge the ordinary human instincts which direct people in what they want to present and what they want to hide.

If the novelist is an impersonator, then what about the autobiography? What is the relationship, for example, between the deaths of the parents, which are so important in the last two Zuckerman novels, and the death of your own parents?

Why not ask about the relationship between the death of my parents and the death of Gabe Wallach's mother, the germinating incident in my 1962 novel, *Letting Go*? Or ask about the death and funeral of the father, at the heart of my first published story, "The Day It Snowed," which appeared in the *Chicago Review* in 1955? Or ask about the death of Kepesh's mother, wife of the owner of a Catskill hotel, which is the turning point in *The Professor of Desire*? The terrible blow of the death of a parent is something I began writing about long before any parent of mine had died. Novelists are frequently as interested in what hasn't happened to them as in what has. What may be taken by the innocent for naked autobiography is, as I've been suggesting, more than likely mock-autobiography or hypothetical autobiography or autobiography grandiosely enlarged. We know about the people who walk into the police station and confess to crimes they haven't committed. Well, the false confession appeals to writers, too. Novelists are even interested in what happens to other people and, like liars and con men everywhere, will pretend that something dramatic or awful or hair-raising or splendid that happened to someone else actually happened to them. The physical particulars and moral circumstances of Zuckerman's mother's death have practically nothing to do with the death of my own mother. The death of the mother of one of my dearest friends—whose account of her suffering stuck in my mind long after he'd told me about it—furnished the most telling details for the mother's death in *The Anatomy Lesson*. The black cleaning woman who commiserates with Zuckerman in Miami Beach about his mother's death is modeled on the housekeeper of old friends in Philadelphia, a woman I haven't seen for ten years and who never laid eyes on anybody in my family but me. I was always entranced by her tangy style of speech, and when the right moment came, I used it. But the words in her mouth I invented. Olivia, the black eighty-three-year-old Florida cleaning woman, *c'est moi*.

As you well know, the intriguing biographical issue—and critical issue, for that matter—isn't that a writer will write about some of what has happened to him, but *how* he writes about it, which, when understood properly, takes us a long way to understanding *why* he writes about it. A more intriguing question is why and how he writes about what hasn't happened—how he feeds what's hypothetical or imagined into what's inspired and controlled by recollection, and how what's recollected spawns the overall fantasy. I suggest, by the way, that the best person to ask about the autobiographical relevance of the climactic death of the father in *Zuckerman Unbound* is my own father, who lives in Elizabeth, New Jersey. I'll give you his phone number.

Then what is the relationship between your experience of psychoanalysis and the use of psychoanalysis as a literary strategem?

If I hadn't been analyzed I wouldn't have written *Portnoy's Complaint* as I wrote it, or *My Life as a Man* as I wrote it, nor would *The Breast* resemble itself. Nor would I resemble myself. The experience of psychoanalysis was probably more useful to me as a writer than as a neurotic, although there may be a false distinction there. It's an experience that I shared with tens of thousands of baffled people, and anything that powerful in the private domain that joins a writer to his generation, to his class, to his moment, is tremendously important for him, providing that afterwards he can separate himself enough to examine the experience objectively, imaginatively, in the writing clinic. You have to be able to become your doctor's doctor, even if only to write about patienthood, which was, certainly in part, a subject in *My Life as a Man*. Why patienthood interested me—and as far back as *Letting Go*, written four or five years before my own analysis—was because so many enlightened contemporaries had come to accept the view of themselves as patients, and the ideas of psychic disease, cure, and recovery. You're asking me about the relationship between art and life? It's like the relationship between the eight hundred or so hours that it took to be psychoanalyzed, and the eight or so hours that it would take to read *Portnoy's Complaint* aloud. Life is long and art is shorter.

Can you talk about your marriage?

It took place so long ago that I no longer trust my memory of it. The problem is complicated further by *My Life as a Man*, which diverges so dramatically in so many places from its origin in my own nasty situation that I'm hard put, some twenty-five years later, to sort out the invention of 1975 from the facts of 1959. You might as well ask the author of *The Naked and the Dead* what happened to him in the Philippines. I can only tell you that that was my time as an infantryman, and that *My Life as a Man* is the war novel I wrote some years after failing to receive the Distinguished Service Cross.

Do you have painful feelings on looking back?

Looking back I see these as fascinating years—as people of fifty often do contemplating the youthful adventure for which they paid with a decade of their lives a comfortingly long time ago. I was more aggressive then than I am today, some people were even said to be intimidated by me, but I was an easy target, all the same. We're easy targets at twenty-five, if only someone discovers the enormous bull's-eye.

And where was it?

Oh, where it can usually be found in self-confessed budding literary geniuses. My idealism. My romanticism. My passion to capitalize the L in life. I wanted something difficult and dangerous to happen to me. I wanted a hard time. Well, I got it. I'd come from a small, safe, relatively happy provincial background—my Newark neighborhood in the thirties and forties was just a Jewish Terre Haute—and I'd absorbed, along with the ambition and drive, the fears and phobias of my generation of American Jewish children. In my early twenties, I wanted to prove to myself that I wasn't afraid of all those things. It wasn't a mistake to want to prove that, even though, after the ball was over, I was virtually unable to write for three or four years. From 1962 to 1967 is the longest I've gone, since becoming a writer, without publishing a book. Alimony and recurrent court costs had bled me of every penny I could earn by teaching and writing, and, hardly into my thirties, I was thousands of dollars in debt to my friend and editor, Joe Fox. The loan was to help pay for my analysis, which I needed primarily to prevent me from going out and committing murder because of the alimony and court costs incurred for having served two years in a childless marriage. The image that teased me during those years was of a train that had been shunted onto the wrong track. In my early twenties, I had been zipping right along there, you know—on schedule, express stops only, final destination clearly in mind; and then suddenly I was on the wrong track, speeding off into the wilds. I'd ask myself, "How the hell do you get this thing back on the right track?" Well, you can't. I've continued to be surprised, over the years, whenever I discover myself, late at night, pulling into the wrong station.

But not getting back on the same track was a great thing for you, presumably.

John Berryman said that for a writer any ordeal that doesn't kill him is terrific. The fact that his ordeal did finally kill him doesn't make what he was saying wrong.

What do you feel about feminism, particularly the feminist attack on you?

What is it?

The force of the attack would be, in part, that the female characters are unsympathetically treated, for instance that Lucy Nelson in When She Was Good *is hostilely presented.*

Don't elevate that by calling it a "feminist" attack. That's just stupid reading. Lucy Nelson is a furious adolescent who wants a decent life. She is presented as better than her world and conscious of being better. She is confronted and opposed by men who typify deeply irritating types to many women. She is the protector of a passive, defenseless mother whose vulnerability drives her crazy. She happens to be raging against aspects of middle-class American life that the new militant feminism was to identify as the enemy only a few years after Lucy's appearance in print—hers might even be thought of as a case of premature feminist rage. *When She Was Good* deals with Lucy's struggle to free herself from the terrible disappointment engendered in a daughter by an irresponsible father. It deals with her hatred of the father he was and her yearning for the father he couldn't be. It would be sheer idiocy, particularly if this *were* a feminist attack, to contend that such powerful feelings of loss and contempt and shame do not exist in the daughters of drunks, cowards, and criminals. There is also the helpless Mama's boy Lucy marries, and her hatred of his incompetence and professional innocence. Is there no such thing in the world as marital hatred? That will come as news to all the rich divorce lawyers, not to mention Thomas Hardy and Gustave Flaubert. By the way, is Lucy's father treated "hostilely" because he's a drunk and a petty thief who ends up in jail? Is Lucy's husband treated "hostilely" because he happens to be a big baby? Is the uncle who tries to destroy Lucy "hostilely" treated because he's a brute? This is a novel about a wounded daughter who has more than sufficient cause to be enraged with the men in her life. She is only "hostilely" presented if it's an act of hostility to recognize that young women can be wounded and young women can be enraged. I'd bet there are even some enraged and wounded women who are feminists. You know, the dirty little secret is no longer sex; the dirty little secret is hatred and rage. It's the tirade that's taboo. Odd that this should be so a hundred years after Dostoyevsky (and fifty after Freud), but nobody nice likes to be identified with the stuff. It's the way folks used to feel about fellatio in the good old days. "Me? Never heard of it. Disgusting." But is it "hostile," really, to take a look at the ferocity of the emotion they call "hostility"? *When She Was Good* is not serving the cause—that's true. The anger of this young woman isn't presented to be endorsed with a hearty "Right on!" that will move the populace to action. The nature of the anger is examined, as is the depth of the wound. So are the consequences of the anger, for Lucy as for everyone. I hate to have to be the one to say it, but the portrait isn't without its poignancy. I don't mean by poignancy what the compassionate book reviewers call "compassion." I mean you see the suffering that real rage is.

But supposing I say to you that nearly all the women in the books are there to obstruct, or to help, or to console the male characters. There's the woman who cooks and consoles and is sane and calming, or the other kind of woman, the dangerous maniac, the obstructor. They occur as means of helping or obstructing Kepesh or Zuckerman or Tarnopol. And that could be seen as a limited view of women.

Let's face it, some women who are sane also happen to know how to cook. So do some of the dangerous maniacs. Let's leave out the sin of cooking. A great book on the order of *Oblomov* could be written about a man allying himself with woman after woman who gorge him with marvelous meals, but I haven't written it. If your description of the "sane," "calm," and "consoling" woman applies to anyone, it's to Claire Ovington in *The Professor of Desire*, with whom Kepesh establishes a tender liaison some years after the breakup of his marriage. Now, I'd have no objection to your writing a novel about this relationship from the point of view of Claire Ovington— I'd be intrigued to see how she saw it—so why do you take a slightly critical tone about my writing the novel from the point of view of David Kepesh?

There's nothing wrong with the novel's being written from David Kepesh's point of view. What might cause difficulties for some readers is that Claire, and the other women in the novel, are there to help or hinder him.

I'm not pretending to give you anything other than his sense of his life with this young woman. My book doesn't stand or fall on the fact that Claire Ovington is calm and sane, but on whether I am able to depict what calmness and sanity are like, and what it is to have a mate—and why it is one would want a mate—who possesses those and other virtues in abundance. She is also vulnerable to jealousy when Kepesh's ex-wife turns up uninvited, and she carries with her a certain sadness about her family background. She isn't there "as a means" of helping Kepesh. She *helps* him—and he helps her. *They are in love.* She is there because Kepesh has fallen in love with a sane and calm and consoling woman after having been unhappily married to a difficult and exciting woman he was unable to handle. Don't people do that? Someone more doctrinaire than you might tell me that the state of being in love, particularly of being passionately in love, is no basis for establishing permanent relationships between men and women. But, alas, people, even people of intelligence and experience, *will* do it—have done it and seem intent on going on doing it— and I am not interested in writing about what people *should* do for the good of the human race and pretending that's what they *do* do, but writing about what they do indeed do, lacking the programmatic efficiency of the infallible theorists. The irony of Kepesh's situation is that having found the calm and consoling woman he can live with, a woman of *numerous* qualities, he then finds his desire for her perversely seeping away, and realizes that unless this involuntary diminution of passion can be arrested, he'll become alienated from the best thing in his life. Doesn't that happen either? From what I hear this damn seeping away of desire happens all the time and is extremely distressing to the people involved. Look, I didn't invent the loss of desire, and I didn't invent the lure of passion, and I didn't invent sane companions, and I didn't invent maniacs. I'm sorry if my men don't have the correct feelings about women, or the universal range of feelings about women, or the feelings about women that it will be okay for men to have in 1995, but I do insist that there is some morsel of truth in my depiction of what it might be like for a man to be a Kepesh, or a Portnoy, or a breast.

Why have you never reused the character of Portnoy in another book, the way that you have used Kepesh and Zuckerman?

But I did use Portnoy in another book. *Our Gang* and *The Great American Novel* are Portnoy in another book. Portnoy wasn't a character for me, he was an explosion, and I wasn't finished exploding after *Portnoy's Complaint*. The first thing I wrote after *Portnoy's Complaint* was a long story called "On the Air" that appeared in Ted Solotaroff's *American Review*. John Updike was here a while ago and while we were all having dinner one night, he said, "How come you've never reprinted that story?" I said, "It's too disgusting." John laughed. He said, "It is, it's a truly disgusting story." And I said, "I didn't know what I was thinking about when I wrote it." And that is true to some degree—I didn't want to know; the idea was *not* to know. But I also did know. I looked in the arsenal and found another dynamite stick, and I thought, "Light the fuse and see what happens." I was trying to blow up more of myself. This phenomenon is known to students of literary survey courses as the writer changing his style. I was blowing up a lot of old loyalties and inhibitions, literary as well as personal. I think this may be why so many Jews were incensed by *Portnoy's Complaint*. It wasn't that they'd never heard about kids masturbating before, or about Jewish family fighting. It was, rather, that if they couldn't even control someone like me anymore, with all my respectable affiliations and credentials, all my Seriousness of Purpose, something had gone wrong. After all, I wasn't Abbie Hoffman or Lenny Bruce, I was a university teacher who had published in *Commentary*. But at the time it seemed to me that the next thing to be serious about was not being so goddamn serious. As Zuckerman reminds Appel, "Seriousness can be as stupid as anything else."

Weren't you also looking for a fight, writing Portnoy's Complaint?

I'd found a fight without looking for it long before that. They never really got off my ass for publishing *Goodbye, Columbus*, which was considered in some circles to be my *Mein Kampf*. Unlike Alexander Portnoy, my education in petit bourgeois morality didn't come at home, but after I'd left home and begun to publish my first short stories. My own household environment as a youngster was much closer to Zuckerman's than to Portnoy's. It had its constraints, but there was nothing resembling the censorious small-mindedness and shame-ridden xenophobia that I ran into from the official Jews who wanted me to shut up. The moral atmosphere of the Portnoy household, in its repressive aspects, owes a lot to the response of persistent voices within the official Jewish community to my debut. They did much to help make it seem auspicious.

You've been talking about the opposition to Portnoy's Complaint. *What about the recognition—how did its enormous success affect you?*

It was too big, on a larger and much crazier scale than I could begin to deal with, so I took off. A few weeks after publication, I boarded a bus at the Port Authority terminal for Saratoga Springs, and holed up at Yaddo, the writer's colony, for three months. Precisely what Zuckerman should have done after *Carnovsky*—but he hung around, the fool, and look what happened to him. He would have enjoyed Yaddo more than he enjoyed Alvin Pepler. But it made *Zuckerman Unbound* funnier keeping him in Manhattan, and it made my own life easier, not being there.

Do you dislike New York?

I lived there from 1962 until I moved to the country after *Portnoy's Complaint,* and I wouldn't trade those years for anything. New York *gave* me *Portnoy's Complaint* in a way. When I was living and teaching in Iowa City and Princeton, I didn't ever feel so free as I did in New York, in the sixties, to indulge myself in comic performance, on paper and with friends. There were raucous evenings with my New York friends, there was uncensored shamelessness in my psychoanalytic sessions, there was the dramatic, stagey atmosphere of the city itself in the years after Kennedy's assassination—all this inspired me to try out a new voice, a fourth voice, a less page-bound voice than the voice of *Goodbye, Columbus,* or of *Letting Go,* or of *When She Was Good.* So did the opposition to the war in Vietnam. There's always something behind a book to which it has no seeming connection, something invisible to the reader which has helped to release the writer's initial impulse. I'm thinking about the rage and rebellious-ness that were in the air, the vivid examples I saw around me of angry defiance and hysterical opposition. This gave me a few ideas for my act.

Did you feel you were part of what was going on in the sixties?

I felt the power of the life around me. I believed myself to be feel-ing the full consciousness of a place—this time New York—for the first time really since childhood. I was also, like others, receiving a stunning education in moral, political, and cultural possibilities from the country's eventful public life and from what was happening in Vietnam.

But you published a famous essay in Commentary *in 1960 called "Writing American Fiction" about the way that intellectuals or thinking people in America felt that they were living in a foreign country, a country in whose communal life they were not involved.*

Well, that's the difference between 1960 and 1968. (Being pub-lished in *Commentary* is another difference.) Alienated in America, a stranger to its pleasures and preoccupations—that was how many young people like me saw their situation in the fifties. It was a per-fectly honorable stance, I think, shaped by our literary aspirations and modernist enthusiasms, the high-minded of the second post-

immigrant generation coming into conflict with the first great erup-
tion of postwar media garbage. Little did we know that some twenty
years later the philistine ignorance on which we would have liked to
turn our backs would infect the country like Camus's plague. Any
satirist writing a futuristic novel who had imagined a President Reagan during the Eisenhower years would have been accused of perpe-
trating a piece of crude, contemptible, adolescent, anti-American
wickedness, when, in fact, he would have succeeded, as prophetic
sentry, just where Orwell failed; he would have seen that the grotesquerie to be visited upon the English-speaking world would not be
an extension of the repressive Eastern totalitarian nightmare but a
proliferation of the Western farce of media stupidity and cynical
commercialism—American-style philistinism run amok. It wasn't
Big Brother who'd be watching us from the screen, but we who'd be
watching a terrifyingly powerful world leader with the soul of an
amiable, soap opera grandmother, the values of a civic-minded Bev-
erly Hills Cadillac dealer, and the historical background and intellectual equipment of a high school senior in a June Allyson musical.

*What happened to you later, in the seventies? Did what was happening in
the country continue to mean much to someone like you?*

I have to remember what book I was writing and then I can
remember what happened to me—though what was happening to
me was largely the book I was writing. Nixon came and went in '73,
and while Nixon was coming and going I was being driven quite
crazy by *My Life as a Man*. In a way I had been writing that book on
and off since 1964. I kept looking for a setting for the sordid scene in
which Maureen buys a urine specimen from a poor pregnant black
woman in order to get Tarnopol to think he's impregnated her. I
thought of it first as a scene for *When She Was Good*, but it was all
wrong for Lucy and Roy in Liberty Center. Then I thought it might

go into *Portnoy's Complaint,* but it was too malevolent for that kind of comedy. Then I wrote cartons and cartons of drafts of what eventually turned out to be *My Life as a Man*—eventually, after I finally realized that my solution lay in the very problem I couldn't overcome: my inability to find the setting appropriate to the sordid event, rather than the sordid event itself, was really at the heart of the novel. Watergate made life interesting when I wasn't writing, but from nine to five every day I didn't think too much about Nixon or about Vietnam. I was trying to solve the problem of this book. When it seemed I never would, I stopped and wrote *Our Gang;* when I tried again and still couldn't write it, I stopped and wrote the baseball book; then while finishing the baseball book, I stopped to write *The Breast.* It was as though I were blasting my way through a tunnel to reach the novel that I couldn't write. Each of one's books *is* a blast, clearing the way for what's next. It's all one book you write anyway. At night you dream six dreams. But *are* they six dreams? One dream prefigures or anticipates the next, or somehow concludes what hasn't yet even been fully dreamed. Then comes the next dream, the corrective of the dream before—the alternative dream, the antidote dream— enlarging upon it, or laughing at it, or contradicting it, or trying just to get the dream *right.* You can go on trying all night long.

After Portnoy, *after leaving New York, you moved to the country. What about rural life? Obviously it was used as material in* The Ghost Writer.

I might never have become interested in writing about a reclusive writer if I hadn't first had my own small taste of E. I. Lonoff's thirty-five years of rural splendor. I need something solid under my feet to kick off my imagination. But aside from giving me a sense of the Lonoffs' lives, the country existence hasn't offered anything as yet in the way of subject. Probably it never will and I should get the hell out. Only I happen to love living there, and I can't make *every* choice conform to the needs of my work.

What about England, where you spend part of each year? Is that a possible source of fiction?

Ask me twenty years from now. That's about how long it took Isaac Singer to get enough of Poland out of his system—and to let enough of America in—to begin, little by little, as a writer, to see and depict his upper Broadway cafeterias. If you don't know the fantasy life of a country, it's hard to write fiction about it that isn't just description of the decor, human and otherwise. Little things trickle through when I see the country dreaming out loud—in the theater, at an election, during the Falklands crisis, but I know nothing really about what means what to people here. It's very hard for me to understand who people are, even when they tell me, and I don't even know if that's *because* of who they are or because of me. I don't know who is impersonating what, if I'm necessarily seeing the real thing or just a fabrication, nor can I easily see where the two overlap. My perceptions are clouded by the fact that I speak the language. I believe I know what's being said, you see, even if I don't. Worst of all, I don't hate anything here. What a relief it is to have no culture-grievances, not to have to hear the sound of one's voice taking positions and having opinions and recounting all that's wrong! What bliss—but for the writing that's no asset. Nothing drives me crazy here, and a writer *has* to be driven crazy to help him to *see*. A writer needs his poisons. The antidote to his poisons is often a book. Now if I *had* to live here, if for some reason I were forbidden ever to return to America, if my position and my personal well-being were suddenly to become permanently bound up with England, well, what was maddening and meaningful might begin to come into focus, and yes, in about the year 2005, maybe 2010, little by little I'd stop writing about Newark and I would dare to set a story at a table in a wine bar on Kensington Park Road. A story about an elderly exiled foreign writer, in this instance reading not the *Jewish Daily Forward* but the *Herald Tribune*.

In these last three books, the Zuckerman novels, there has been a reiteration of the struggle with Jewishness and Jewish criticism. Why do you think these books go over the past as much as they do? Why is that happening now?

In the early seventies, I began to be a regular visitor to Czechoslovakia. I went to Prague every spring and took a little crash course in political repression. I'd only known repression firsthand in somewhat more benign and covert forms—as psychosexual constraint or as social restriction. I knew less about anti-Semitic repression from personal experience than I did about the repressions Jews practiced upon themselves, and upon one another, as a consequence of the history of anti-Semitism. Portnoy, you remember, considers himself just such a practicing Jew. Anyway, I became highly attuned to the differences between the writer's life in totalitarian Prague and in freewheeling New York, and I decided, after some initial uncertainty, to focus on the unreckoned consequences of a life in art in the world that I knew best. I realized that there were already many wonderful and famous stories and novels by Henry James and Thomas Mann and James Joyce about the life of the artist, but none I knew of about the comedy that an artistic vocation can turn out to be in the U.S.A. When Thomas Wolfe tackled the subject he was rather rhapsodic. Zuckerman's struggle with Jewishness and Jewish criticism is seen in the context of his comical career as an American writer, ousted by his family, alienated from his fans, and finally at odds with his own nerve endings. The Jewish quality of books like mine doesn't really reside in their subject matter. Talking about Jewishness hardly interests me at all. It's a kind of sensibility that makes, say, *The Anatomy Lesson* Jewish, if anything does: the nervousness, the excitability, the arguing, the dramatizing, the indignation, the obsessiveness, the touchiness, the play-acting—above all the *talking*. The talking and the shouting. Jews will go on, you know. It isn't what it's talking *about* that makes a book Jewish—it's that the book won't shut up.

The book won't leave you alone. Won't let up. Gets too close. "Listen, listen—that's only the half of it!" I knew what I was doing when I broke Zuckerman's jaw. For a Jew a broken jaw is a terrible tragedy. It was to avoid this that so many of us went into teaching rather than prizefighting.

Why is Milton Appel, the good, high-minded Jew who was a guru for Zuckerman in his early years, a punching-bag in The Anatomy Lesson, *someone that Zuckerman wants to desanctify?*

If I were not myself, if someone else had been assigned the role of being Roth and writing his books, I might very well, in this other incarnation, have been his Milton Appel.

Is Zuckerman's rage at Milton Appel the expression of a kind of guilt on your part?

Guilt? Not at all. As a matter of fact, in an earlier draft of the book, Zuckerman and his young girlfriend Diana took exactly opposite positions in their argument about Appel. She, with all her feisty inexperience, said to Zuckerman, "Why do you let him push you around, why do you take this shit sitting down?" and Zuckerman, the older man, said to her, "Don't be ridiculous, Dear, calm down, he doesn't matter." There was the real autobiographical scene, and it had no life at all. I had to absorb the rage into the main character even if my own rage on this topic had long since subsided. By being true to life I was actually ducking the issue. So I reversed their positions, and had the twenty-year-old college girl telling Zuckerman to grow up, and gave Zuckerman the tantrum. Much more fun. I wasn't going to get anywhere with a Zuckerman as eminently reasonable as myself.

So your hero always has to be enraged or in trouble or complaining.

My hero has to be in a state of vivid transformation or radical displacement. "I am not what I am—I am, if anything, what I am not!" The litany begins something like that.

How conscious are you as you are writing of whether you are moving from a third- to a first-person narrative?

It's not conscious or unconscious—the movement is spontaneous.

But how does it feel, to be writing in the third person as opposed to the first person?

How does it feel looking through a microscope, when you adjust the focus? Everything depends upon how close you want to bring the naked object to the naked eye. And vice versa. Depends on what you want to magnify, and to what power.

But do you free yourself in certain ways by putting Zuckerman in the third person?

I free myself to say about Zuckerman what it would be inappropriate for him to say about himself in quite the same way. The irony would be lost in the first person, or the comedy; I can introduce a note of gravity that might be jarring coming from him. The shifting within a single narrative from the one voice to the other is how a reader's moral perspective is determined. It's something like this that we all want to do in ordinary conversation when we employ the indefinite pronoun "one" in speaking of ourselves. Using "one" places your observation in a looser relationship to the self that's uttering it. Look, sometimes it's more telling to let him speak for himself, sometimes it's more telling to speak about him; sometimes it's more telling to narrate obliquely, sometimes not. *The Ghost Writer* is narrated in the first person, probably because what's being described is largely a world Zuckerman's discovered outside of himself, the book of a young explorer. The older and more scarred he gets, the more *inward*-looking he gets, the further out *I* have to get. The crisis of solipsism he suffers in *The Anatomy Lesson* is better seen from a bit of a distance.

Do you direct yourself as you are writing to make distinctions between what is spoken and what is narrative?

I don't "direct" myself. I respond to what seem the liveliest possibilities. There's no necessary balance to be achieved between what is spoken and what is narrated. You go with what's alive. Two thousand pages of narrative and six lines of dialogue may be just the ticket for one writer, and two thousand pages of dialogue and six lines of narrative the solution for another.

Do you ever take long chunks that have been dialogue and make them into narrative, or the other way around?

Sure. I did that with the Anne Frank section of *The Ghost Writer.* I had trouble getting that right. When I began, in the third person, I was somehow *revering* the material. I was taking a high elegiac tone in telling the story of Anne Frank surviving and coming to America. I didn't know where I was going so I began by doing what you're supposed to do when writing the life of a saint. It was the tone appropriate to hagiography. Instead of Anne Frank gaining new meaning within the context of my story, I was trying to draw from the ready store of stock emotions that everybody is supposed to have about her. It's what even good actors sometimes will do during the first weeks of rehearsing a play—gravitate to the conventional form of presentation, cling to the cliché while anxiously waiting for something authentic to take hold. In retrospect, my difficulties look somewhat bizarre, because just what Zuckerman was fighting against, I was in fact succumbing to—the officially authorized and most consoling legend. I tell you, no one who later complained that in *The Ghost Writer* I had abused the memory of Anne Frank would have batted an eye had I let those banalities out into the world. That would have been just fine; I might even have got a citation. But I couldn't have given myself any prizes for it. The difficulties of telling a Jewish story—How should it be told? In what tone? To whom should it be told? To what end? Should it be told at all? —was finally to become *The Ghost Writer*'s theme. But before it became a theme, it apparently had to be an ordeal. It often happens, at least with me, that the struggles that generate a book's moral life are naively enacted upon the body of the book during the early, uncertain stages of writing. That *is* the ordeal, and it ended when I took that whole section and recast it in the first person—Anne Frank's story told by Amy Bellette. The victim wasn't herself going to talk about her plight in the voice of "The March of Time." She hadn't in the *Diary*, so why should she in life? I didn't want this section to *appear* as first-person narration, but I knew that by passing it through the first-person sieve, I stood a good chance of getting rid of this terrible tone, which wasn't hers, but mine. I did get rid of it. The impassioned cadences, the straining emotions, the somber, overdramatized, archaic diction—I cleared it all out, thanks to Amy Bellette. Rather straightforwardly, I then cast the section *back* into the third person, and then I was able to get to work on it—to write rather than to rhapsodize or eulogize.

How do you think you have influenced the environment, the culture, as a writer?

Not at all. If I had followed my early college plans to become an attorney, I don't see where it would matter to the culture.

Do you say that with bitterness or with glee?

Neither. It's a fact of life. In an enormous commercial society that demands complete freedom of expression, the culture is a maw. Recently, the first American novelist to receive a special Congressional Gold Medal for his "contribution to the nation" was Louis L'Amour. It was presented to him at the White House by the President. The only other country in the world where such a writer would receive his government's highest award is the Soviet Union. In a totalitarian state, however, *all* culture is dictated by the regime; fortunately we Americans live in Reagan's and not Plato's Republic, and aside from their stupid medal, culture is almost entirely ignored. And that is preferable by far. As long as those on top keep giving the honors to Louis L'Amour and couldn't care less about anything else, everything will be just fine. When I was first in Czechoslovakia, it occurred to me that I work in a society where as a writer everything goes and nothing matters, while for the Czech writers I met in Prague, nothing goes and everything matters. This isn't to say I wished to change places. I didn't envy them their persecution and the way in which it heightens their social importance. I didn't even envy them their seemingly more valuable and serious themes. The trivialization, in the West, of much that's deadly serious in the East is itself a subject, one requiring considerable imaginative ingenuity to transform into compelling fiction. To write a serious book that doesn't signal its seriousness with the rhetorical cues or thematic gravity that's traditionally associated with seriousness is a worthy undertaking too. To do justice to a spiritual predicament that is *not* blatantly shocking and monstrously horrible, that does *not* elicit universal compassion, or occur on a large historical stage, or on the grandest scale of twentieth-century suffering—well, that's the lot that has fallen to those who write where everything goes and nothing matters. I recently heard the critic George Steiner, on English television, denouncing contemporary Western literature as utterly worthless and without quality, and claiming that the great documents of the human soul, the masterpieces, could only arise from souls being crushed by regimes like those in Czechoslovakia. I wonder then why all the writers I know in Czechoslovakia loathe the regime and passionately wish that it would disappear from the face of the earth. Don't they understand, as Steiner does, that this is their chance to be great? Sometimes one or two writers with colossal brute strength do manage, miraculously, to survive and, taking the system as their subject, to make art of a very high order out of their persecution. But most of them who remain sealed up inside totalitarian states are, as writers, destroyed by the system. That system doesn't make masterpieces; it makes coronaries, ulcers, and asthma, it makes alcoholics, it makes depressives, it makes bitterness and desperation and insanity. The writers are intellectually disfigured, spiritually demoralized, physically sickened, and culturally bored. Frequently they are silenced completely. Nine-tenths of the best of them will never do their best work just because of the system. The writers nourished by this system are the party hacks. When such a system prevails for two or three generations, relentlessly grinding away at a community of writers for twenty, thirty, or forty years, the obsessions become fixed, the language grows stale, the readership slowly dies out from starvation, and the existence of a national literature of originality, variety, vibrancy (which is very different from the brute survival of a single powerful voice) is nearly impossible. A literature that has the misfortune of remaining isolated underground for too long will inevitably become provincial, backwards, even naive, despite the fund of dark experience that may inspire it. By contrast, our work here hasn't been deprived of authenticity because as writers we haven't been stomped on by a totalitarian government. I don't know of any Western writer, aside from George Steiner, who is so grandiosely and sentimentally deluded about human suffering—and "masterpieces"—that he's come back from behind the Iron Curtain thinking himself devalued because he hasn't had to contend with such a wretched intellectual and literary environment. If the choice is between Louis L'Amour and our literary freedom and our extensive, lively national literature on the one hand, and Solzhenitsyn and that cultural desert and crushing suppression on the other, I'll take L'Amour.

But don't you feel powerless as a writer in America?

Writing novels is not the road to power. I don't believe that, in my society, novels effect serious changes in anyone other than the handful of people who are writers, whose own novels are of course seriously affected by other novelists' novels. I can't see anything like that happening to the ordinary reader, nor would I expect it to.

What do novels do then?

To the ordinary reader? Novels provide readers with something to read. At their best writers change the *way* readers read. That seems to me the only realistic expectation. It also seems to me quite enough. Reading novels is a deep and singular pleasure, a gripping and mysterious human activity that does not require any more moral or political justification than sex.

But are there no other aftereffects?

You asked me if I thought my fiction had changed anything in the culture and the answer is no. Sure there's been some scandal, but people are scandalized all the time; it's a way of life for them. It doesn't mean a thing. If you ask if I *want* my fiction to change anything in the culture, the answer is still no. What I want is to possess my readers while they are reading my book—if I can, to possess them in ways that other writers don't. Then let them return, just as they were, to a world where everybody else is working to change, persuade, tempt, and control them. The best readers come to fiction to be free of all that noise, to have set loose in them the consciousness that's otherwise conditioned and hemmed in by all that *isn't* fiction. This is something that every child, smitten by books, understands immediately, though it's not at all a childish idea about the importance of reading.

Last question. How would you describe yourself? What do you think you are like, compared with those vividly transforming heroes of yours?

I am like somebody who is trying vividly to transform himself out of himself and into his vividly transforming heroes. I am very much like somebody who spends all day writing.

Interview on *Zuckerman*

Many critics and reviewers persist in writing about Roth rather than his fiction. Why this persistence after all these years?

If that's so, it may have to do with the intensity with which my fiction has focused upon the self-revealing dilemmas of a single central character whose biography, in certain obvious details, overlaps with mine and who is then assumed "to be" me.

The Ghost Writer was automatically described in the press as "autobiographical" because the narrator, Nathan Zuckerman, is an American-Jewish writer my age, born in Newark, whose earliest writing elicits a protest from some Jewish readers. But, as a matter of fact, that about constitutes the similarity between my history and Zuckerman's in that book. The unsettling opposition from his father that young Zuckerman confronts and that propels the moral plot of *The Ghost Writer* I happen to have been spared; the intelligent, fatherly interest taken in his work by a renowned older writer whose New England houseguest he's lucky enough to be at twenty-three resembles no experience of mine starting out in the fifties; nor have I ever met a woman to whom I have been romantically drawn because

An interview with Asher Z. Milbauer and Donald G. Watson for their book *Reading Philip Roth* (St. Martin's Press, 1985).

149

she resembled Anne Frank or whom I mentally transformed into Anne Frank and endowed with her status in order to try to clear myself of Jewish charges of self-hatred and anti-Semitism.

Though some readers may have trouble disentangling my life from Zuckerman's, *The Ghost Writer*—along with the rest of *Zuckerman Bound* and *The Counterlife*—is an imaginary biography, an invention stimulated by themes in my experience to which I've given considerable thought but the result of a writing process a long way from the methods, let alone the purposes, of autobiography. If an avowed autobiographer transformed *his* personal themes into a detailed narrative embodying a reality distinct and independent from his own day-to-day history, peopled with imaginary characters conversing in words never spoken, given meaning by a sequence of events that had never taken place, we wouldn't be surprised if he was charged with representing as his real life what was an outright lie.

May I quote John Updike? Asked about my Zuckerman books, he said to an interviewer "Roth's inventing what looks a like *roman-à-clef* but is not."

But if your books are misread, other than by John Updike, isn't that more or less the fate of most good writing? Don't you expect to be misread?

That novelists serve readers in ways that they can't anticipate or take into account while writing doesn't come as news to someone who spent eight years with *Zuckerman Bound*. That's the story told on nearly every one of its 800 pages, from the opening scene, when Nathan the budding writer enters Lonoff's living room seeking absolution from sins committed in his juvenilia against his family's self-esteem, to its conclusion on the day that, as an established writer in his forties, he is forced to surrender to the Prague police the wholly harmless Yiddish stories that they've decided to impound as subversive.

The only reading resembling the ideal reading that a writer

yearns for is the writer's reading of himself. Every other reading is something of a surprise—to use your word, a "misreading," if what's meant isn't reading that's shallow and stupid but that's fixed in its course by the reader's background, ideology, sensibility, etc.

To be misread in any way that bears thinking about, however, a writer has to be *read* as well. But *those* misreadings, conferred by skillful, cultivated, highly imaginative, widely read misreaders can be instructive, even when quite bizarre—witness Lawrence on American literature; or Freud, the all-time most influential misreader of imaginative literature. So are those misreaders the censors influential, though for other reasons. And *are* the Soviet censors necessarily misreading, in Solzhenitsyn's fiction, his political aims? Though censors may appear to be the most narrow-minded and perverse of all misreaders, at times they may be more discerning about the socially injurious implications of a book than the most tolerantly open-minded audience.

Serious misreading has little to do with a text's impenetrability; geniuses misread nursery rhymes—all that's required is for the genius to have his own fish to fry.

In the light of this, what about an audience? Do you think you have one, and, if so, what does it mean to you?

I've had two audiences, a general audience and a Jewish audience. I have virtually no sense of my impact upon the general audience, nor do I really know who these people are. By a general audience I don't refer to anything vast. Despite the popularity of *Portnoy's Complaint*, the number of Americans who may have read, with any real attention, half of my books—as opposed to those who have read one or two—can't number more than 50,000, if that. I don't think anymore about them when I'm at work than they think about me when they're at work. They're as remote as the onlookers are to a chess player concentrating on the board and his opponent's game.

On the other hand, an unknowable audience of 50,000 judicious readers (or inventive misreaders) whose serious, silent attention I freely command is a great satisfaction. The enigmatic interchange between a silent book and a silent reader has struck me, ever since childhood, as a unique transaction. As far as I'm concerned, it's what the public side of the novelist's vocation has to come down to.

Counterbalancing the general audience has been a Jewish audience, affording me the best of both worlds. With my Jewish audience I feel intensely their expectations, disdain, delight, criticism, their wounded self-love, their healthy curiosity—what I imagine the writer's awareness of an audience is in the capital of a small country where culture is thought to mean as much as politics, where culture *is* politics: some little nation perpetually engaged in evaluating its purpose, contemplating its meaning, joking away its shame, and sensing itself imperiled in one way or another.

Why do you irritate Jews so much?

Do I any longer? Certainly "so much" must be an exaggeration by now, though one that I've helped unintentionally to perpetuate because of the writer's predicament in *Zuckerman Bound*. After fifteen books I may have become much less irritating than the Zuckerman I've depicted, largely because the Jewish generation that didn't go for me is by now less influential and the rest are no longer ashamed, if they ever were, of how Jews behave in my fiction.

Because it *was* shame—theirs—that had a lot to do with that conflict. But now that everybody's more confident about the right of Jews to have sexual thoughts and engage in authorized and unauthorized erotic practices, I think that stuff is over. On the whole, Jewish readers aren't quite so responsive to other people's ideas (real or imaginary) of what constitutes socially acceptable Jewish behavior and don't appear to be obsessively worried that damaging perceptions of them can be indelibly imprinted on the public mind through a work of fiction and that these will set off an anti-Semitic reaction. American Jews are less intimidated by Gentiles than they were when I began publishing in the 1950s, they are more sophisticated about anti-Semitism and its causes, and they are less hedged in by suffocating concepts of normalcy.

This is because they are not so preoccupied as they once were with the problematic nature of assimilation and are justifiably less troubled by ethnic disparities in the new American society of the last fifteen years—a society created by a massive influx of over twenty million people far less assimilable than themselves, about eighty-five percent of them non-Europeans, whose visible presence has reestablished polygenesis as a glaring and unalterable fact of our national life. When the cream of Miami is the Cuban bourgeoisie, and the best students at M.I.T. are Chinese, and not a candidate can stand before a Democratic presidential convention without flashing his racial or ethnic credentials—when *everybody* sticks out and doesn't seem to mind—perhaps Jews are less likely to worry about *their* sticking out, less likely *to* stick out.

In addition to the shame I fomented there was the menace I was said to pose by confirming the beliefs of the committed Jew-hater and mobilizing the anti-Semitism latent in the Gentile population generally. Years ago, the eminent scholar of Jewish mysticism Gershom Scholem published an attack on *Portnoy's Complaint* in an Israeli newspaper, predicting that not I but the Jews would pay the price for that book's impudence. I learned about Scholem's article only recently in Israel—a university professor from Tel Aviv summarized Scholem's argument for me and asked what I thought of it. I said that history had proved Scholem wrong: more than fifteen years had passed since the publication of *Portnoy's Complaint* and not a single Jew had paid for the book anything other than the few dollars it cost in the bookstore. The professor's reply? "Not yet," he said, "but the Gentiles will make use of it when the time is right."

The Jews I still irritate are for the most part like the Israeli professor; for them the danger of abetting anti-Semitism overrides nearly every other consideration.

Of course there must be many Jews as well as Gentiles who don't care for my books because they think that I don't know how to write fiction. Nothing wrong with that. I'm pointing rather to a psychological or ideological orientation, a view of politics and history that *had* to make *Portnoy's Complaint* anathema to a certain group of readers. Though the example of the Israeli professor might seem to suggest otherwise, this particular Jewish orientation seems to me to be disappearing just *because* of the existence of Israel and its effect upon American Jewish self-confidence.

I'm not referring to the pride that may be inspired in American Jews by Israeli military might. It's not images of Israel triumphant or naïve notions of Israeli moral infallibility that have signaled to American Jews that they needn't any longer be too tightly constrained by protective self-censorship, but just the opposite, their awareness of Israel as an openly discordant, divisive society with conflicting political goals and a self-questioning conscience, a Jewish society that makes no effort to conceal its imperfections from itself and that couldn't conceal them from the world if it wanted to. The tremendous publicity to which Israeli Jews are exposed—and to which they're not unaddicted—has many causes, not all of them benign, but certainly one effect of unashamed Israeli self-divulging has been to lead American Jews to associate a whole spectrum of behavior with which they themselves may have preferred not to be publicly identified, with people perceived as nothing if *not* Jews.

To move to a more general subject, do you think of fiction as a way of knowing the world or of changing the world?

As a way of knowing the world as it's not otherwise known. A lot can be known about the world without the help of fiction, but nothing else engenders fiction's kind of knowing because nothing else makes the world *into* fiction. What you know from Flaubert or Beckett or Dostoyevsky is never a great deal more than you knew before about adultery or loneliness or murder—what you know is *Madame Bovary, Molloy,* and *Crime and Punishment.* Fiction derives from that unique mode of scrutiny called imagination, and its wisdom is inseparable *from* the imagination. The intelligence of even the most intelligent novelist is often debased, and at the least distorted, when it's isolated from the novel that embodies it; without intending to, it addresses the mind alone rather than suffusing a wider consciousness, and however much prestige it may be accorded as "thought," ceases to be a way of knowing the world as it's not otherwise known. Detached from the fiction, a novelist's wisdom is often so much talk.

Novels *do* influence behavior, shape opinion, alter conduct—a book can, of course, change somebody's life—but that's because of a choice made by the reader to use the fiction for purposes of his own (purposes that might appal the novelist) and not because the novel is incomplete without the reader's taking action. The 1967 conference near Prague organized by Czech intellectuals around themes in Kafka turned out to be a political stepping-stone to Dubček's reform government and the Prague Spring of 1968; nonetheless, it was not something Kafka invited, could have foreseen, or would necessarily have enjoyed. Ways of knowing the world that he entitled *The Trial* and *The Castle*—which look to most people like no way of knowing anything—were exploited by these Czech intellectuals as a means of organizing a perception of *their* world persuasive enough to augment a political movement already under way to loosen the bonds of Soviet totalitarianism.

You sound as though you really prefer that fiction should change nothing.

Everything changes everything—nobody argues with that. My point is that whatever changes fiction may appear to inspire have usually to do with the goals of the reader and not of the writer.

There is something that writers do have the power to change and that they work to change every day, and that's writing. A writer's responsibility is to the integrity of his own kind of discourse.

Do you feel that the importance, if not even the integrity, of fictional discourse is threatened by rivals like film and television and the headlines, which propose entirely different ways of knowing the world? Haven't the popular media all but usurped the scrutinizing function that you attribute to the literary imagination?

Fiction that has a scrutinizing function isn't merely threatened, it's been swept away in America as a serious way of knowing the world, almost as much within the country's small cultural elite as among the tens of millions for whom television is the only source of knowing anything. Animated talk about tenth-rate movies by first-rate people has almost displaced discussion of any comparable length or intensity about a book. Talking about movies in the relaxed, impressionistic way that movies invite being talked about is not only the unliterate man's literary life but the literary life of the literate as well. It appears to be easier for even the best-educated people to articulate how they know the world from a pictured story than for them to confidently tell you what they make of a verbal narrative—which goes some way to explaining why what the verbal narrative knows has itself become less knowable. It requires concentration of a kind that has become too difficult for people or too boring or both.

The popular media have usurped literature's scrutinizing function—usurped it and trivialized it. The momentum of the American mass media is toward the trivialization of everything. The trivialization of everything is of no less importance for Americans than repression is for Eastern Europeans, and if the problem has not achieved the same notoriety at the PEN Club as political repression, it's because it flows out of political *freedom*. The threat to a civilized America isn't the censorship of this or that book in some atypical school district somewhere; it's not the government's attempt to suppress or falsify this or that piece of information. It's the *superabundance* of information, the circuits *burgeoning* with information—it's the censorship of *nothing*. The trivialization of everything results from exactly what they do *not* have in Eastern Europe or the Soviet Union—the freedom to say anything and to sell anything however one chooses.

There are now writers in the West tempted to think that it might really be better for their work if they were oppressed in Moscow or Warsaw rather than free in London or Paris. It's as though without an authoritarian environment imaginative possibilities are curtailed and one's literary seriousness is open to question. Unfortunately for writers who may be afflicted with such longings, the intellectual situation for thinking Americans in no telling way mirrors, parallels, or resembles what is horrifying for thoughtful people in the Soviet orbit. There is, however, a looming American menace that evokes its own forms of deprivation and suffering, and that's the creeping trivialization of everything in a society where freedom of expression is anything but compressed.

The Czech writer Josef Skvorecky, who now lives in Toronto, has said, "To be a bad writer in Eastern Europe, you *really* have to be bad." He means that in those countries the political origins of people's suffering are plainly visible in everyday life and the predicament is constantly staring them in the face; personal misfortune is inevitably colored by politics and history, and no individual drama is seemingly without social implications. What Skvorecky wryly suggests is that there is almost a chemical affinity between the consequences of oppression and the genre of the novel; what I'm saying is that in the less graspable consequences of our unprecedented Western freedom there may well be a subject for imaginative scrutiny of no less gravity. Our society doesn't lack for imaginative possibilities because it isn't plagued by the secret police. That it isn't always as easy to be interesting in our part of the world as it is in Skvorecky's occupied country may only mean that to be a good writer in the West and of the West you have to be very, *very* good.

Was it not a problem for your generation of writers to establish the serious-ness of your fiction without resorting to or falling back upon the established conventions of seriousness, be they the realism of James or the modernism of Joyce?

That's a problem for every generation. Ambitious young writers are always tempted to imitate those verified by authority; the influ-ence of an established writer on a beginning writer has usually to do with the search for credentials. Finding a voice and a subject of one's own, however, entails making fiction that may well prompt the writer's first readers to think, "But he can't be serious," as opposed to "This is very serious indeed." The lesson of modernism isn't encap-sulated in a technique that's "Joycean" or a vision that's "Kafkaesque"; it originates in the revolutionary sense of seriousness that's exempli-fied in the fiction of Joyce, Kafka, Beckett, Céline—even of Proust—fiction that to an unknowing reader probably bears the earmark less of seriousness than of high eccentricity and antic obsession. By now the methods of these outlandish writers have themselves become the conventions of seriousness, but that it no way dilutes their mes-sage, which isn't "Make it new," but "Make it serious in the least likely way."

Has the "least likely way" for you been your kind of comedy?

Comedy has been my most likely way. I could do it no other way, though it did require time to work up confidence to take the instinct for comedy seriously, to let it contend with my earnestness and finally take charge. It's not that I don't trust my uncomic side or that I don't have one; it's that the uncomic side more or less resembles everyone else's. Through the expressive gradations of comedy I can best imagine what I know.

Yet isn't Zuckerman, in The Anatomy Lesson, *afraid that he is not "serious" enough, afraid that for all his physical ailments he is not "suffering" sufficiently? Isn't that why he wants to enroll in medical school and, in* The Prague Orgy, *travels to Eastern Europe?*

Yes. His comic predicament results from the repeated attempt to escape his comic predicament. Comedy is what Zuckerman is bound by—what's laughable in *Zuckerman Bound* is his insatiable desire to be a serious man taken seriously by all the serious men like his father and his brother and Milton Appel. A stage direction that appears in *The Prague Orgy* could have been the trilogy's title: *Enter Zuckerman, a serious person.* Coming to terms with the profane realities of what he had assumed to be one of the world's sacred professions is for him a terrific ordeal. His superseriousness is what the comedy's *about.*

Zuckerman Bound opens with a pilgrimage to the patron saint of seriousness, E. I. Lonoff; it ends, as you point out, at the shrine of suffering, Kafka's occupied Prague. Imagining himself married to Anne Frank is the earliest escape that he attempts to contrive from the seriousness that first challenges his youthful illusions about a dignified role in the world. Judge Leopold Wapter, Alvin Pepler, the Czech secret police, a crippling, unexplained pain in the neck—all are representatives of impious life encroaching upon that seriousness he had once believed to be inherent to his calling. But what most successfully subverts the calling's esteem is his sizeable talent for depicting impious life: it's Zuckerman who gives his dignity the most trouble.

The denouement of the trilogy begins midway through the third volume, when, on the way to Chicago to become a doctor—for those Jews who most disapprove of him, the supreme embodiment of professional seriousness—Zuckerman adopts the disguise of a pornographer and, abandoning whatever claim he believes he still may have to be taken seriously, transforms himself into a vessel of the profane. Well, it's a long way from pretending to be the husband of Anne Frank in E.I. Lonoff's sanctum sanctorum to proclaiming himself publisher of *Lickety Split*. Like a good modernist writer, Zuckerman the pornographer imagines at last the least likely way to dramatize the serious lesson taught him by the chastening ordeal of unhallowed existence.

I realize that this sort of ordeal, as suffered by the high-minded, looks like an old, obsessional theme if you think of Gabe Wallach in *Letting Go* or David Kepesh in *The Breast* and *The Professor of Desire*. The ordeal of an unhallowed existence is also what Portnoy's complaining about.

Are you complaining about it—is that why it's an old, obessional theme?

Obsessional themes evolve from astonishment as much as from grievance. A writer is beset not so much by the theme as by an underlying *naïveté* in the face of it. The novelist suffers from serious ignorance of his obsessional theme. He lays siege to it time and again because the obsessional theme is the one he least understands—he knows it so well that he knows how little he knows.

We realize that you are reluctant to appear to be explicating a book prior to its publication. However, without "explaining" it away, can you comment generally on the unusual form for The Counterlife, *which is certainly unlike anything you've done before?*

Normally there is a contract between the author and the reader that gets torn up only at the end of the book. In this book the contract gets torn up at the end of each chapter: a character who is dead and buried is suddenly alive, a character who is assumed to be alive is, in fact, dead, and so on. This is not the ordinary Aristotelian narrative that readers are accustomed to reading or that I am accustomed to writing. It isn't that it lacks a beginning, middle, and ending; there are too *many* beginnings, middles, and endings. It is a book where you never get to the bottom of things—rather than concluding with all the questions answered, it leaves everything suddenly open to question. Because one's original reading is always being challenged and the book progressively undermines its own fictional assumptions, the reader is constantly cannibalizing his own reactions.

In many ways it's everything that people don't want in a novel. Primarily what they want is a story in which they can be made to believe; otherwise they don't want to be bothered. They agree, in accordance with the standard author-reader contract, to believe in the story they are being told—and then in *The Counterlife* they are being told a contradictory story. "I'm interested in what's going on," says the reader, "only now, suddenly, there are three things going on. Which is real and which is false? Which are you asking me to believe in? Why do you bother me like this?"

Which is real and which is false? All are equally real and equally false.

Which are you asking me to believe in? All/none.

Why do you bother me like this? Because there is nothing unusual about somebody's changing his story. People constantly change their story—one runs into that every day. But last time you told me—." "Well, that was last time—this is this time." There is nothing "modernist," "postmodernist," or the least bit avant-garde about that approach. We are writing fictitious versions of our lives *all* the time, contradictory but mutually entangling stories that, however subtly or grossly falsified, constitute our hold on reality and are the closest thing we have to the truth.

Why do I bother you like this? Because life doesn't necessarily have a course, a simple sequence, a predictable pattern. The bothersome form is intended to dramatize that obvious fact. The narratives are all awry but they have a unity; it is expressed in the title—the idea of a counterlife, of counterlives, counterliving. Life, like the novelist, has a powerful transforming urge.

TWO

Writing American Fiction

Several winters back, while I was living in Chicago, the city was shocked and mystified by the death of two teenage girls. So far as I know, the populace is mystified still; as for the shock, Chicago is Chicago, and one week's dismemberment fades into the next's. The victims this particular year were sisters. They went off one December night to see an Elvis Presley movie, for the sixth or seventh time we are told, and never came home. Ten days passed, and fifteen and twenty, and then the whole bleak city, every street and alley, was being searched for the missing Grimes girls, Pattie and Babs. A girl friend had seen them at the movie, a group of boys had caught a glimpse of them afterward getting into a black Buick, another group said a green Chevy, and so on and so forth, until one day the snow melted and the unclothed bodies of the two girls were discovered in a roadside ditch in a forest preserve west of Chicago. The coroner said he didn't know the cause of death, and then the newspapers took over. One paper ran a drawing of the girls on the back page, in bobby socks and Levi's and babushkas: Pattie and Babs a foot tall, and in four colors, like Dixie Dugan on Sundays. The mother of the two girls wept herself right into the arms of a local newspaper lady,

Originally a speech delivered at Stanford University, which co-sponsored with *Esquire* magazine a symposium on "Writing in America Today." (1960)

who apparently set up her typewriter on the Grimeses' front porch and turned out a column a day, telling us that these had been good girls, hard-working girls, average girls, churchgoing girls, et cetera. Late in the evening one could watch television interviews featuring schoolmates and friends of the Grimes sisters: the teenage girls look around, dying to giggle; the boys stiffen in their leather jackets. "Yeah, I knew Babs, yeah, she was all right, yeah, she was popular . . ." On and on, until at last comes a confession. A skid-row bum of thirty-five or so, a dishwasher, a prowler, a no-good named Benny Bedwell, admits to killing both girls, after he and a pal cohabited with them for several weeks in various flea-bitten hotels. Hearing the news, the weeping mother tells the newspaper lady that the man is a liar—her girls, she insists now, were murdered the night they went off to the movie. The coroner continues to maintain (with rumblings from the press) that the girls show no signs of having had sexual intercourse. Meanwhile, everybody in Chicago is buying four papers a day, and Benny Bedwell, having supplied the police with an hour-by-hour chronicle of his adventures, is tossed in jail. Two nuns, teachers of the girls at the school they attended, are sought out by the newspapermen. They are surrounded and questioned, and finally one of the sisters explains all. "They were not exceptional girls," the sister says, "they had no hobbies." About this time, some good-natured soul digs up Mrs. Bedwell, Benny's mother, and a meeting is arranged between this old woman and the mother of the slain teenagers. Their picture is taken together, two overweight, overworked American ladies, quite befuddled but sitting up straight for the photographers. Mrs. Bedwell apologizes for her Benny. She says, "I never thought any boy of mine would do a thing like that." Two weeks later, maybe three, her boy is out on bail, sporting several lawyers and a new one-button-roll suit. He is driven in a pink Cadillac to an out-of-town motel where he holds a press conference. Yes, he is the victim of police brutality. No, he is not a murderer; a degenerate maybe, but even that is changing. He is going to become a carpenter (a carpenter!) for the Salvation Army, his lawyers say. Immediately, Benny is asked to sing (he plays the guitar) in a Chicago night spot for two thousand dollars a week, or is it ten thousand? I forget. What I remember is that suddenly, into the mind of the onlooker, or newspaper reader, comes The Question: is this all public relations? But of course not—two girls are dead. Still, a song begins to catch on in Chicago, "The Benny Bedwell Blues." Another newspaper launches a weekly contest: "How Do You Think the Grimes Girls Were Murdered?" and a prize is given for the best answer (in the opinion of the judges). And now the money begins to flow; donations, hundreds of them, start pouring in to Mrs. Grimes from all over the city and the state. For what? From whom? Most contributions are anonymous. Just the dollars, thousands and thousands of them—the *Sun-Times* keeps us informed of the grand total. Ten thousand, twelve thousand, fifteen thousand. Mrs. Grimes sets about refinishing and redecorating her house. A stranger steps forward, by the name of Shultz or Schwartz—I don't really remember—but he is in the appliance business and he presents Mrs. Grimes with a whole new kitchen. Mrs. Grimes, beside herself with appreciation and joy, turns to her surviving daughter and says, "Imagine me in that kitchen!" Finally, the poor woman goes out and buys two parakeets (or maybe another Mr. Shultz presents them as a gift); one parakeet she calls Babs, the other Pattie. At just about this point, Benny Bedwell, doubtless having barely learned to hammer a nail in straight, is extradited to Florida on the charge of having raped a twelve-year-old girl there. Shortly thereafter I left Chicago myself, and so far as I know, though Mrs. Grimes hasn't her two girls, she has a brand-new dishwasher and two small birds.

And what is the moral of the story? Simply this: that the American writer in the middle of the twentieth century has his hands full in trying to understand, describe, and then make *credible* much of American reality. It stupefies, it sickens, it infuriates, and finally it is even a kind of embarrassment to one's one meager imagination. The actuality is continually outdoing our talents, and the culture tosses up figures almost daily that are the envy of any novelist. Who, for example, could have invented Charles Van Doren? Roy Cohn and David Schine? Sherman Adams and Bernard Goldfine? Dwight David Eisenhower?

Several months back, most of the country heard one of the candidates for the Presidency of the United States say something like, "Now if you feel that Senator Kennedy is right, then I sincerely believe you should vote for Senator Kennedy, and if you feel that I am right, I humbly submit that you vote for me. Now I feel, and this is certainly a personal opinion, that I am right . . ." and so on. Though it did not appear this way to some thirty-four million voters, it still seems to me a little easy to ridicule Mr. Nixon, and it is not for that reason that I have bothered to paraphrase his words here. If one was at first amused by him, one was ultimately astonished. Perhaps as a satiric literary creation, he might have seemed "believable," but I myself found that on the TV screen, as a real public figure, a political fact, my mind balked at taking him in. Whatever else the television debates produced in me, I should point out, as a literary curiosity, they also produced professional envy. All the machinations over make-up and rebuttal time, all the business over whether Mr. Nixon should look at Mr. Kennedy when he replied, or should look away— all of it was so beside the point, so fantastic, so weird and astonishing, that I found myself beginning to wish I had invented it. But then, of course, one need not have been a fiction writer to wish that *someone* had invented it, and that it was not real and with us.

The daily newspapers, then, fill us with wonder and awe (is it possible? is it happening?), also with sickness and despair. The fixes, the scandals, the insanity, the idiocy, the piety, the lies, the noise . . . Recently, in *Commentary*, Benjamin DeMott wrote that the "deeply lodged suspicion of the times [is] namely, that events and individuals are unreal, and that power to alter the course of the age, of my life and your life, is actually vested nowhere." There seems to be, said

DeMott, a kind of "universal descent into unreality." The other night—to give a benign example of the descent—my wife turned on the radio and heard the announcer offering a series of cash prizes for the three best television plays of five minutes' duration written by children. It is difficult at such moments to find one's way around the kitchen. Certainly few days go by when incidents far less benign fail to remind us of what DeMott is talking about. When Edmund Wilson says that after reading *Life* magazine he feels he does not belong to the country depicted there, that he does not live in this country, I understand what he means.

However, for a writer of fiction to feel that he does not really live in his own country—as represented by *Life* or by what he experiences when he steps out the front door—must seem a serious occupational impediment. For what will his subject be? His landscape? One would think that we might get a high proportion of historical novels or contemporary satire—or perhaps just nothing. No books. Yet almost weekly one finds on the best-seller list another novel which is set in Mamaroneck or New York City or Washington, with characters moving through a world of dishwashers and TV sets and advertising agencies and senatorial investigations. It all *looks* as though the writers are turning out books about our world. There is *Cash McCall* and *The Man in the Gray Flannel Suit* and *Marjorie Morningstar* and *The Enemy Camp* and *Advise and Consent,* and so on. But what is noteworthy is that these books aren't very good. Not that the writers aren't sufficiently horrified with the landscape to suit me— quite the contrary. They are generally full of concern for the world about them; finally, however, they just don't imagine the corruption and vulgarity and treachery of American public life any more profoundly than they imagine human character—that is, the country's private life. All issues are generally solvable, suggesting that they are not so much awe-struck or horror-struck as they are provoked by some topical controversy. "Controversial" is a common word in the critical language of this literature, as it is, say, in the language of the TV producer.

It is hardly news that in best-sellerdom we frequently find the hero coming to terms and settling down in Scarsdale, or wherever, knowing himself. And on Broadway, in the third act, someone says, "Look, why don't you just love each other?" and the protagonist, throwing his hand to his forehead, cries, "God, why didn't *I* think of that!" and before the bulldozing action of love, all else collapses— verisimilitude, truth, and interest. It is like "Dover Beach" ending happily for Matthew Arnold, and for us, because the poet is standing at the window with a woman who understands him. If the literary investigation of our era were to become solely the property of Wouk, Weidman, Sloan Wilson, Cameron Hawley, and Broadway's *amor-vincit-omnia* boys it would be unfortunate indeed—like leaving sex to the pornographers, where again there is more to what is happening than first meets the eye.

But the times have not yet been given over completely to lesser minds and talents. There is Norman Mailer. And he is an interesting example of a writer in whom our era has provoked such a magnificent disgust that dealing with it in fiction has almost come to seem, for him, beside the point. He has become an actor in the cultural drama, the difficulty of which is that it leaves one with less time to be a writer. For instance, to defy the civil-defense authorities and their H-bomb drills, you have to take off a morning from the typewriter and go down and stand outside of City Hall; then, if you're lucky and they toss you in jail, you have to give up an evening at home and your next morning's work as well. To defy Mike Wallace, or challenge his principle-less aggression, or simply use him or straighten him out, you must first be a guest on his program*—there's one

---

*In the late fifties and early sixties, Mike Wallace, now a seasoned CBS correspondent, ran an exceedingly abrasive TV interview show; I appeared there to be cross-examined by him after *Goodbye, Columbus* won a National Book Award.

night shot. Then you may well spend the next two weeks (I am speaking from memory) disliking yourself for having gone, and then two more writing an article attempting to explain why you did it and what it was like. "It's the age of the slob," says a character in William Styron's new novel. "If we don't watch out they're going to drag us under. . . ." And the dragging under can take many forms. We get, from Mailer, for instance, a book like *Advertisements for Myself,* a chronicle for the most part of why I did it and what it was like—and who I have it in for: his life as a substitute for his fiction. An infuriating, self-indulgent, boisterous, mean book, not much worse than most advertising we have to put up with—but, taken as a whole, curiously moving in its revelation of despair so great that the man who bears it, or is borne by it, seems for the time being to have given up on making an imaginative assault upon the American experience, and has become instead the champion of a kind of public revenge. However, what one champions one day may make one its victim the next; once having written *Advertisements for Myself,* I don't see that you can write it again. Mailer probably now finds himself in the unenviable position of having to put up or shut up. Who knows— maybe it's where he wanted to be. My own feeling is that times are tough for a fiction writer when he takes to writing letters to his newspaper rather than those complicated, disguised letters to himself, which are stories.

The last is not intended to be a sententious, or a condescending remark, or even a generous one. However one suspects Mailer's style or his motives, one sympathizes with the impulse that leads him to want to be a critic, a reporter, a sociologist, a journalist, or even the Mayor of New York. For what is particularly tough about the times is writing about them, as a serious novelist or storyteller. Much has been made, much of it by the writers themselves, of the fact that the American writer has no status, no respect, and no audience. I am pointing here to a loss more central to the task itself, the loss of a subject; or, to put it another way, a voluntary withdrawal of interest by the fiction writer from some of the grander social and political phenomena of our times.

Of course there have been writers who have tried to meet these phenomena head-on. It seems to me I have read several books or stories in the past few years in which one character or another starts to talk about "The Bomb," and the conversation usually leaves me feeling less than convinced, and in some extreme instances, with a certain amount of sympathy for fallout; it is like people in college novels having long talks about what kind of generation they are. But what then? What can the writer do with so much of the American reality as it is? Is the only other possibility to be Gregory Corso and thumb your nose at the whole thing? The attitude of the Beats (if such a phrase has meaning) is not entirely without appeal. The whole thing is a joke. America, ha-ha. But that doesn't put very much distance between Beatdom and its sworn enemy, best-sellerdom—not much more than what it takes to get from one side of a nickel to the other: for is America, ha-ha, really any more than America, hoo-ray, stood upon its head?

Now it is possible that I am exaggerating the serious writer's response to our cultural predicament and his inability or unwillingness to deal with it imaginatively. There seems to me little, in the end, to prove an assertion about the psychology of a nation's writers, outside, that is, of their books themselves. In this case, unfortunately, the bulk of the evidence is not books that *have* been written but the ones that have been left unfinished, and those that have not even been considered worth the attempt. Which is not to say that there have not been certain literary signs, however, certain obsessions and innovations, to be found in the novels of our best writers, supporting the notion that the social world has ceased to be as suitable or as manageable a subject as it once may have been.

Let me begin with some words about the man who, by reputation at least, is *the* writer of the age. The response of college students to the work of J. D. Salinger indicates that perhaps he, more than anyone else, has not turned his back on the times but, instead, has managed to put his finger on whatever struggle of significance is going on today between self and culture. *The Catcher in the Rye* and the recent stories in *The New Yorker* having to do with the Glass family surely take place in the immediate here and now. But what about the self, what about the hero? The question is of particular interest here, for in Salinger, more than in most of his contemporaries, the figure of the writer has lately come to be placed directly in the reader's line of vision, so that there is a connection, finally, between the attitudes of the narrator as, say, brother to Seymour Glass, and as a man who writes by profession.

And what of Salinger's heroes? Well, Holden Caulfield, we discover, winds up in an expensive sanitarium. And Seymour Glass commits suicide finally, but prior to that he is the apple of his brother's eye—and why not? He has learned to live in this world—but how? By not living in it. By kissing the soles of little girls' feet and throwing rocks at the head of his sweetheart. He is a saint, clearly. But since madness is undesirable and sainthood, for most of us, out of the question, the problem of how to live *in* this world is by no means answered; unless the answer is that one cannot. The only advice we seem to get from Salinger is to be charming on the way to the loony bin. Of course, Salinger is under no obligation to supply advice of any sort to writers or readers—still, I happen to find myself growing more and more curious about this professional writer, Buddy Glass, and how *he* manages to coast through life in the arms of sanity.

There is in Salinger the suggestion that mysticism is a possible road to salvation; at least some of his characters respond well to an intensified, emotional religious belief. Now my own reading in Zen is minuscule, but as I understand it from Salinger, the deeper we go into this world, the further we can get away from it. If you contemplate a potato long enough, it stops being a potato in the usual sense; unfortunately, however, it is the usual sense that we have to deal with from day to day. For all his loving handling of the world's objects there seems to me, in Salinger's Glass family stories as in *The Catcher*, a spurning of life as it is lived in the immediate world—this place and time is viewed as unworthy of those few precious people who have been set down in it only to be maddened and destroyed.

A spurning of our world—though of a different order—occurs in the work of another of our most gifted writers, Bernard Malamud. Even when Malamud writes a book about baseball, *The Natural*, it is not baseball as it is played in Yankee Stadium but a wild, wacky game, where a player who is instructed to knock the cover off the ball promptly steps up to the plate and does just that: the batter swings and the inner core of the ball goes looping out to center field, where the confused fielder commences to tangle himself in the unwinding sphere; then the shortstop runs out and, with his teeth, bites the center fielder and the ball free from one another. Though *The Natural* is not Malamud's most successful book, it is at any rate our introduction to his world, which is by no means a replica of our own. There are really things called baseball players, of course, and really things called Jews, but there much of the similarity ends. The Jews of *The Magic Barrel* and the Jews of *The Assistant* are not the Jews of New York City or Chicago. They are Malamud's invention, a metaphor of sorts to stand for certain possibilities and promises, and I am further inclined to believe this when I read the statement attributed to Malamud which goes, "All men are Jews." In fact, we know this is not so; even the men who are Jews aren't sure they're Jews. But Malamud, as a writer of fiction, has not shown specific interest in the anxieties and dilemmas and corruptions of the contemporary American Jew, the Jew we think of as characteristic of our times. Rather, his people live in a timeless depression and a placeless Lower East Side; their society is not affluent, their predicament is not cultural. I am not saying—one cannot, of Malamud—that he has spurned life or an examination of its difficulties. What it is to be human, and to be humane, is his deepest concern. What I do mean to point out is that he does not—or has not yet—found the *contemporary* scene a proper or sufficient backdrop for his tales of heartlessness and heartache, of suffering and regeneration.

Now, Malamud and Salinger cannot, of course, be considered to speak for all American writers, and yet their fictional response to the world about them—what they choose to emphasize or ignore—is of interest to me simply because they are two of the best. Of course there are plenty of other writers around, capable ones too, who do not travel the same roads; however, even among these others, I wonder if we may not be witnessing a response to the times, less apparently dramatized perhaps than the social detachment in Salinger and Malamud, but there in the body of the work nonetheless.

Let us take up the matter of prose style. Why is everybody so bouncy all of a sudden? Those who have been reading Saul Bellow, Herbert Gold, Arthur Granit, Thomas Berger, and Grace Paley will know to what I am referring. Writing recently in *The Hudson Review,* Harvey Swados said that he saw developing "a nervous muscular prose perfectly suited to the exigencies of an age which seems at once appalling and ridiculous. These are metropolitan writers, most of them are Jewish, and they are specialists in a kind of prose-poetry that often depends for its effectiveness as much on how it is ordered, or how it looks on the printed page, as it does on what it is expressing. This is risky writing . . ." Swados added, and perhaps it is in its very riskiness that we can discover some kind of explanation for it. I'd like to compare two short descriptive passages, one from Bellow's *The Adventures of Augie March,* the other from Gold's new novel, *Therefore Be Bold,* in the hope that the differences revealed will be educational.

As numerous readers have already pointed out, the language of *Augie March* combines literary complexity with conversational ease, joins the idiom of the academy with the idiom of the streets (not all streets—certain streets); the style is special, private, energetic, and though it can at times be unwieldy, it generally serves Bellow brilliantly. Here, for instance, is a description of Grandma Lausch:

> With the [cigarette] holder in her dark little gums between which all her guile, malice, and command issued, she had her best inspirations of strategy. She was as wrinkled as an old paper bag, an autocrat, hard-shelled and jesuitical, a pouncy old hawk of a Bolshevik, her small ribboned gray feet immobile on the shoekit and stool Simon had made in the manual-training class, dingy old wool Winnie [the dog] whose bad smell filled the flat on the cushion beside her. If wit and discontent don't necessarily go together, it wasn't from the old woman that I learned it.

Herbert Gold's language has also been distinctly special, private, energetic. One notices in the following passage from *Therefore Be Bold* that here too the writer begins by recognizing a physical similarity between the character to be described and some unlikely object, and from there, as in Bellow's Grandma Lausch passage, attempts to wind up, via the body, making a discovery about the soul. The character described is named Chuck Hastings.

> In some respects he resembled a mummy—the shriveled yellow skin, the hands and head too large for a wasted body, the bottomless eye sockets of thought beyond the Nile. But his agile Adam's apple and point-making finger made him less the Styx-swimmer dog-paddling toward Coptic limbos than a high school intellectual intimidating the navel-eyed little girls.

First, the grammar itself has me baffled: ". . . bottomless eye sockets of thought beyond the Nile." Is the thought beyond the Nile, or the eye sockets? What does it mean to be beyond the Nile anyway? These grammatical difficulties have little in common with the ironic inversion with which Bellow's description begins: "With the holder in her dark little gums between which all her guile, malice, and command issued . . ." Bellow goes on to describe Grandma Lausch as an "autocrat," "hard-shelled," "jesuitical," "a pouncy old hawk of a Bolshevik"—imaginative certainly, but tough-minded, *exact*, not primarily exhibitionistic. Of Gold's Chuck Hastings, however, we learn, "His agile Adam's apple and point-making finger made him less the Styx-swimmer dog-paddling toward Coptic limbos," etc. . . . Language in the service of the narrative, or literary regression in the service of the ego? In a recent review of *Therefore Be Bold,* Granville Hicks quoted this very paragraph in praise of Gold's style. "This is high-pitched," Mr. Hicks admitted, "but the point is that Gold keeps it up and keeps it up." I take it the sexual pun is not deliberate; nevertheless, it might serve as a reminder that showmanship and passion are not one and the same. What we have here is not stamina or vitality but reality taking a back seat to personality—and not the personality of the imagined character, but of the writer who is doing the imagining. Bellow's description seems to arise out of a writer's firm grasp of his character: Grandma Lausch *is.* Behind the description of Chuck Hastings there seems to me something else that is being said: Herbert Gold is. Look at me, I'm writing.

Now, I am not trying to sell selflessness here. Rather, I am suggesting that this nervous muscular prose that Swados talks about may perhaps have something to do with the unfriendly relations that exist between the writer and the culture. The prose suits the age, Swados suggests, and I wonder if it does not suit it, in part, because it rejects it. The writer thrusts before our eyes—it is in the very ordering of his sentences—*personality*, in all its separateness and specialness. Of course, the mystery of personality may be nothing less than a writer's ultimate concern; and certainly when the muscular prose is revealing of character and evocative of an environment—as in *Augie March*—it can be wonderfully effective; at its worst, however, as a form of literary onanism, it seriously curtails the fictional possibilities, and may perhaps be thought of as a symptom of the writer's loss of the community—of what is *outside* himself—as subject.

True, the bouncy style can be understood in other ways as well. It is not surprising that most of the practitioners Swados points to are Jewish. When writers who do not feel much of a connection to Lord Chesterfield begin to realize that they are under no real obligation to try and write like that distinguished old stylist, they are likely enough to go out and be bouncy. Also, there is the matter of the spoken language which these writers have heard, as our statesmen might put it, in the schools, the homes, the churches and the synagogues of the nation. I would even say that when the bouncy style is not an attempt to dazzle the reader, or one's self, but to incorporate into American literary prose the rhythms, nuances, and emphases of urban and immigrant speech, the result can sometimes be a language of new and rich emotional subtleties, with a kind of backhanded charm and irony all its own, as in Grace Paley's book of stories *The Little Disturbances of Man*.

But whether the practitioner is Gold, Bellow, or Paley, there is a further point to make about the bounciness: it is an expression of pleasure. However, a question: If the world is as crooked and unreal as it feels to me it is becoming, day by day; if one feels less and less power in the face of this unreality; if the inevitable end is destruction, if not of all life, then of much that is valuable and civilized in life—then why in God's name is the writer pleased? Why don't all our fictional heroes wind up in institutions, like Holden Caulfield, or suicides, like Seymour Glass? Why is it that so many of them—not just in books by Wouk and Weidman but in Bellow, Gold, Styron, and others—wind up affirming life? For surely the air is thick these days with affirmation, and though we shall doubtless get our annual editorial this year from *Life* calling for affirmative novels, the fact is that more and more books by serious writers seem to end on a note of celebration. Not just the tone is bouncy, the moral is bouncy too. In *The Optimist,* another of Gold's novels, the hero, having taken his lumps, cries out in the book's last line, "More. More. More! More! More!" Curtis Harnack's novel, *The Work of an Ancient Hand,* ends with the hero filled with "rapture and hope" and saying aloud, "I believe in God." And Saul Bellow's *Henderson the Rain King* is a book given over to celebrating the regeneration of the heart, blood, and general health of its hero. Yet it is of some importance, I think, that the regeneration of Henderson takes place in a world that is thoroughly and wholly imagined, *but that does not really exist.* It is not the tumultuous Africa of the newspapers and the United Nations discussions that Eugene Henderson visits. There is nothing here of nationalism or riots or apartheid. But why should there be? There is the world, and there is also the self. And the self, when the writer turns upon it all his attention and talent, is revealed to be a most remarkable thing. First off, it exists, it's real. *I am,* the self cries out, and then, taking a nice long look, it adds, *and I am beautiful.*

At the conclusion to Bellow's book, his hero, Eugene Henderson, a big, sloppy millionaire, is returning to America, coming home from a trip to Africa, where he has been plague fighter, lion tamer, and rainmaker; he is bringing back with him a real lion. Aboard the plane he befriends a small Persian boy, whose language he cannot understand. Still, when the plane lands at Newfoundland, Henderson takes the child in his arms and goes out onto the field. And then:

> Laps and laps I galloped around the shining and riveted body of the plane, behind the fuel trucks. Dark faces were looking from within. The great, beautiful propellers were still, all four of them. I guess I felt it was my turn now to move, and so went running—leaping, leaping, pounding, and tingling over the pure white lining of the gray Arctic silence.

And so we leave Henderson, a very happy man. Where? In the Arctic. This picture has stayed with me since I read the book a year ago: of a man who finds energy and joy in an imagined Africa, and celebrates it on an unpeopled, ice-bound vastness.

Earlier I quoted from Styron's new novel, *Set This House on Fire*. Now Styron's book, like Bellow's, also tells of the regeneration of an American who leaves his own country and goes abroad for a while to live. But where Henderson's world is wildly removed from our own, Kinsolving, Styron's hero, inhabits a place we immediately recognize. The book is thick with detail that twenty years from now will probably require extensive footnotes to be thoroughly understood. The hero is an American painter who has taken his family to live in a small town on the Amalfi coast. Cass Kinsolving detests America, and himself. Throughout most of the book he is taunted, tempted, and disgraced by Mason Flagg, a fellow countryman, who is rich, boyish, naïve, licentious, indecent, cruel, and stupid. Kinsolving, by way of his attachment to Flagg, spends most of the book choosing between living and dying, and at one point, in a tone that is characteristic, says this about his expatriation:

> . . . the man I had come to Europe to escape [why he's] the man in all the car advertisements, you know, the young guy waving there—he looks so beautiful and educated and everything, and he's got it *made*, Penn State and a blonde there, and a smile as big as a billboard. And he's going places. I mean electronics. Politics. What they call communication. Advertising. Saleshood. Outer space. God only knows. And he's as ignorant as an Albanian peasant.

However, despite all his disgust with what American public life can do to a man's private life, Kinsolving, like Henderson, comes back to America at the end, having opted for existence. But the America that we find him in seems to me to be the America of his childhood, and (if only in a metaphoric way) of everyone's childhood: he tells his story while he fishes from a boat in a Carolina stream. The affirmation at the conclusion is not as go-getting as Gold's "More! More!" or as sublime as Harnack's "I believe in God," or as joyous as Henderson's romp on the Newfoundland airfield. "I wish I could tell you that I had found some belief, some rock . . ." Kinsolving says, "but to be truthful, you see, I can only tell you this: that as for being and nothingness, the only thing I did know was that to choose between them was simply to choose being . . ." Being. Living. Not where one lives or with whom one lives—but *that* one lives.

And what does all of this add up to? It would, of course, drastically oversimplify the art of fiction to suggest that Saul Bellow's book or Herbert Gold's prose style arise ineluctably out of our distressing cultural and political predicament. Nonetheless, that the communal predicament *is* distressing weighs upon the writer no less, and perhaps even more, than upon his neighbor—for to the writer the community is, properly, both subject and audience. And it may be that when this situation produces not only feelings of disgust, rage, and melancholy but impotence too, the writer is apt to lose heart and turn finally to other matters, to the construction of wholly imaginary worlds, and to a celebration of the self, which may, in a variety of ways, become his subject, as well as the impetus that establishes the perimeters of his technique. What I have tried to point out is that the vision of self as inviolable, powerful, and nervy, self imagined as the only seemingly real thing in an unreal-seeming environment, has given some of our writers joy, solace, and muscle. Certainly to have come through a serious personal struggle intact, simply to have survived, is nothing to be made light of, and it is for just this reason that Styron's hero manages to engage our sympathies right down to the end. Still, when the survivor cannot choose but be ascetic, when the self can only be celebrated as it is excluded from society, or as it is exercised and admired in a fantastic one, we then do not have much reason to be cheery. Finally, for me there is something unconvincing about a regenerated Henderson up on the pure white lining of the world dancing around that shining airplane. Consequently, it is not with this scene that I should like to conclude, but instead with the image of his hero that Ralph Ellison presents at the end of *Invisible Man*. For here too the hero is left with the simple stark fact of himself. He is as alone as a man can be. Not that he hasn't gone out into the world; he has gone out into it, and out into it, and out into it—but at the end he chooses to go underground, to live there and to wait. And it does not seem to him a cause for celebration either.

Some New Jewish Stereotypes

I find that I am suddenly living in a country in which the Jew has come to be—or is allowed for now to think he is—a cultural hero. Only recently on the radio I heard a disc jockey introducing the theme song from the new movie *Exodus*. The words were to be sung by Pat Boone. The disc jockey made it clear that this was the "only authorized version of the song." Authorized by what? For whom? Why? No further word from the d.j. Only a silence crackling with piety, and then Mr. Boone, singing out of something less than a whirlwind—

> This land is mind,
> God gave this land to me!

I do not know whether I am moving up or down the cultural ladder, or simply sideways, when I recall that there has been the song "Exodus," preceded by the movie *Exodus,* preceded by the novel *Exodus.* However you slice it, there does not seem to be any doubt that

---

Originally a speech delivered at Loyola University (Chicago) for a symposium on "The Needs and Images of Man," sponsored jointly by the Anti-Defamation League of B'nai B'rith and Loyola. (1961)

the image of the Jew as patriot, warrior, and battle-scarred belliger-
ent is rather satisfying to a large segment of the American public.

In an interview in the *New York Post,* Leon Uris, the author of the
novel, claims that his image of the Jewish fighter is a good deal closer
to the truth than images of Jews presented by other Jewish writers. I
take it I am one of the others to whom Mr. Uris is referring—the *Post*
clipping was mailed to me by a woman demanding some explanation for the "anti-Semitism and self-hatred" that she found in a collection of my short fiction that had just been published. What Uris
told his interviewer, Joseph Wershba, was this:

> There is a whole school of Jewish American writers, who
> spend their time damning their fathers, hating their moth-
> ers, wringing their hands and wondering why they were
> born. This isn't art or literature. It's psychiatry. These writ-
> ers are professional apologists. Every year you find one of
> their works on the best seller lists. Their work is obnoxious
> and makes me sick to my stomach.
>
> I wrote *Exodus* because I was just sick of apologizing—
> or feeling that it was necessary to apologize. The Jewish
> community of this country has contributed far more greatly
> than its numbers—in art, medicine, and especially literature.
>
> I set out to tell a story of Israel. I am definitely biased. I
> am definitely pro-Jewish.
>
> An author goes through everything his readers do. It was
> a revelation to me, too, when I was researching *Exodus* in
> Europe and in Israel. And the revelation was this: that we
> Jews are not what we have been portrayed to be. In truth,
> we have been fighters.

"In truth, we have been fighters." So bald, stupid, and uninformed
is the statement that it is not even worth disputing. One has the feeling that, single-handed, Uris has set out to counter with his new

image of the Jew, the older one that comes down to us in those several stories, the punch line of which is, "Play nice, Jakie—don't fight." However, there is not much value in swapping one simplification for the other. What Uris might do, when he is not having revelations by way of "researching" novels, is to read a new book called *Dawn,* by Elie Wiesel. Wiesel is not an American-Jewish writer; he is a Hungarian Jew now living in New York, and his first book, *Night,* was an autobiographical account of his experiences as a fifteen-year-old boy in Auschwitz and Buchenwald, those concentration camps, he writes, which "consumed my faith forever . . . murdered my God and my soul and turned my dreams to dust." *Dawn,* the second book, has for its background the Jewish terrorist activities in Palestine that preceded the establishment of the State of Israel. The hero is assigned the task of executing a British major who has been taken hostage by the Jewish terrorists; the novel deals with the terrible hours the hero spends prior to the execution. I should like to tell Uris that Wiesel's Jew is not so proud to discover himself in the role of a fighter, nor is he able to find justification for himself in some traditional Jewish association with pugnacity or bloodletting. But actually it turns out that there is really no need to tell Uris anything of the sort; if we can believe a news item that we find in *Time* magazine, he already knows more than he lets on in the *New York Post.*

In Manhattan, *Time* reports,

> Captain Yehiel Aranowicz, 37 . . . one-time master of the blockade-running Israeli refugee ship "Exodus," reported some reservations back home about the best selling (4,000,000 copies to date) novel inspired by his 1947 heroics. "Israelis," he said, "were pretty disappointed in the book, to put it lightly. The types that are described in it never existed in Israel. The novel is neither history nor literature." . . . In Encino, California, *Exodus'* author Leon Uris rebutted: "You may quote me as saying, 'Captain who?' and that's all I

have to say. I'm not going to pick on a lightweight. Just look
at my sales figures."

Admittedly, it is not safe to indict a man solely on the basis of
what *Time* quotes him as having said; it may even be *Time*'s pleasure
to titillate its readers with a classic stereotype—the Jewish hustler
who will sell anything for a price. There was a time when this image
was helpful to certain Gentiles in dealing with the Jew. Now there is
another way of dealing with him—there is the image that Mr. Uris
has sold, the image millions have read about in his book and other
millions will see flickering on the screen.

There is Leon Uris to make the Jew and Jewishness acceptable,
appealing, and attractive, and there is that famous optimist and
cracker-barrel philosopher, Harry Golden. The image of the Jew
that Harry Golden presents has been analyzed to a turn in Theodore
Solotaroff's recent essay in *Commentary*, "Harry Golden and the
American Audience." Mr. Solotaroff points out that in Golden's
three books, *For 2¢ Plain, Only in America,* and *Enjoy, Enjoy!* he "satisfied both Jewish nostalgia and Gentile curiosity," that "he presents
with depressing clarity certain very real problems and conditions of
our society in the past decade—a society characterized by its well-
intentioned but soft, sloppy, equivocal thinking about itself. . . . Gar-
nished with a little Manischewitz horseradish the perplexed banalities
of the middle class come back to [the reader] as the wisdom of the
ages."

Solotaroff thinks of horseradish; in matters Goldenian, I am
a schmaltz man myself. It is interesting to observe that Golden,
in replying to Solotaroff's comments, manages himself to lay the
schmaltz on with one hand while at the same time trying to wipe it
away with the other. In his newspaper, *The Carolina Israelite,* Golden
writes that Solotaroff is dead wrong in accusing him of glamorizing
life in the New York ghetto. With characteristic restraint and logic,
Golden explains: "We Jews . . . not only had a society, but, quite

frankly, a Jewish city, and this sense of community is what lends memories of the old East Side its glamour, and it is for this reason that the bulk of American Jewry up in the middle class lick their fingers over everything I write about the Lower East Side of New York. Sentiment alone could never sustain such amazingly wide-spread interest." The word is spelled sentimentality, and if *it* can't produce widespread interest, what can?

Popular Jewish interest in Golden and in Uris isn't hard to understand. For one thing, there is the pleasure of recognition, the plain and simple kick that comes of seeing the words "kugel" and "latkes" in print. Then there is the romance of oneself: The Hebrew Hero on the one hand, the Immigrant Success on the other. Harry Golden, a self-confessed Horatio Alger, furnishes us with the names of the judges, movie stars, scientists, and comedians who have risen from the Jewish Lower East Side to fame and fortune. But what of the Gentile interest? Four million people have bought copies of *Exodus;* two million, copies of *Only in America;* they can't all have been Jews. Why this Gentile interest in Jewish characters, history, manners, and morals? How does Pat Boone come to be singing the "only authorized version" anyway? Why not Moishe Oysher or Eddie Fisher?

One explanation Solotaroff offers for Golden's appeal is that, among other things, Golden presents to his readers a world characterized by "vividness, energy, aspiration, discipline, and finally the warmth of life—that is, precisely those qualities which are said to be declining in the modern middle-class family and suburb." And there does seem to be fascination these days with the idea of Jewish emotionalism. People who have more sense than to go up to Negroes and engage them in conversation about "rhythm" have come up to me and asked about my "warmth." They think it is flattering—and they think it is true.

I do not believe that they think it is complicated; that warmth, when it does appear, does not just radiate itself—at the center there is usually a fire.

There are several Jewish graduate students in a class I teach at the Writing Workshop of the State University of Iowa, and during this last semester three of them wrote stories about a Jewish childhood; and in all three the emotional pitch of the drama ran very high. Curiously, or perhaps not so curiously, in each story the hero is a Jewish boy, somewhere between ten and fifteen, who gets excellent grades in school and is always combed and courteous. The stories, all told in the first person, have to do with a friendship that grows up between the hero and a Gentile neighbor or schoolmate. The Gentile is from a slightly lower class—Italian-American, in one instance, Tom Sawyer-American in another—and he leads the Jewish boy, who is of the middle class, into the world of the flesh. The Gentile boy has himself already had some kind of sexual experience. Not that he is much older than his Jewish sidekick—he has had a chance to find his way to adventure because his parents pay hardly any attention to him at all: they are divorced, or they drink, or they are uneducated and say "goddamn" all the time, or they just don't seem to be around that much to care. This leaves their offspring with plenty of time to hunt for girls. The Jewish boy, on the other hand, is watched—he is watched at bedtime, at study time, and especially at mealtime. Who he is watched by is his mother. The father we rarely see, and between him and the boy there seems to be little more than a nodding acquaintance. The old man is either working or sleeping or across the table, silently stowing it away. Still, there is a great deal of warmth in these families—especially when compared to the Gentile friend's family—and almost all of it is generated by the mother. And it does not strike the young hero the way it strikes Harry Golden and his audience. The fire that warms can also burn and asphyxiate: what the hero envies the Gentile boy is his parents' *indifference,* and largely, it would seem, because of the opportunities it affords him for sexual adventure. Religion here is understood, not as the key to the mysteries of the divine and the beyond, but to the mystery of the sensual and the erotic, the wonder of laying a hand on the girl down the street. The warmth these Jewish storytellers want then is the warmth to which the Gentiles seem (to them) to have such easy access, just as the warmth that Harry Golden's Gentiles envy him for is the warmth he tells them that Jews come by practically as a matter of course.

I hasten to point out that in these short stories the girls to whom the Gentile friend leads the young narrator are never Jewish. The Jewish women are mothers and sisters. The sexual yearning is for the Other. The dream of the shiksa—counterpart to the Gentile dream of the Jewess, often adjectivally described as "melon-breasted." (See Thomas Wolfe.) I do not mean, by the way, to disparage the talent of these writing students by comparing their interest in a Jewish boy's dreams with the kind of dreaminess you find in Golden: what the heroes of these stories invariably learn—as the Gentile comrades disappear into other neighborhoods or into maturity—are the burdensome contradictions of their own predicament.

Golden and Uris burden no one with anything. Indeed, much of their appeal is that they help to dissipate guilt, real and imagined. It turns out that the Jews are not poor innocent victims after all—all the time they were supposed to be being persecuted, they were having a good time being warm to one another and having their wonderful family lives. What they were developing—as one reviewer quoted by Solotaroff says of Harry Golden—was their "lovely Jewish slant on the world."

Ah, that lovely Jewish slant—its existence surely can soothe the conscience: for if the victim is not a victim, then the victimizer is probably not a victimizer either. Along with the other comforts Golden offers, there is a kind of escape hatch for Gentiles who, if they have not been practicing anti-Semites, have at any rate been visited with distrustful, suspicious feelings about Jews, feelings which they are told they ought not to have. Golden assures them (as he assures the Jews) that we are a happy, optimistic, endearing people, and also that we live in a top-notch country—is not his career proof that bigotry does not corrode and corrupt the American system? There he is, a Jew—and one who speaks up, mind you—a respected citizen in a Southern city. Wonderful! And not in Sweden either, or in Italy, or in the Philippines. Only—Golden tells them—in America!

This may be pleasant therapy for certain anxious, well-meaning Gentiles, in that they do not have to continue to feel guilty for crimes for which they do not in fact bear any responsibility; it may even unburden some halfhearted anti-Semites who don't like Jews because they don't like themselves for not liking Jews. But I do not see that it is very respectful to the Jews and the hard facts of their history. Or even to the validity of Gentile suspiciousness. For why shouldn't the Gentiles have suspicions? The fact is that, if one is committed to being a Jew, then he believes that on the most serious questions pertaining to man's survival—understanding the past, imagining the future, discovering the relation between God and humanity—that he is right and the Christians are wrong. As a believing Jew, he must certainly view the breakdown in this century of moral order and the erosion of spiritual values in terms of the inadequacy of Christianity as a sustaining force for the good. However, who would care to say such things to his neighbor? Rather, what we witness daily in American life is the "socialization of the anti-social . . . the acculturation of the anti-cultural . . . the legitimization of the subversive." These phrases are Lionel Trilling's; he has used them to describe the responses many of his students have to the more extreme elements in modern literature. His words have for me an even broader cultural relevance: I refer to the swallowing up of difference that goes on around us continuously, that deadening "tolerance" that robs—and is designed to rob—those who differ, diverge, or rebel of their powers. Instead of being taken seriously as a threat, a man is effectively silenced by being made popular. They are presently holding beatnik parties in the suburbs—which does not convince me that all men are brothers. On the contrary, they are strangers; that comes home to me every day when I read the newspaper. They are strangers, and just as often they are enemies, and it is because that is how things are that it behooves us, not "to love one another" (which from all evidence appears to be asking for the moon), but to practice no violence and treachery upon one another, which, it would seem, is difficult enough.

But of course the Jews *have* done violence. It is the story of their violence that Leon Uris is so proud to tell to America. Its appeal to American Jews is not hard to understand, but again, what of the Gentiles? Why all the piety about the "only authorized version" of a popular song? Why is the song even popular? the movie? the book? So persuasive and agreeable is the *Exodus* formulation to so many in America that I am inclined to wonder if the burden that it is working to remove from the nation's consciousness is nothing less than the memory of the holocaust itself, the murder of six million Jews, in all its raw, senseless, fiendish horror. As though, say, a popular song or movie were to come along some day soon to enable us to dispose of that other troublesome horror, the murder of the citizens of Hiroshima. In the case of Hiroshima, we might perhaps be told a story and given a song to sing about the beautiful modern city that has risen from the ashes of atomic annihilation, about how much more prosperous, healthy, and enterprising life is in the new city than it was in the one that vanished. But be that as it may—and who in this go-getting land is to say that it may not be soon enough?— now there is Golden to assure us that even ghettoized Jews were really happy, optimistic, and warm (as opposed to aggrieved, pessimistic, and xenophobic), and there is Uris to say that you don't have to worry about Jewish vulnerability and victimization after all, the Jews can take care of themselves. They *have* taken care of themselves. One week *Life* magazine presents on its cover a picture of Adolf Eichmann; weeks later, a picture of Sal Mineo as a Jewish freedom fighter. A crime to which there is no adequate human response, no grief, no compassion, no vengeance that is sufficient seems, in part then, to have been avenged. And when the scales appear at last to begin to balance, there cannot but be a sigh of relief. The Jew is no longer looking out from the wings on the violence of our age, nor is he its favorite victim; now he is a participant. Fine then. Welcome aboard. A man with a gun and a hand grenade, a man who kills for his God-given rights (in this case, as the song informs us, God-given *land*) cannot sit so easily in judgment of another man when he kills for what God has given *him*, according to his accounting and inventory.

Mr. Uris's discovery that the Jews are fighters fills him with pride; it fills any number of his Jewish readers with pride as well, and his Gentile readers less perhaps with pride than with relief. However, the hero of *Dawn*, Elie Wiesel's novel about the Jewish terrorists, is visited with less comforting and buoyant emotions. He is overcome with shame and confusion and a sense that he is locked hopelessly and forever in a tragic nightmare. No matter how just he tells himself are the rights for which he murders, nothing in his or his people's past is able to make firing a bullet into another man anything less ghastly than it is. He has seen and suffered so much, in Buchenwald and Auschwitz, that it is with a final sense of the death of what he thought he was that he pulls the trigger on the British officer and becomes another of the executioners in our violent century. He is one of those Jews, like Job, who wonder why they were born.

Writing About Jews

1

Ever since some of my first stories were collected in 1959 in a volume called *Goodbye, Columbus,* my work has been attacked from certain pulpits and in certain periodicals as dangerous, dishonest, and irresponsible. I have read editorials and articles in Jewish community newspapers condemning these stories for ignoring the accomplishments of Jewish life, or, as Rabbi Emanuel Rackman recently told the convention of the Rabbinical Council of America, for creating a "distorted image of the basic values of Orthodox Judaism," and even, he went on, for denying the non-Jewish world the opportunity of appreciating the "overwhelming contribution which Orthodox Jews are making in every avenue of modern endeavor. . . ." Among the letters I receive from readers, there have been a number written by Jews accusing me of being anti-Semitic and "self-hating," or, at least, tasteless; they argue or imply that the sufferings of the Jews throughout history, culminating in the murder of six million by the Nazis, have made certain criticisms of Jewish life insulting and triv-

---

This essay evolved from remarks delivered in 1962 and 1963 at the University of Iowa Hillel House, the Hartford, Conn., Jewish Community Center, and Yeshiva University. (1963)

ïal. Furthermore, it is charged that such criticism as I make of Jews—or apparent criticism—is taken by anti-Semites as justification of their attitudes, as "fuel" for their fires, particularly as it is a Jew himself who seemingly admits to habits and behavior that are not exemplary, or even normal and acceptable. When I speak before Jewish audiences, invariably there have been people who have come up to me afterward to ask, "Why don't you leave us alone? Why don't you write about the Gentiles?"—"Why must you be so critical?"—"Why do you disapprove of us so?"—this last question asked as often with incredulity as with anger; and often by people a good deal older than myself, asked as of an erring child by a loving but misunderstood parent.

It is difficult, if not impossible, to explain to some of the people claiming to have felt my teeth sinking in that in many instances they haven't been bitten at all. Not always, but frequently, what readers have taken to be my disapproval of the lives lived by Jews seems to have to do more with their own moral perspective than with the one they would ascribe to me: at times they see wickedness where I myself had seen energy or courage or spontaneity; they are ashamed of what I see no reason to be ashamed of, and defensive where there is no cause for defense.

Not only do they seem to me often to have cramped and untenable notions of right and wrong, but looking at fiction as they do—in terms of "approval" and "disapproval" of Jews, "positive" and "negative" attitudes toward Jewish life—they are likely not to see what it is that the story is really about.

To give an example. A story I wrote called "Epstein" tells of a sixty-year-old man who has an adulterous affair with the lady across the street. In the end, Epstein, who is the hero, is caught—caught by his family, and caught and struck down by exhaustion, decay, and disappointment, against all of which he had set out to make a final struggle. There are Jewish readers, I know, who cannot figure out why I found it necessary to tell this story about a Jewish man: don't other people commit adultery too? Why is it the Jew who must be shown cheating?

But there is more to adultery than cheating: for one thing, there is the adulterer himself. For all that some people may experience him as a cheat and nothing else, he usually experiences himself as something more. And generally speaking, what draws most readers and writers to literature is this "something more"—all that is beyond simple moral categorizing. It is not my purpose in writing a story of an adulterous man to make it clear how right we all are if we disapprove of the act and are disappointed in the man. Fiction is not written to affirm the principles and beliefs that everybody seems to hold, nor does it seek to guarantee the appropriateness of our feelings. The world of fiction, in fact, frees us from the circumscriptions that society places upon feeling; one of the greatnesses of the art is that it allows both the writer and the reader to respond to experience in ways not always available in day-to-day conduct; or, if they are available, they are not possible, or manageable, or legal, or advisable, or even necessary to the business of living. We may not even know that we have such a range of feelings and responses *until* we have come into contact with the work of fiction. This does not mean that either reader or writer no longer brings any judgment to bear upon human action. Rather, we judge at a different level of our being, for not only are we judging with the aid of new feelings but without the necessity of having to act upon judgment. Ceasing for a while to be upright citizens, we drop into another layer of consciousness. And this expansion of moral consciousness, this exploration of moral fantasy, is of considerable value to a man and to society.

I do not care to go at length here into what a good many readers take for granted are the purposes and possibilities of fiction. I do want to make clear, however, to those whose interests may not lead them to speculate much on the subject, a few of the assumptions a writer may hold—assumptions such as lead me to say that I do not write a story to make evident whatever disapproval I may feel for adulterous men. I write a story of a man who is adulterous to reveal the condition of such a man. If the adulterous man is a Jew, then I am revealing the condition of an adulterous man who is a Jew. Why tell that story? Because I seem to be interested in how—and why and when—a man acts counter to what he considers to be his "best self," or what others assume it to be, or would like it to be. The subject is hardly "mine"; it interested readers and writers for a long time before it became my turn to be engaged by it too.

One of my readers, a man in Detroit, was himself not too engaged and suggested in a letter to me that he could not figure out why I was. He posed several questions which I believe, in their very brevity, were intended to disarm me. I quote from his letter without his permission.

The first question: "Is it conceivable for a middle-aged man to neglect business and spend all day with a middle-aged woman?" The answer is yes.

Next he asks: "Is it a Jewish trait?" I take it he is referring to adultery and not facetiously to the neglecting of business. The answer is: "Who said it was?" Anna Karenina commits adultery with Vronsky, with consequences more disastrous than those Epstein brings about. Who thinks to ask, "Is it a Russian trait?" It is a decidedly human possibility. Even though the most famous injunction against it is reported as being issued, for God's own reasons, to the Jews, adultery has been one of the ways by which people of *all* faiths have sought pleasure—or freedom, or vengeance, or power, or love, or humiliation . . .

The next in the gentleman's series of questions to me is: "Why so much *shmutz*?" Is he asking, Why is there dirt in the world? Why is there disappointment? Why is there hardship, ugliness, evil, death? It would be nice to think these were the questions he had in mind when he asks, "Why so much *shmutz*?" But all he is really asking is, "Why so much *shmutz* in that story?" This is what the story adds up to for him. An old man discovers the fires of lust are still burning in him? *Shmutz!* Disgusting! Who wants to hear that kind of stuff! Struck as he is by nothing but the dirty aspects of Epstein's troubles, the gentleman from Detroit concludes that I am narrow-minded.

So do others. Narrow-mindedness, in fact, was the charge that a New York rabbi, David Seligson, was reported in *The New York Times* recently as having brought against me and other Jewish writers who, he told his congregation, dedicated themselves "to the exclusive creation of a melancholy parade of caricatures." Rabbi Seligson also disapproved of *Goodbye, Columbus* because I described in it a "Jewish adulterer . . . and a host of other lopsided schizophrenic personalities." Of course, adultery is not a characteristic symptom of schizophrenia, but that the rabbi should see it this way, as a sign of a diseased personality, indicates to me that we have different notions as to what health is. After all, it may be that *life* produces a melancholy middle-aged businessman like Lou Epstein, who in Dr. Seligson's eyes looks like another in a parade of caricatures. I myself find Epstein's adultery an unlikely solution to his problems, a pathetic, even doomed response, and a comic one too, since it does not even square with the man's own conception of himself and what he wants; but none of this *unlikeliness* leads me to despair of his sanity, or humanity. I suppose it is tantamount to a confession from me of lopsided schizophrenia to admit that the character of Epstein happened to have been conceived with considerable affection and sympathy. As I see it, one of the rabbi's limitations is that he cannot recognize a bear hug when one is being administered right in front of his eyes.

The *Times* report continues: "The rabbi said he could only 'wonder about' gifted writers, 'Jewish by birth, who can see so little in the tremendous saga of Jewish history.'" But I don't imagine the rabbi "wonders" about me any more than I wonder about him: that wondering business is only the voice of wisdom that is supposed to be making itself heard, always willing to be shown the light, if, of course, there is any; but I can't buy it. Pulpit fair-mindedness only hides the issue—as it does here in the rabbi's conclusion, quoted by the *Times:* "'That they [the Jewish writers in question] must be free to write, we would affirm most vehemently; but that they would know their own people and tradition, we would fervently wish.'"

However, the issue is not knowledge of one's "people." At least, it is not a question of who has more historical data at his fingertips, or is more familiar with Jewish tradition, or which of us observes more customs and rituals. It is even possible, needless to say, to "know" a good deal about tradition, and to misunderstand what it is that tradition signifies. The story of Lou Epstein stands or falls not on how much I know about tradition but on how much I know and understand about Lou Epstein. Where the history of the Jewish people comes down in time and place to become the man whom I called Epstein, that is where my knowledge must be sound. But I get the feeling that Rabbi Seligson wants to rule Lou Epstein *out* of Jewish history. I find him too valuable to forget or dismiss, even if he is something of a *grubber yung* and probably more ignorant of history than the rabbi believes me to be.

Epstein is pictured not as a learned rabbi, after all, but as the owner of a small paper-bag company; his wife is not learned either, and neither is his mistress; consequently, a reader should not expect to find in this story knowledge on my part, or the part of the characters, of the *Sayings of the Fathers;* he has every right to expect that I be close to the truth as to what might conceivably be the attitudes of a Jewish man of Epstein's style and history toward marriage, family life, divorce, and fornication. This story is called "Epstein" because Epstein, not the Jews, is the subject; where the story is weak I think I know by this time; but the rabbi will never find out until he comes at the thing in terms of what *it* wants to be about, rather than what he would like it to be about.

Obviously, though, his interest is not in the portrayal of character; what he wants in my fiction is, in his words, a "balanced portrayal of Jews as we know them." I even suspect that something called "balance" is what the rabbi would advertise as the most significant characteristic of Jewish life; what Jewish history comes down to is that at long last we have in our ranks one of everything. But his assumptions about the art of fiction are what I should like to draw particular attention to. In his sermon Rabbi Seligson says of Myron Kaufmann's *Remember Me to God* that it can "hardly be said to be recognizable as a Jewish sociological study." But Mr. Kaufmann, as a novelist, probably had no intention of writing a sociological study, or—for this seems more like what the rabbi really yearns for in the way of reading—a nice positive sampling. *Madame Bovary* is hardly recognizable as a sociological study either, having at its center only a single, dreamy, provincial Frenchwoman, and not one of every other kind of provincial Frenchwoman too; this does not, however, diminish its brilliance as a novel, as an exploration of Madame Bovary herself. Literary works do not take as their subjects characters and events which have impressed a writer primarily by the *frequency* of their appearance. For example, how many Jewish men, as we know them, have come nearly to the brink of plunging a knife into their only son because they believed God had demanded it of them? The story of Abraham and Isaac derives its meaning from something other than its being a familiar, recognizable, everyday occurrence. The test of any literary work is not how broad is its range of representation—for all that breadth may be characteristic of a kind of narrative—but the depth with which the writer reveals whatever he has chosen to represent.

To confuse a "balanced portrayal" with a novel is finally to be led into absurdities. "Dear Fyodor Dostoevsky—All the students in our school, and most of the teachers, feel that you have been unfair to us. Do you call Raskolnikov a balanced portrayal of students as we know them? Of Russian students? Of poor students? What about those of us who have never murdered anyone, who do our schoolwork every night?" "Dear Mark Twain—None of the slaves on our plantation has ever run away. But what will our owner think when he reads of Nigger Jim?" "Dear Vladimir Nabokov—The girls in our class . . ." and so on. What fiction does and what the rabbi would like it to do are two entirely different things. The concerns of fiction are not those of a statistician—or of a public-relations firm. The novelist asks himself, "What do people think?"; the PR man asks, "What *will* people think?" But I believe this is what is actually troubling the rabbi when he calls for his "balanced portrayal of Jews": What will people think?

Or, to be exact: What will the goyim think?

2

This was the question raised—and urgently—when another story of mine, "Defender of the Faith," appeared in *The New Yorker* in April 1959. The story is told by Nathan Marx, an army sergeant just rotated back to Missouri from combat duty in Germany, where the war has ended. As soon as he arrives, he is made first sergeant in a training company, and immediately is latched on to by a young recruit who tries to use his attachment to the sergeant to receive kindnesses and favors. The attachment, as he sees it, is that they are both Jews. As the story progresses, what the recruit, Sheldon Grossbart, comes to demand are not mere considerations but privileges to which Marx does not think he is entitled. The story is about one man who uses his own religion, and another's uncertain conscience, for selfish ends; but mostly it is about this other man, the narrator, who, because of the ambiguities of being a member of his religion, is involved in a taxing, if mistaken, conflict of loyalties.

I don't now, however, and didn't while writing, see Marx's problem as nothing more than "Jewish": confronting the limitations of charity and forgiveness in one's nature—having to draw a line between what is merciful and what is just—trying to distinguish between apparent evil and the real thing, in one's self and others—these are problems for most people, regardless of the level at which they are perceived or dealt with. Yet, though the moral complexities are not exclusively a Jew's, I never for a moment considered that the characters in the story should be anything other than Jews. Someone else might have written a story embodying the same themes, and similar events perhaps, and had at its center Negroes or Irishmen; for me there was no choice. Nor was it a matter of making Grossbart a Jew and Marx a Gentile, or vice versa; telling half the truth would have been much the same here as telling a lie. Most of those jokes beginning "Two Jews were walking down the street" lose a little of their punch if one of the Jews, or both, is disguised as an Englishman or a Republican. Similarly, to have made any serious alteration in the Jewish factuality of "Defender of the Faith," as it began to fill itself out in my imagination, would have so unsprung the tensions I felt in the story that I would no longer have had left a story that I wanted to tell, or one I believed myself able to.

Some of my critics must wish that this had happened, for in going ahead and writing this story about Jews, what else did I do but confirm an anti-Semitic stereotype? But to me the story confirms something different, if no less painful, to its readers. To me Grossbart is not something we can dismiss solely as an anti-Semitic stereotype; he is a Jewish fact. If people of bad intention or weak judgment have converted certain facts of Jewish life into a stereotype of The Jew, that does not mean that such facts are no longer important in our lives, or that they are taboo for the writer of fiction. Literary investigation may even be a way to redeem the facts, to give them the weight and value that they should have in the world, rather than the disproportionate significance they obviously have for some misguided or vicious people.

Sheldon Grossbart, the character I imagined as Marx's antagonist, has his seed in fact. He is not meant to represent The Jew, or Jewry, nor does the story indicate that the writer intends him to be understood that way by the reader. Grossbart is depicted as a single blundering human being, one with force, self-righteousness, cunning, and, on occasion, even a little disarming charm; he is depicted as a man whose lapses of integrity seem to him so necessary to his survival as to convince him that such lapses are actually committed in the name of integrity. He has been able to work out a system whereby his own sense of responsibility can suspend operation, what with the collective guilt of the others having become so immense as to have seriously altered the conditions of trust in the world. He is represented not as the stereotype of The Jew, but as a Jew who acts like the stereotype, offering back to his enemies their vision of him, answering the punishment with the crime. Given the particular kinds of humiliations and persecutions that the nations have practiced on the Jews, it argues for far too much nobility to deny not only that Jews like Grossbart exist but that the temptations to Grossbartism exist in many who perhaps have more grace, or will, or are perhaps only more cowed, than the simple frightened soul that I imagined weeping with fear and disappointment at the end of the story. Grossbart is not The Jew; but he is a fact of Jewish experience and well within the range of its moral possibilities.

And so is his adversary, Marx, who is, after all, the story's central character, its consciousness and its voice. He is a man who calls himself a Jew more tentatively than does Grossbart; he is not sure what it means—means for *him*—for he is not unintelligent or without conscience; he is dutiful, almost to a point of obsession, and confronted by what are represented to him as the needs of another Jew, he does not for a while know what to do. He moves back and forth from feelings of righteousness to feelings of betrayal, and only at the end, when he truly does betray the trust that Grossbart tries to place in him, does he commit what he has hoped to all along: an act he can believe to be honorable.

Marx does not strike me, nor any of the readers I heard from, as unlikely, incredible, "made-up"; the verisimilitude of the characters and their situation was not what was called into question. In fact, an air of convincingness that the story was believed to have caused a number of people to write to me, and *The New Yorker,* and the Anti-Defamation League, protesting its publication.

Here is one of the letters I received after the story was published:

Mr. Roth:

With your one story, "Defender of the Faith," you have done as much harm as all the organized anti-Semitic organizations have done to make people believe that all Jews are cheats, liars, connivers. Your one story makes people—the general public—forget all the great Jews who have lived, all the Jewish boys who served well in the armed services, all the Jews who live honest hard lives the world over. . . .

Here is one received by *The New Yorker:*

Dear Sir:

. . . We have discussed this story from every possible angle and we cannot escape the conclusion that it will do irreparable damage to the Jewish people. We feel that this story presented a distorted picture of the average Jewish soldier and are at a loss to understand why a magazine of your fine reputation should publish such a work which lends fuel to anti-Semitism.

Clichés like "this being Art" will not be acceptable. A reply will be appreciated.

Here is a letter received by the officials of the Anti-Defamation League, who, because of the public response, telephoned to ask if I wanted to talk to them. The strange emphasis of the invitation, I thought, indicated the discomfort they felt at having to pass on messages such as this:

Dear ———,

What is being done to silence this man? Medieval Jews would have known what to do with him. . . .

The first two letters I quoted were written by Jewish laymen, the last by a rabbi and educator in New York City, a man of prominence in the world of Jewish affairs.

The rabbi was later to communicate directly with me. He did not mention that he had already written to the Anti-Defamation League to express regret over the decline of medieval justice, though he was careful to point out at the conclusion of his first letter his reticence in another quarter. I believe I was supposed to take it as an act of mercy: "I have not written to the editorial board of *The New Yorker,*" he told me. "I do not want to compound the sin of informing. . . ."

Informing. There was the charge so many of the correspondents had made, even when they did not want to make it openly to me, or to themselves. I had informed on the Jews. I had told the Gentiles what apparently it would otherwise have been possible to keep secret from them: that the perils of human nature afflict the members of our minority. That I had also informed them it was possible for there to be such a Jew as Nathan Marx did not seem to bother anybody; if I said earlier that Marx did not seem to strike my correspondents as unlikely, it is because he didn't strike them at all. He might as well not have been there. Of the letters that I read, just one mentioned Marx, and only to point out that I was no less blameworthy for portraying the Sergeant as a "white Jew," as he was described by my correspondent, a kind of Jewish Uncle Tom.

But even if Marx were that and only that, a white Jew, and Grossbart a black one, did it in any way follow that because I had examined the relationship between them—another concern central to the story which drew barely a comment from my correspondents—that I had then advocated that Jews be denationalized, deported, persecuted, murdered? Well, no. Whatever the rabbi may believe privately, he did not indicate to me that he thought I was an anti-Semite. There was a suggestion, however, and a grave one, that I had acted like a fool. "You have earned the gratitude," he wrote, "of all who sustain their anti-Semitism on such conceptions of Jews as ultimately led to the murder of six million in our time."

Despite the sweep there at the end of the sentence, the charge made is actually up at the front: I "earned the gratitude . . ." But of whom? I would put it less dramatically but maybe more exactly: of those who are predisposed to misread the story—out of bigotry, ignorance, malice, or even innocence. If I did earn their gratitude, it was because they failed to see, even to look for, what I was talking about . . . Such conceptions of Jews as anti-Semites hold, then, and as they were able to confirm by misunderstanding my story, are the same, the rabbi goes on to say, as those which "ultimately led to the murder of six million in our time."

"Ultimately"? Is that not a gross simplification of the history of the Jews and the history of Hitler's Germany? People hold serious grudges against one another, vilify one another, deliberately misunderstand one another, but they do not always, as a consequence, *murder* one another, as the Germans murdered the Jews, and as other Europeans allowed the Jews to be murdered, or even helped the slaughter along. Between prejudice and persecution there is usually, in civilized life, a barrier constructed by the individual's convictions and fears, and the community's laws, ideals, values. What "ultimately" caused this barrier to disappear in Germany cannot be explained only in terms of anti-Semitic misconceptions; surely what must also be understood here is the intolerability of Jewry, on the one hand, and its usefulness, on the other, to the Nazi ideology and dream.

By simplifying the Nazi-Jewish relationship, by making *prejudice* appear to be the primary cause of annihilation, the rabbi is able to make the consequences of publishing "Defender of the Faith" in *The New Yorker* seem very grave indeed. He doesn't appear to be made at all anxious, however, by the consequences of his own position. For what he is suggesting is that some subjects must not be written about, or brought to public attention, because it is possible for them to be misunderstood by people with weak minds or malicious instincts. Thus he consents to put the malicious and weak-minded in a position of determining the level at which open communication on these subjects will take place. This is not fighting anti-Semitism but submitting to it: that is, submitting to a restriction of consciousness as well as communication, because being conscious and being candid are too risky.

In his letter the rabbi calls my attention to that famous madman who shouts "Fire!" in a "crowded theater." He leaves me to complete the analogy myself: by publishing "Defender of the Faith" in *The New Yorker:* (1) I am shouting; (2) I am shouting "Fire!"; (3) there is no fire; (4) all this is happening in the equivalent of a "crowded theater." The crowded theater: there is the risk. I should agree to sacrifice the freedom essential to my vocation, and even to the general well-being of the culture, because—because of what? The "crowded theater" has absolutely no relevance to the situation of the Jew in America today. It is a grandiose delusion. It is not a metaphor describing a cultural condition but a revelation of the nightmarish visions that plague people as demoralized as the rabbi appears to be: rows endless, seats packed, lights out, doors too few and too small, panic and hysteria just under the skin . . . No wonder he says to me finally, "Your story—in Hebrew—in an Israeli magazine or newspaper—would have been judged exclusively from a literary point of view." That is, ship it off to Israel. But please don't tell it here, now.

Why? So that "they" will not commence persecuting Jews again? If the barrier between prejudice and persecution collapsed in Germany, this is hardly reason to contend that no such barrier exists in our country. And if it should ever begin to appear to be crumbling, then we must do what is necessary to strengthen it. But not by putting on a good face; not by refusing to admit to the intricacies and impossibilities of Jewish lives; not by pretending that Jews have existences less in need of, and less deserving of, honest attention than the lives of their neighbors; not by making Jews invisible. The solution is not to convince people to like Jews so as not to want to kill them; it is to let them know that they cannot kill them even if they despise them. And how to let them know? Surely repeating over and over to oneself, "It can happen here," does little to prevent "it" from happening. Moreover, ending persecution involves more than stamping out persecutors. It is necessary, too, to unlearn certain responses to them. All the tolerance of persecution that has seeped into the Jewish character—the adaptability, the patience, the resignation, the silence, the self-denial—must be squeezed out, until the only response there is to any restriction of liberties is "No, I refuse."

The chances are that there will always be some people who will despise Jews, just so long as they continue to call themselves Jews; and, of course, we must keep an eye on them. But if some Jews are dreaming of a time when they will be accepted by Christians as Christians accept one another—if *this* is why certain Jewish writers should be silent—it may be that they are dreaming of a time that cannot be, and of a condition that does not exist this side of one's dreams. Perhaps even the Christians don't accept one another as they are imagined to in that world from which Jews may believe themselves excluded solely because they are Jews. Nor are the Christians going to feel toward Jews what one Jew may feel toward another. The upbringing of the alien does not always alert him to the whole range of human connections which exists between clannish solidarity on the one hand and exclusion or rejection on the other. Like those of most men, the lives of Jews no longer take place in a world that is just *landsmen* and enemies. The cry "Watch out for the goyim!" at times seems more the expression of an unconscious wish than of a warning: Oh that they were out there, so that we could be together in here! A rumor of persecution, a taste of exile, might even bring with it that old world of feelings and habits—something to replace the new world of social accessibility and moral indifference, the world which tempts all our promiscuous instincts, and where one cannot always figure out what a Jew is that a Christian is not.

Jews are people who are not what anti-Semites say they are. That was once a statement out of which a man might begin to construct an identity for himself; now it does not work so well, for it is difficult to act counter to the ways people expect you to act when fewer and fewer people define you by such expectations. The success of the struggle against the defamation of Jewish character in this country has itself made more pressing the need for a Jewish self-consciousness that is relevant to this time and place, where neither defamation nor persecution are what they were elsewhere in the past. For those Jews who choose to continue to call themselves Jews, and find reason to do so, there are courses to follow to prevent it from ever being 1933 again that are more direct, reasonable, and dignified than beginning to act as though it already is 1933—*or as though it always is.* But the death of all those Jews seems to have taught my correspondent, a rabbi and a teacher, little more than to be discreet, to be foxy, to say this but not that. It has taught him nothing other than how to remain a victim in a country where he does not have to live like one if he chooses. How pathetic. And what an insult to the dead. Imagine: sitting in New York in the 1960's and piously summoning up the "six million" to justify one's own timidity.

Timidity—and paranoia. It does not occur to the rabbi that there are Gentiles who will read the story intelligently. The only Gentiles the rabbi can imagine looking into *The New Yorker* are those who hate Jews and those who don't know how to read very well. If there are others, they can get along without reading about Jews. For to suggest that one translate one's stories into Hebrew and publish them in Israel is to say, in effect: "There is nothing in our lives we need to tell the Gentiles about, unless it has to do with how well we manage. Beyond that, it's none of their business. We are important to no one but ourselves, which is as it should be (or better be) anyway." But indicate that moral crisis is something to be hushed up is not, of course, to take the prophetic line; nor is it a rabbinical point of view that Jewish life is of no significance to the rest of mankind.

Even given his own kind of goals, however, the rabbi is not very farsighted or imaginative. What he fails to see is that the stereotype as often arises from ignorance as from malice; deliberately keeping Jews out of the imagination of Gentiles, for fear of the bigots and their stereotyping minds, is really to invite the invention of stereotypical ideas. A book like Ralph Ellison's *Invisible Man,* for instance, seems to me to have helped many whites who are not anti-Negro, but who do hold Negro stereotypes, to surrender their simpleminded notions about Negro life. I doubt, however, that Ellison, describing as he does not just the squalor Negroes must put up with but certain bestial aspects of his Negro characters as well, has converted one Alabama redneck or one United States senator over to the cause of desegregation; nor could the novels of James Baldwin cause Governor Wallace to conclude anything more than that Negroes are just as hopeless as he's always known them to be. As novelists, neither Baldwin nor Ellison are (to quote Mr. Ellison on himself) "cogs in the machinery of civil rights legislation." Just as there are Jews who feel that my books do nothing for the Jewish cause, so there are Negroes, I am told, who feel that Mr. Ellison's work has done little for the Negro cause and probably has harmed it. But that seems to place the Negro cause somewhat outside the cause of truth and justice. That many blind people are still blind does not mean that Ellison's book gives off no light. Certainly those of us who are willing to be taught, and who needed to be, have been made by *Invisible Man* less stupid than we were about Negro lives, including those lives that a bigot would point to as affirming his own half-baked, inviolable ideas.

3

But it is the treachery of the bigot that the rabbi appears to be worried about and that he presents to me, to himself, and probably to his congregation, as the major cause for concern. Frankly, I think those are just the old words coming out, when the right buttons are pushed. Can he actually believe that on the basis of my story anyone is going to start a pogrom, or keep a Jew out of medical school, or even call some Jewish schoolchild a kike? The rabbi is entombed in his nightmares and fears; but that is not the whole of it. He is also hiding something. Much of this disapproval of "Defender of the Faith" because of its effect upon Gentiles seems to me a coverup for what is really objected to, what is immediately painful—and that is its direct effect upon certain Jews. "You have hurt a lot of people's feelings because you have revealed something they are ashamed of." That is the letter the rabbi did not write but should have. I would have argued then that there are things of more importance—even to these Jews—than those feelings that have been hurt, but at any rate he would have confronted me with a genuine fact, with something I was actually responsible for, and which my conscience would have had to deal with, as it does.

For the record, all the letters I saw that came in about "Defender of the Faith" were from Jews. Not one of those people whose gratitude the rabbi believes I earned wrote to say, "Thank you," nor was I invited to address any anti-Semitic organizations. When I did begin to receive speaking invitations, they were from Jewish ladies' groups, Jewish community centers, and from all sorts of Jewish organizations, large and small.

And I think this bothers the rabbi too. Some Jews are hurt by my work; but some are interested. At the rabbinical convention I mentioned earlier, Rabbi Emanuel Rackman, a professor of political science at Yeshiva University, reported to his colleagues that certain

Jewish writers were "assuming the mantle of self-appointed spokes-men and leaders for Judaism." To support his remark he referred to a symposium held in Israel this last June at which I was present; as far as I know, Rabbi Rackman was not. If he had been there, he would have heard me make it quite clear that I did not want to, did not intend to, and was not able to speak *for* American Jews; I surely did not deny, and no one questioned the fact, that I spoke *to* them, and I hope to others as well. The competition that Rabbi Rackman imag-ines himself to be engaged in hasn't to do with who will presume to lead the Jews; it is really a matter of who, in addressing them, is going to take them more seriously—strange as that may sound—with who is going to see them as something more than part of the mob in a crowded theater, more than helpless and threatened and in need of reassurance that they are as "balanced" as anyone else. The question really is, who is going to address men and women like men and women, and who like children. If there are Jews who have begun to find the stories the novelists tell more provocative and pertinent than the sermons of some of the rabbis, perhaps it is because there are regions of feeling and consciousness in them which cannot be reached by the oratory of self-congratulation and self-pity.

The Story of Three Stories

The three stories of mine that Larry Arrick has chosen to adapt and direct for the stage—and that, taken together, he calls *Unlikely Heroes*—are among the first I wrote and published. As a result I am no longer on intimate or even particularly friendly terms with them. This isn't to say that I find the stories wholly without merit, or that, from the heights of my professionalism, I am ready to dismiss them out of hand as juvenilia. For one thing, there are no such heights, only new stages in the writer's perennial apprenticeship. Each new project makes one into a beginner again, though a different sort of beginner in the seventies than in the fifties. My point is simply that fourteen years and five books of fiction have come and gone since these stories were everything to me, and I would be a mawkish, deluded parent if I were to feel toward them in their awkward adolescence as I did in their darling infancy.

At seventy-nine, Tolstoy told a youthful admirer, "I have completely forgotten my earlier work." Not quite half the titan's age, I am able to recall the tiny apartment across from Stagg Field on Chicago's South Side where, fourteen years ago, I sat at my desk

This piece appeared in the Arts and Leisure section of *The New York Times* a few days before the New York opening of *Unlikely Heroes,* a dramatization by Larry Arrick of three stories from *Goodbye, Columbus.* (1971)

writing these stories, yet I am largely out of touch by now with the interests that generated them and determined their spirit and tone. I remember some sentences here and there as mine, but it has already begun to seem that a stranger imagined the story as a whole.

The pressures of personal history and literary idealism that cause a first book to be written are apt to be like none that a writer is ever to experience again. The example of the great writers will probably never be stronger (for good and bad) and his own virgin forest of memory, fantasy, and obsession may never again be so vast. Then there is the exuberance of being a literary orphan. Not as yet informed that he is a realistic writer, or a Jewish writer, or an academic writer, or a controversial writer, he is not tempted either to satisfy the expectation or to subvert it. An embarrassment of riches—and yet, with it all, the fledgling invariably winds up writing somewhat like the bad poet described by T. S. Eliot, who is "usually unconscious where he ought to be conscious, and conscious where he ought to be unconscious."

In my own earliest work I attempted to transform into fiction something of the small world in which I had spent the first eighteen years of my life. The stories did not draw so much upon immediate personal experience or the history of my own family as upon the ethos of my highly self-conscious Jewish neighborhood, which had been squeezed like some embattled little nation in among ethnic rivals and antagonists, peoples equally proud, ambitious, and xeno-phobic, and equally baffled and exhilarated by the experience of being fused into a melting pot. It was to this nation-neighborhood—this demi-Israel in a Newark that was our volatile Middle East—that I instinctively turned for material at the beginning of my writing career, and to which I returned, ten years later, when I tried to distill from that Newark Jewish community the fictional, or folkloric, fam-ily that I called the Portnoys.

Of the three stories dramatized in *Unlikely Heroes*, "Epstein" is the most strongly rooted in that vanishing world. It is the story of an aging Jewish businessman, married and lonely lo these many years, who is jolted by a sexual pang into the bed of the buxom widow across the street. For his terminal bravery he receives a venereal rash and, if that isn't enough in the way of somatic retribution, a nearly fatal heart attack. I wrote "Epstein" when I was twenty-four, ten years after my father had recounted a similar tale of neighborhood adultery during dinner one night—mealtime being Scheherazade-time in our kitchen. At fourteen I had been delighted to hear that scandalous passion had broken out on our decent, law-abiding street, but my pleasure derived especially from the blend of comedy and sympathy with which the story had been told. A decade later, when I set out to make fiction from this delicious bit of neighborhood gossip, I tried to be faithful to the point of view of the original narrator, which seemed to me morally astute and, in its unself-righteous gaiety and lustiness, endearing. In writing I of course shifted the story's intestines around to get at what I took to be the vital organs—and then tacked on a special cardiac seizure to give the story the brutal edge that Mr. Reality had strangely neglected to impart on this occasion.

With "Defender of the Faith" and "Eli, the Fanatic"—the other stories adapted by Arrick for *Unlikely Heroes*—I began to move out of the old neighborhood, relying less upon the ethos and atmosphere of a place than upon a state of mind, a sense of self, which for lack of a better term is frequently called "Jewishness." Written immediately after "Epstein," these two stories turned out to be something of a departure from those stories of Jewish life upon which many readers, myself included, had been raised, particularly in the immediate postwar years. Instead of telling of a Jew who is persecuted by a Gentile because he is a Jew—a subject treated variously in *Gentleman's Agreement* by Laura Z. Hobson, *Focus* by Arthur Miller, and *The Victim* by Saul Bellow—each of my two stories was about a Jew persecuted for being a Jew *by another Jew.*

I did not realize at the time that I had turned the familiar subject of anti-Semitism somewhat on its head, and that, in writing of the harassment of Jew by Jew rather than Jew by Gentile, I was pressing readers to alter a system of responses to "Jewish" fiction to which they had perhaps become more than a little accustomed. Had I been fully alert to the demand being made and the expectations being bucked, I might not have been so bewildered by the charges of "anti-Semitism" and "self-hatred" that were brought against me by any number of Jewish readers following the publication in *The New Yorker*, in 1959, of "Defender of the Faith." Only five thousand days after Buchenwald and Auschwitz it was asking a great deal of people still frozen in horror by the Nazi slaughter of European Jewry to consider, with ironic detachment, or comic amusement, the internal politics of Jewish life. In some instances, understandably, it was asking the impossible.

It remains to be seen now how much or how little uneasiness these three stories will arouse in an audience that has lived through the turbulence of the intervening decade—and how much or how little pleasure they may provide.

The Newark Public Library

What will the readers of Newark do if the City Council goes ahead with its money-saving plan to shut down the public library system on April 1? Will they loot the stacks the way Newarkers looted appliance stores in the riot of 1967? Will police be called in to Mace down thieves racing off with the *Encyclopaedia Britannica?* Will scholars take up sniping positions at reference-room windows and school-children seize the main Washington Street building in order to complete their term papers? If the City Council locks up the books, will library card holders band together to "liberate" them?

I suppose one should hope not. Apparently there must be respect for Law and Order, even where there is none for aspiration and curiosity and quiet pleasure, for language, learning, scholarship, intelligence, reason, wit, beauty, and knowledge.

When I was growing up in Newark in the forties, we assumed

In February 1969, after riots had already destroyed much of Newark's black slums, the City Council voted to strike from the city budget the $2.8 million required to finance the Newark Museum and the Newark Public Library. Hundreds of Newark residents vehemently opposed this move, which would have shut down two exceptional civic institutions. In the face of the protest, the council eventually rescinded their decision. My piece appeared on the editorial page of *The New York Times* about two weeks after the announcement of the budget cutback. (1969)

that the books in the public library belonged to the public. Since my family did not own many books, or have the money for a child to buy them, it was good to know that solely by virtue of my municipal citizenship I had access to any book I wanted from that grandly austere building downtown on Washington Street, or from the branch library I could walk to in my neighborhood. No less satisfying was the idea of communal ownership, property held in common for the common good. Why I had to care for the books I borrowed, return them unscarred and on time, was because they weren't mine alone, they were everybody's. That idea had as much to do with civilizing me as any I was ever to come upon in the books themselves.

If the idea of a *public* library was civilizing, so was the place, with its comforting quiet, its tidy shelves, its knowledgeable, dutiful employees who weren't teachers. The library wasn't simply where one had to go to get the books, it was a kind of exacting haven to which a city youngster willingly went for his lesson in restraint and his training in self-control. And then there was the lesson in order, the enormous institution itself serving as instructor. What trust it inspired—in both oneself and in systems—first to decode the catalogue card, then to make it through the corridors and stairwells into the open stacks, and there to discover, exactly where it was supposed to be, the desired book. For a ten-year-old to find he actually can steer himself through tens of thousands of volumes to the very one he wants is not without its satisfactions. Nor did it count for nothing to carry a library card in one's pocket; to pay a fine; to sit in a strange place, beyond the reach of parent and school, and read whatever one chose, in anonymity and peace; finally, to carry home across the city and even into bed at night a book with a local lineage of its own, a family tree of Newark readers to which one's name had now been added.

In the forties, when the city was still largely white, it was simply an unassailable fact of life that the books were "ours" and that the public library had much to teach us about the rules of civilized life, as well as civilized pleasures to offer. It is strange (to put it politely) that now, when Newark is mostly black, the City Council (for fiscal reasons, we are told) has reached a decision that suggests that the books don't really belong to the public after all, and that what a library provides for the young is no longer essential to an education. In a city seething with social grievances there is, in fact, probably little that could be *more* essential to the development and sanity of the thoughtful and ambitious young than access to those books. For the moment the Newark City Council may have solved its fiscal problem; it is too bad, however, that the councilmen are unable to calculate the frustration, cynicism, and rage that this insult must inevitably generate, and to imagine what shutting down its libraries may cost the community in the end.

My Baseball Years

In one of his essays George Orwell writes that, though he was not very good at the game, he had a long, hopeless love affair with cricket until he was sixteen. My relations with baseball were similar. Between the ages of nine and thirteen, I must have put in a forty-hour week during the snowless months over at the neighborhood playfield—softball, hardball, and stickball pick-up games—while simultaneously holding down a full-time job as a pupil at the local grammar school. As I remember it, news of two of the most cataclysmic public events of my childhood—the death of President Roosevelt and the bombing of Hiroshima—reached me while I was out playing ball. My performance was uniformly erratic; generally okay for those easygoing pick-up games, but invariably lacking the calm and the expertise that the naturals displayed in stiff competition. My taste, and my talent, such as it was, was for the flashy, whiz-bang catch rather than the towering fly; running and leaping I loved, all the do-or-die stuff—somehow I lost confidence waiting and waiting for the ball lofted right at me to descend. I could never make the high school team, yet I remember that, in one of the two years I vainly (in both senses of the word) tried out, I did a good enough imitation of

Written at the invitation of *The New York Times,* to appear on the Op-Ed page on the opening day of the baseball season. (1973)

a baseball player's *style* to be able to fool (or amuse) the coach right down to the day he cut the last of the dreamers from the squad and gave out the uniforms.

Though my disappointment was keen, my misfortune did not necessitate a change in plans for the future. Playing baseball was not what the Jewish boys of our lower-middle-class neighborhood were expected to do in later life for a living. Had I been cut from the high school itself, *then* there would have been hell to pay in my house, and much confusion and shame in me. As it was, my family took my chagrin in stride and lost no more faith in me than I actually did in myself. They probably would have been shocked if I had made the team.

Maybe I would have been too. Surely it would have put me on a somewhat different footing with this game that I loved with all my heart, not simply for the fun of playing it (fun was secondary, really), but for the mythic and aesthetic dimension that it gave to an American boy's life—particularly to one whose grandparents could hardly speak English. For someone whose roots in America were strong but only inches deep, and who had no experience, such as a Catholic child might, of an awesome hierarchy that was real and felt, baseball was a kind of secular church that reached into every class and region of the nation and bound millions upon millions of us together in common concerns, loyalties, rituals, enthusiasms, and antagonisms. Baseball made me understand what patriotism was about, at its best.

Not that Hitler, the Bataan Death March, the battle for the Solomons, and the Normandy invasion didn't make of me and my contemporaries what may well have been the most patriotic generation of schoolchildren in American history (and the most willingly and successfully propagandized). But the war we entered when I was eight had thrust the country into what seemed to a child—and not only to a child—a struggle to the death between Good and Evil. Fraught with perilous, unthinkable possibilities, it inevitably nourished a patriotism grounded in moral virtue and bloody-minded hate, the patriotism that fixes a bayonet to a Bible. It seems to me that through baseball I was put in touch with a more humane and tender brand of patriotism, lyrical rather than martial or righteous in spirit, and without the reek of saintly zeal, a patriotism that could not so easily be sloganized, or contained in a high-sounding formula to which you had to pledge something vague but all-encompassing called your "allegiance."

To sing the National Anthem in the school auditorium every week, even during the worst of the war years, generally left me cold. The enthusiastic lady teacher waved her arms in the air and we obliged with the words: "See! Light! Proof! Night! There!" But nothing stirred within, strident as we might be—in the end, just another school exercise. It was different, however, on Sundays out at Ruppert Stadium, a green wedge of pasture miraculously walled in among the factories, warehouses, and truck depots of industrial Newark. It would, in fact, have seemed to me an emotional thrill forsaken if, before the Newark Bears took on the hated enemy from across the marshes, the Jersey City Giants, we hadn't first to rise to our feet (my father, my brother and I—along with our inimical countrymen, the city's Germans, Italians, Irish, Poles, and, out in the Africa of the bleachers, Newark's Negroes) to celebrate the America that had given to this unharmonious mob a game so grand and beautiful.

Just as I first learned the names of the great institutions of higher learning by trafficking in football pools for a neighborhood bookmaker rather than from our high school's college adviser, so my feel for the American landscape came less from what I learned in the classroom about Lewis and Clark than from following the major-league clubs on their road trips and reading about the minor leagues in the back pages of *The Sporting News*. The size of the continent got through to you finally when you had to stay up to 10:30 p.m. in New Jersey to hear via radio "ticker-tape" Cardinal pitcher Mort Cooper throw the first strike of the night to Brooklyn shortstop Pee Wee Reese out in "steamy" Sportsman's Park in St. Louis, Missouri. And however much we might be told by teacher about the stockyards and the Haymarket riot, Chicago only began to exist for me as a real place, and to matter in American history, when I became fearful (as a Dodger fan) of the bat of Phil Cavarretta, first baseman for the Chicago Cubs.

Not until I got to college and was introduced to literature did I find anything with a comparable emotional atmosphere and aesthetic appeal. I don't mean to suggest that it was a simple exchange, one passion for another. Between first discovering the Newark Bears and the Brooklyn Dodgers at seven or eight and first looking into Conrad's *Lord Jim* at age eighteen, I had done some growing up. I am only saying that my discovery of literature, and fiction particularly, and the "love affair"—to some degree hopeless, but still earnest—that has ensued, derives in part from this childhood infatuation with baseball. Or, more accurately perhaps, baseball—with its lore and legends, its cultural power, its seasonal associations, its native authenticity, its simple rules and transparent strategies, its longueurs and thrills, its spaciousness, its suspensefulness, its heroics, its nuances, its lingo, its "characters," its peculiarly hypnotic tedium, its mythic transformation of the immediate—was the literature of my boyhood.

Baseball, as played in the big leagues, was something completely outside my own life that could nonetheless move me to ecstasy and to tears; like fiction it could excite the imagination and hold the attention as much with minutiae as with high drama. Mel Ott's cocked leg striding into the ball, Jackie Robinson's pigeon-toed shuffle as he moved out to second base, each was to be as deeply affecting over the years as that night—"inconceivable," "inscrutable," as any night Conrad's Marlow might struggle to comprehend—the night that Dodger wild man, Rex Barney (who never lived up to "our" expectations, who should have been "our" Koufax), not only went the distance without walking in half a dozen runs, but, of all things, threw a no-hitter. A thrilling mystery, marvelously enriched by the fact that a light rain had fallen during the early evening, and Barney, figuring the game was going to be postponed, had eaten a hot dog just before being told to take the mound.

This detail was passed on to us by Red Barber, the Dodger radio sportscaster of the forties, a respectful, mild Southerner with a subtle rural tanginess to his vocabulary and a soft country-parson tone to his voice. For the adventures of "dem bums" of Brooklyn—a region then the very symbol of urban wackiness and tumult—to be narrated from Red Barber's highly alien but loving perspective constituted a genuine triumph of what my English professors would later teach me to call "point of view." James himself might have admired the implicit cultural ironies and the splendid possibilities for oblique moral and social commentary. And as for the detail about Rex Barney eating his hot dog, it was irresistible, joining as it did the spectacular to the mundane, and furnishing an adolescent boy with a glimpse of an unexpectedly ordinary, even humdrum, side to male heroism.

Of course, in time, neither the flavor and suggestiveness of Red Barber's narration nor "epiphanies" as resonant with meaning as Rex Barney's pre-game hot dog could continue to satisfy a developing literary appetite; nonetheless, it was just this that helped to sustain me until I was ready to begin to respond to the great inventors of narrative detail and masters of narrative voice and perspective like James, Conrad, Dostoevsky, and Bellow.

Cambodia: A Modest Proposal

Only a few weeks before Prince Sihanouk was ousted as Chief of State last spring, and the way was open for the brutal war in Vietnam to spread westward into Cambodia, I was a visitor in that unlucky country. I'd come to see the temple ruins at Angkor, but during my stay also traveled some fifteen miles south to the great inland lake that looks on the map, at least these days, like a large tear falling across the face of Cambodia. The lake is about fifty miles long and five feet deep and empties into the Tonle Sap River, which joins at Pnompenh with the Mekong flowing down from Laos. In the summer, Mekong flood waters cause the Tonle Sap to flow backward, and the water and the fish of the Great Lake of Cambodia to spread over hundreds of square miles of dry land. The thousands of Cambodians who fish these waters for a livelihood dwell only a few feet above their prey in small bamboo huts raised up on stilts.

The day I drove down to the Great Lake the temperature was over a hundred, and once off the main road, the Land Rover had to dig for several miles through a path deep with dust before it emerged onto the soft mud of a village of forty or fifty of these bamboo huts.

I visited Cambodia in March 1970, two months before President Nixon ordered the "incursion" by American and South Vietnamese troops that touched off the full-scale Cambodian war. The proposal appeared in *Look* magazine. (1970)

When the rains came, the villagers would be moving from house to house by sampan rather than on bare feet through the slime.

In the village I hired two local boys and their boat and went out with them onto the lake. From the muck of the landing we moved down a narrow brownish channel between a few "stores" up on stilts, past some houseboats that had window boxes with flowers growing in them and were obviously the dwellings of the village affluent, and then onto the vast motionless body of water, whose farthest encampment of bamboo huts looked from that distance like a brown insect skimming between water and sky. There was nothing *but* that encampment to separate the water from the sky. Where a horizon should have been, there was a seamless, gray intensity of light.

The farther out on the lake we went, the greater the distance between the little settlements that were arranged, some twenty huts in a row, on either side of what on land we call a street. Occasionally we passed a hut set completely off by itself, looking in its isolation as though it might be the habitation of the last member of the human race, or the first. The possessions of each household appeared to consist of a sampan, fishing nets, straw baskets for fish and rice, and a water jug. Some houses were fronted by small open platforms serving as porches; on a few of these platforms greens of some sort were growing in tubs.

That was it. That was *all*. No telephone wires, no electric power lines, no cars, no garages, no lawn mowers and no lawns, no screens or screen doors, no carpeting, no sofas, no armchairs, no washers, no dryers, no flameless electric water heaters, no ping-pong tables, no sauna-belt waistline reducers, no Norelcos, no golf carts, no *Today* show in the morning, no *Tonight* show at night, no wardrobes for summer, winter, spring, and fall, no maxis, no minis—instead, a dry season and a rainy season, the sun and a stretch of horizonless water.

That was it—life as spare and barren and repetitious as it must have been when the ancestors of these villagers first raised their dwellings on piles in order to survive the monsoon flood. Millions of Cambodians live this way, if not in the fishing settlements along the fifty-mile stretch of lake, then equally unblessed on the rice field that is the Cambodian plain.

And sure as hell, I thought, the day is going to come when the bombers fly in over the heads of these lake dwellers in order to "save" them. From what? Watching the solitary fishermen push by in their sampans, I could not imagine what there was that could be taken away from them, other than their toil and their arduous lives. Their freedom? They are the slaves of the sun and the monsoon, and always have been. Who in his right mind would plunge this country of peasants into yet another battle for "minds and hearts"? Who in his right mind would ever drop anything on these people other than food, medicine, and clothing?

And then it occurred to me: Why don't we try it?

Here is a modest proposal for winning the war in Indochina that came to me while drifting out on the Great Lake of Cambodia only weeks before that country too began to bleed: instead of bombs, how about dropping goods on Southeast Asia? Wasn't it for the welfare and well-being of these impoverished Asians that we entered this fray to begin with? And if goods are not at the heart of the matter, what is? "Democracy"? Why not just give them what they need, rather than what we want them to need, which often appears largely to be us. To be sure, we have our winning ways: the free-fire zone, the relocation camp, the search-and-destroy mission, the defoliants, the napalm, etc. At times one wonders how they can possibly resist us—but then these are inscrutable people.

Admittedly, if the government were to adopt my proposal and commence bombing with food and refrigerators, vaccines and shoes, it would very likely make the United States the laughingstock of Asia, for we would be dropping this stuff on people who don't start off loving and admiring us very much, and who, from the way they are behaving, look as though they are stubbornly determined to refuse to learn how. To some we might even appear to be the biggest fools in the history of the world; yet isn't that preferable, speaking strictly in terms of our image abroad, to being considered the world's biggest scourge? Of course, there will be those who laugh when the guerrillas enter a village we have bombarded with goods and haul them away to their encampments. Let them: we'll just fly in the next day with another payload. We can pound away at a village for days on end if that's what it takes to inundate the place with goods. Furthermore, a thousand pairs of boots dropped daily for a week is still cheaper than a single one-thousand-pound bomb. So not only will we be shodding these barefooted Indochinese but there will be an enormous dollar-saving—and thereby certainly the last laugh will be ours.

In order, however, to make it as difficult as possible for the revolutionary bands to appropriate the peasants' goods for themselves, I suggest that we hunt out the enemy and bomb him with goods first. Keep the Communist soldiers busy opening *their* packages, and meanwhile move swiftly in and dump a load on the villagers. As for that odd Asian peasant we read about in the papers, who is said to take flight when an American plane swoops low over his rice paddy in order to start saving him, let's make him feel like the fool he is to flee his Uncle Sam. Instead of spraying him with bullets, drop a sack of flour at his feet. That'll make him stop and think.

Of course there is no denying that if the government adopts my proposal there are going to be casualties. This is still war, and somebody is bound to be hit on the head with a pair of shoes, or, what's worse, with a bag of rice, which could hurt. To be wholly candid, it is not unlikely that, given the massive nature of the bombardment I have in mind, somewhere in Southeast Asia a child is going to be crushed to death by an air conditioner dropped from the sky. Our pilots are the most highly skilled in the world, and needless to say every precaution would be taken to avoid this sort of tragic mishap—leaflets beforehand to warn of an air-conditioner drop, and perhaps even specially demarcated air-conditioner drop zones. But in the end we must recognize that those in the air are no less human than those on the ground, and human beings make errors. I could not in good conscience make this proposal without also making perfectly clear the serious risk that is involved.

As a consequence, I do not expect this proposal to go unopposed. Ours is a compassionate republic that detests violence, and there will be those in public life who will contend that I have impugned the national honor by suggesting that our nation would assume responsibility for the death of a single innocent child, regardless of how magnanimous our overall mission. Let me say that I do not doubt the sincerity of those who for religious, moral, and patriotic reasons take such a position. I would want quickly to assure them that I too am opposed to the crushing and killing of an innocent Asian child under an American air conditioner. I would go even further and say that I am categorically opposed to the crushing of any child anywhere under an air conditioner, *even a Communist child*. I like to think that I am a humane man. Nonetheless, we must be steadfast in our high national purpose, which has not to do with saving some child somewhere from a falling air conditioner but rather with saving *all* the people of Indochina from a foe whose viciousness and inhumanity exceed the imagination of the American public. And chances are that, with something as heavy as an air conditioner, the child would never know what hit him anyway.

Our Castle

Like any number of stunned citizens, I have in recent days been looking for something to help me understand the latest shock to the political system and the national conscience, the "full, free, and absolute pardon" granted by President Ford to former President Nixon, "for all offenses against the United States." *Now* where are we? It has occurred to me that at least for the moment, and perhaps for some years to come, we are in something like the world of Kafka's *Castle*.

To be sure, Franz Kafka's novels, *The Castle* and *The Trial*, have come to provide a model that is frequently overworked or misapplied. At the popular level, the novels have given way to a word, "Kafkaesque," which by now is plastered indiscriminately on almost any baffling or unusually opaque event that is not easily translatable into the going simplifications. Kafkaesque has certainly never seemed, until now, a word that might add appreciably to an understanding of the Watergate years, even if any number of the characters and events that have surfaced along the way have partaken of that eerie

---

This piece was prompted by President Ford's announcement on Sunday morning, September 8, 1974—a month after he had taken office—that he was giving an unconditional pardon to his predecessor for any crimes he may have committed while he was President of the United States. (1974)

mix, formerly associated with dreams, of the grave and the bizarre, the horrifying and the ridiculous, that gives Kafka's novels their special resonance and saliency.

Likewise, the attempt to determine President Nixon's culpability did not, strictly speaking, have much to do with the plight of Joseph K., the accused isolate of *The Trial*. Nixon protested his innocence no less vehemently, and his talent for self-delusion and self-pity undoubtedly enabled him to see himself in a predicament very like Joseph K.'s, as it is described in the opening sentence of *The Trial*: "Someone must have traduced [Richard N.], for without having done anything wrong he was arrested one fine morning." Nonetheless, unlike Kafka's doomed hero, the former President was never without the power to defy and obstruct the tribunals that would call him to judgment. And "'The End'" that President Ford has told us he "must write" for Richard N.'s suffering is the very one that eluded poor Joseph K., despite his equally fervent efforts to bring his own famous case to precisely this conclusion.

And yet it is just this seemingly un-Kafkaesque ending that has now given to Watergate its Kafkaesque dimension. President Ford, so very deliberate about closing the Watergate story—"My conscience tells me that only I, as President, have the constitutional power to firmly shut and seal this book"—has actually, like some latter-day Kafka, imagined a final chapter wholly in the modernist literary tradition that scorns conventional unravelings and clarifying judgments as so much Mother Goosery, and insists instead upon the ungraspable, the impenetrable, on all that is tediously ambiguous. That human affairs can be settled and managed, even to some large degree understood, is an idea that is as uncongenial to the imagination of the good-natured Middle Western President as it was to the depressed and tormented Prague Jew. Story writing, it now seems, makes even stranger bedfellows than politics. Kafka! thou shouldst be living at this hour: the White House hath need of a new Press Secretary.

As I see it, there is still another telling Kafkaesque dimension to Watergate now that President Ford has written his version of The End. It is the enormousness of the frustration that has taken hold in America ever since Compassionate Sunday, the sense of waste, futility, and hopelessness that now attaches to the monumental efforts that had been required just to begin to get at the truth. And along with the frustration, the sickening disappointment of finding in the seat of power neither reason, nor common sense, nor horse sense—and certainly not charity or courage—but moral ignorance, blundering authority, and witless, arbitrary judgment.

It is as though the American public, having for a decade been cast in one painful or degrading role after another—Kennedy's orphans, Johnson's patriots, Nixon's patsies—has now been assigned to play the part of the Land Surveyor K. in Kafka's *Castle*. In this novel, the Land Surveyor, full of hope and energy, enters a village under the jurisdiction of a labyrinthian bureaucracy whose headquarters is a rather inaccessible castle looming over the landscape. How eager the Land Surveyor is to get permission from the Chief of the Castle bureaucracy—a Mr. Klamm of unascertainable competence—to get down to work and achieve a purposeful social existence. How willing he is to bend over backward to live on friendly terms with the powers that be, imperfect as they are. His early hours in the Castle village bring to mind the touching atmosphere that prevailed in these parts during the thirty-day honeymoon with our Mr. Klamm. How willing! How eager! And how innocent.

For, with all the will in the world to get on with the job, what the Land Surveyor discovers is that he can't—the Castle won't let him. He is blocked at every turn by authorities to whose inscrutable edicts and bizarre decrees he is beholden, but whose motives and methods defy his every effort to make sense of them. And that the Klamm who is running the whole bewildering operation happens not to be a criminal does not make the Land Surveyor's frustrations any less enervating to the body or the spirit.

Imagining the Erotic: Three Introductions

1. Alan Lelchuk

For half of its five hundred pages, Alan Lelchuk's first novel, *American Mischief* (which I have just read in manuscript), is a brilliant and original comedy on the subject of the immediate present: i.e., what disheartens Bellow in *Mr. Sammler's Planet,* what provokes Kate Millett in *Sexual Politics,* what causes Malamud to cry "Mercy" for half a page at the conclusion of *The Tenants.* The fresh and intriguing aspect of Lelchuk's book is obviously not the concern with obsession, extremism, outlandishness, and injustice; it is, rather, *the robust delight* that the contemplation of confusion arouses in him. Like the Cambridge professor and "erogonist" Dean Bernard Kovell, whose creation is Lelchuk's triumph—like Basil Seal in Waugh's comedy of cultural breakdown, from which the author borrows the ironic (and mischievous) noun of his own title—it appears to be Alan Lelchuk's great good luck to be on hand for the Dissolution. He gets a kick out of it all, which isn't to suggest that he is simply malicious or perverse, that he is anything like cynical or nihilistic, or that the blood

My contribution to a 1972 *Esquire* colloquium entitled "Which Writer Under Thirty-Five Has Your Attention and What Has He Done to Get It?" *American Mischief* was published by Farrar, Straus and Giroux in 1973.

coursing through this book is cold, thin, or blue. Since this is a birth notice and not a eulogy, I *will* record that the newborn possesses a mean, pricky streak that at times leads him to be contemptuous in excess of the evidence. But by and large, like another Brooklyn Jew and literary roughneck whose ferocity tends to obscure his sweetness (often enough by design), Lelchuk is voracious rather than vicious; and rude and gruff as his appetite for the contradictory and the bewildering can make him, he is not at all a novelist to gloat over our uncertainties. Rude and gruff, he can also be nicely ironic (and, in the next breath, perfectly innocent), and therein lies much of this cocky snake charmer's charm, as is the case too with the sword swallower of the literary bazaar, Mr. Mailer.

The first half of *American Mischief*—the comic and remarkable half—consists almost entirely of the words (some sixty thousand well-chosen ones) of Dean Bernard Kovell of Mass (or as he would have it) Ass Ave. No novelist has written with such knowledge and eloquence of the consequences of carnal passion in Massachusetts since *The Scarlet Letter* (Updike and his Tarbox cunnilinguist notwithstanding). Hawthorne gave us Hester Prynne, the brave adulteress of Puritan Boston, whose cunt, to paraphrase an ancient, was her fate. Lelchuk introduces us to Kovell and Cambridge Now: the feverish literary dean (author of a book on Gissing), whose stupendous appetite for girls with hapless lives and specialized needs leads him to establish a family, or harem, of six damaged mistresses (a desolate young mother, an analyst-seduced analysand, and assorted Radcliffe graduates with wires crossed and fuses blown); and then there is the brainy, Brahmin town, America's Alexandria, turned brothel, opium den, and open mental ward, the "Shanghai of New England," to hear the reeling dean describe it.

Lelchuk, who so revels in contradiction, and for whom contrast provides the organizing principle of his work, should take special delight in the comparison of his accomplishment to Hawthorne's; let him enjoy it. Very soon now the charge of "sexism" will be leveled at him by the Feminist Right, inevitably for demonstrating in his fiction that there are indeed women in America as broken and resentful as the women in America are coming to proclaim themselves to be. Admittedly, Dean Kovell's solution to his mistresses' problems would not necessarily be NOW's or Shirley Chisholm's, but then Humbert Humbert's is not necessarily the most responsible solution to his little female orphan's predicament, nor is Clyde Griffith's the most humane approach to the problem raised by a pregnant proletarian girl friend. Yes, Kovell is a male chauvinist pig, and so is Grushenka a ballbuster and Oblomov a dropout. As Delmore Schwartz once wrote, "Literary criticism is often very inneresting."

Lelchuk's dean is also a campus hero, elevated by the students themselves to a deanship on the strength of his derring-do, as illustrated by the incident in which he is caught in his office going down on a graduate assistant. The Kids love him for the risks he takes. Some seventy pages of the manuscript are bravely given over to excerpts from a four-hour Castroesque (but anti-revolutionary) speech that "Kove" makes to the revolutionary students of Cardozo College when they occupy the college's prestigious art museum, with its collection of de Koonings, Nevelsons, and David Smiths, and the Picassos, Matisses, Kandinskys, and Mirós on loan that month from the Boston Museum. It is an elegant, playful, heartfelt speech, crackling with intelligence and charm, and particularly marvelous because the wild sexual extremist preaches so eloquently to the rebels in behalf of order, restraint, and moderation, reducing himself to tears in the end with his plea for "belief in the species." Thereupon the undergraduates proceed to defecate on the de Koonings and cut the Matisses into ribbons.

Thus ends the remarkable half of *American Mischief.* In what follows, Lelchuk's imagination runs away with him, though not far enough. Events are suddenly momentous and catastrophic: mood darkens; motive darkens; we are in a world of blood and flames—and yet the somber reverberations are too faint, the prose is undistinguished, and the human side of it all is somewhat strained and transparent.

The subject here is not the dean and his family of women but a young student, Lenny Pincus, Cardozo College's Cohn-Bendit, who emerges from the museum uprising with a plan for revolution that earns him a *Time* cover story and the editorial wrath of *The New York Times* (the paper Pincus loathes the way a P.T.A. president loathes *Screw*). Even more extreme in the political realm than is Kovell in the sexual, Pincus, after taking a fourteen-year-old runaway for his moll, murders Norman Mailer (firing the fatal bullet up the author's determinedly virginal anus) and burns down the Widener Library and the Fogg Museum. He then establishes a kind of prison camp on a remote New Hampshire farm, to which he brings, in chains, eminent literary intellectuals for the purpose of brainwashing. They are snatched at gunpoint from the platform of a Hofstra literary symposium (what a sly dreamer this Lelchuk is) and transported in U-Haul trucks by Pincus's Cambridge guerrilla band. And then still more, before Pincus, always a bookish Trotsky to the blacks and Puerto Ricans he commands, is betrayed by his cadre to the FBI and apprehended in a Cambridge hideout.*

American Mischief ends with Pincus in jail. "And whoever claims that criminals are interesting men," the young murderer writes in his diary, "should be condemned to live among them . . ." These final pages on the subject of pain are generally poignant, but as of this date, Lelchuk is not quite Dostoevsky. His imagination, relentless and extreme—and, one feels, accurately prophetic—when it comes to dreaming up offenses against society, is not equal to the task of dreaming up the offender himself. Pincus the political revolutionary is only intermittently in focus and of a piece, and never so thorough-

---

*The circumstances of Pincus's arrest were altered by Lelchuk after I had read the manuscript, and in the published novel are somewhat different from what I describe here.

going an ironist, or so convincing a philosopher and psychologist of his own conduct, as is the sexual revolutionary Kovell. But in praise of Lelchuk's ambitiousness, it must be said that Pincus's turbulence is grander and more harrowing than Kovell's, and his spiritual yearnings are meant to be more mysterious and incomprehensible even to himself. Nonetheless, he is neither a Peter Verhovensky or a Raskolnikov.

To judge a thirty-three-year-old first novelist by such standards may at first appear wildly unjust and silly—one thing to flatter him with Hawthorne, another to hang him for not having written *Crime and Punishment* or *The Possessed*. I only draw this comparison because the scrappy first novelist, leading with his chin, would have it that way: Pincus repeatedly mentions Dostoevsky's two monstrous youths, partly to provide himself and the reader with a point of reference, but also, I think, in order to place his own name in nomination for the Bad Boys' Hall of Fame.

However: inconclusive as the second half of *American Mischief* may be (though it, too, has its felicitous pages, as when Pincus compares horrendous passages in Sophocles and Herman Kahn; when Pincus plans and executes the Mailer murder; and when he befriends— if that is the word—the fourteen-year-old innocent named Nugget), there seems to me, in the fictional impulse to join Pincus's story to Kovell's, the sign of the natural. To be sure, the impulse is of the kind that makes brave prose writers tremble: quirky, daring, wrongheaded, but *perhaps* inspired; it is the kind of impulse that the writer who tries simultaneously to be dreamy *and* alert realizes may as easily undermine the entire project as turn up those riches that perhaps—*perhaps*—lie buried in his talent. What is so engaging to me about Lelchuk is that in the midst of his very first book he is already impatient with himself, already so arrogant about what he does well as to be exuberantly hacking and tearing away at himself (before our very eyes, in fact), trying to see what else he can do. I don't doubt that he'll find out, though the battlefield be strewn with chunks of his own tough hide.

2. Milan Kundera

The book that made Milan Kundera famous, and infamous, in Czechoslovakia is a political novel entitled, unjokingly, *The Joke.* A direct and realistic book, openly reflective about the issues it raises— proceeding by means of philosophical thoughtfulness and accurate observation of a fairly broad spectrum of "politicized" citizens, it is something like a cross between Dos Passos and Camus—*The Joke* is largely concerned with the absurdities that wreck the life of a skeptical young Czech party intellectual during the bitter postwar years of Stalinist purges, trials, and other dogmatic enthusiasms. *The Joke* was published in Prague in 1967, at the time when pressure from writers and intellectuals like Kundera against official government repression was building rapidly toward the spirited national uprising that would become known (at first somewhat romantically, then altogether accurately) as the "Prague Spring." "An attempt," Kundera called the doomed reform movement that lasted little more than a season, "to create a socialism without an omnipotent secret police; with freedom of the spoken and written word; with a public opinion of which notice is taken and on which policy is based; with a modern culture freely developing; and with citizens who have lost their fear."

In January 1968, Alexander Dubček's government—the political offspring of the reform movement—came to power and immediately set out to dismantle the totalitarian machinery that had been integral to Communist Party rule since the "Revolution of 1948." According to the inspired slogan of the Dubček government, very

---

Introduction to *Laughable Loves,* a collection of Kundera's stories (Knopf, 1974).

soon now in Czechoslovakia there would be "socialism with a human
face." Instead, soon enough, Soviet tanks appeared in Prague's Old
Town Square, and overnight—the night of August 20, 1968—some
two hundred thousand Russian and other Warsaw Pact soldiers had
occupied Czechoslovakia.

Six years later an eighty-thousand-man Russian army is still there,
largely in the countryside now, hidden from the sight of the demoralized Czechs but close enough to the capital to lend whatever authority is needed to the repressive edicts and punitive decrees of the regime
that the Russians have placed back in power. Alexander Dubček is
reported to be currently employed as an inspector in a trolley factory
in Slovakia. The author of *The Joke*, and of the stories that follow,
also lives in the provinces, in Brno, the city where he was born forty-
five years ago. Along with the other leading intellectuals whose
speeches and writings helped to make the Prague Spring (and who
continue to refuse to "confess" to their "mistakes" so as to receive
official absolution), he is excluded from membership in the post-
occupation writers' union (an undistinguished government-approved
group bearing little resemblance to the outspoken writers' union
that was dissolved by the government when it refused to comply with
Soviet "normalization"); he has been fired from his teaching position
at the Prague Film School; he is forbidden to travel to the West;* his
literary works have been removed from the nation's libraries and
bookstores; his plays have been banned from the theaters; and as a
result of a series of government decrees establishing confiscatory
taxes aimed specifically at ten dissident writers, he now receives less
than 10 percent of the royalties that his books earn in Europe, where
he is a writer of considerable reputation. Recently his new novel, *Life
Is Elsewhere*, received the Prix Médicis as the best foreign novel pub-

---

*Shortly after the publication of this piece, Kundera was permitted to go to
Paris to receive the Prix Médicis Etranger.

lished in France in 1973; the book cannot, however, be published in the country, and in the language, in which it was written.

The Czech novelist and journalist Ludvík Vaculík, who is perhaps considered an even more dangerous political criminal than Kundera by the current Czech rulers, has remarked in an interview (given to a Swiss journalist visiting Prague, and printed subsequently in several Western magazines) that he considers it "unfortunate . . . when foreign cities judge the quality of Czech literary work exclusively by the degree to which it 'settles accounts with illusions about socialism' or by the acerbity with which it stands up to the regime here. I cannot use the foreign book market to stand up to the regime, nor do I want to."

Similarly, the Czech poet and immunologist Miroslav Holub let me know, when we were introduced in Prague in 1973, that he did not care to receive attention from foreign literary visitors simply because he was considered by them to be a "poor Czech." I had just expressed admiration for his Penguin collection of poems, which I'd read at the suggestion of A. Alvarez, the English critic and editor of the Penguin European Poets series. Still, Dr. Holub momentarily bristled, as though it could be that I actually had more sympathy for the predicament in which he and other Czech writers found themselves than for his verse. Only a few months after our first meeting, Holub went on Prague radio and made what was described by the government announcer as a "self-critical confession of the political standpoint he took . . . in the crisis years of 1968 and 1969 . . ." Reading a transcript of Holub's confession of error—a windy, clichéd document in no way like the sharp and elegant poetry—I wondered if this sternly intelligent and theoretically minded poet-scientist, with whom I'd developed something of a friendship during my weeks in Prague, might have been moved to denounce himself on the radio not necessarily to curry favor with the authorities, or because he had finally to yield for personal reasons to government threat and intimidation, or even because he had changed his mind about '68, but rather, perhaps, to discourage once and for all sympathetic judgments about himself or his work that might be thought to arise in response to the conspicuously grave circumstances in which he writes poetry and studies blood.*

I would think that like Holub and Vaculík, Milan Kundera too would prefer to find a readership in the West that was not drawn to his fiction because he is a writer who is oppressed by a Communist regime, especially since Kundera's political novel, *The Joke,* happens to represent only an aspect of his wide-ranging intelligence and talent. To date, Kundera has published, aside from *The Joke,* two plays; three books of poems (one on the subject of women in love, another on a Czech resistance hero of World War II); a study of the modern Czech novelist Vladislav Vančura; and several volumes of short stories which, like the stories collected here, focus largely on the private world of erotic possibilities, rather than on politics and the state. At present, Kundera, whose father was a pianist and rector of the state music conservatory at Brno, is at work on a study of the composer Leoš Janáček, whose strong interest in Moravian folk music Kundera shares. (An earlier book on Janáček was published in 1924 by Max Brod, Kafka's friend and biographer.)

But having written *The Joke,* Kundera, for all his wide-ranging interests, now finds himself an enemy of the state and nothing more—ironically enough, in a position very much like the protagonist of *The Joke,* whose error it is as a young Communist student to

---

*Visiting Prague again, some months after writing this introduction, I learned that though the "self-critical confession" read on the Prague radio was attributed to Holub, the reader's voice was not his, and there are some in the literary community there who would not be surprised to find that the words were not all his either.

send a teasing postcard to his girl friend, making fun of her naïve political earnestness. She happens to be away from him for a few weeks, taking a summer course in the strategies of the revolutionary movement, and seems to Ludvík Jahn not to be missing him quite enough. So, playful lover that he is, he dashes off a message to his ardent young Stalinist:

> Optimism is the opium of the people! The healthy atmosphere stinks! Long live Trotsky!
>
> Ludvík

Well, in Eastern Europe a man should be more careful of the letters he writes, even to his girl friend. For his three joking sentences, Jahn is found guilty by a student tribunal of being an enemy of the state, is expelled from the university and the Party, and is consigned to an army penal corps where for seven years he works in the coal mines. "But, Comrades," says Jahn, "it was only a joke." Nonetheless, he is swallowed up by a state somewhat lacking a sense of humor about itself, and subsequently, having misplaced his own sense of humor somewhere in the mines, he is swallowed up and further humiliated by his plans for revenge.

The Joke is, of course, not so benign in intent as Jahn's postcard. I would suppose that Kundera must himself have known, somewhere along the line, that one day the authorities might confirm the imaginative truthfulness of his book by bringing their own dogmatic seriousness down upon him for writing as he did about the plight of Ludvík Jahn. "Socialist realism," after all, is the approved artistic mode in his country, and as one Prague critic informed me when I asked for a definition, "Socialist realism consists of writing in praise of the government and the party so that even *they* understand it." Oddly (just another joke, really) Kundera's book conforms more to Stalin's own prescription for art: "socialist content in national form." Since two of the most esteemed books written in the nation in question happen to be *The Trial* by Franz Kafka and *The Good Soldier Schweik* by Jaroslav Hašek, Kundera's own novel about a loyal citizen upon whom a terrible joke is played by the powers that be would seem to be entirely in keeping with the spirit of Stalin's injunction. If only Stalin were alive so that Kundera could point out to him this continuity in "national form" and historical preoccupation.

At any rate: that he has received from reality such strong verification for what was, after all, only a literary invention must furnish some consolation to a writer so attuned to harsh irony, and so intrigued by the startling consequences that can flow from playing around.

Erotic play and power are the subjects frequently at the center of the stories that Kundera calls, collectively, *Laughable Loves.* Sexuality as a weapon (in this case, the weapon of he who is otherwise wholly assailable) is to the point of *The Joke* as well: to revenge himself upon the political friend who had turned upon him back in his remote student days, Ludvík Jahn, released from the coal mines at last, coldly conceives a plan to seduce the man's wife. In this decision by Kundera's hero to put his virility in the service of his rage, he displays a kinship to characters in the fiction of Mailer and Mishima—the vengeful husband, for example, in Mishima's *Forbidden Colors,* who engages a beautiful young homosexual to arouse the passion and then break the hearts of women who have betrayed and rejected him; or the Greenwich Village bullfight instructor, in Mailer's "The Time of Her Time," whose furious copulations seem to be aimed at producing pleasure for his partner in the form of punishment. However, what distinguishes Kundera's cocksman from Mailer's or Mishima's is the ease with which his erotic power play is thwarted, and turns into yet another joke at his expense. He is so much more vulnerable in good part because he has been so crippled by ostracism from the Party and imprisonment in the penal corps (compare the limitless social freedom of Mailer's Americans, O'Shaugnessy and Rojack), but also because Kundera, unlike Mailer or Mishima, seems even in a book as bleak and cheerless as *The Joke* to be fundamentally *amused* by the uses to which a man will think to put his sexual member, or the uses to which his member will put him. This amusement, mixed though it is with sympathy and sorrow, leads Kundera away from anything even faintly resembling a mystical belief or ideological investment in the power of potency or orgasm.

In *Laughable Loves,* what I've called Kundera's "amusement" with erotic enterprises and lustful strategies emerges as the mild satire of a story like "The Golden Apple of Eternal Desire," wherein Don Juanism is viewed as a sport played by a man against a team of women, oftentimes without body contact—or, in the wry, rather worldly irony of the Dr. Havel stories, "Symposium" and "Dr. Havel After Ten Years," where Don Juanism is depicted as a way of life in which women of all social stations eagerly and willingly participate as "sexual objects," particularly so with Havel, eminent physician and aging Casanova, who in his prime is matter-of-factly told by a professional colleague: ". . . you're like death, you take everything." Or Kundera's amusement emerges as a kind of detached Chekhovian tenderness in the story about a balding, thirtyish, would-have-been eroticist, who sets about to seduce an aging woman whose body he expects to find repellent, a seduction undertaken to revenge himself upon his own stubborn phallic daydreams. Narrated alternatively from the point of view of the thirty-five-year-old seducer and the fifty-year-old seduced, and with a striking air of candor that borders somehow on impropriety—as though a discreet acquaintance were suddenly letting us in on sexual secrets both seamy and true—this story, "Let the Old Dead Make Room for the Young Dead," seems to me "Chekovian" not merely because of its tone, or its concern with the painful and touching consequences of time passing and old selves dying, but because it is so very good.

In "The Hitchhiking Game," "Nobody Will Laugh," and "Edward

and God," Kundera turns to those jokes he is so fond of contemplating, the ones that begin in whimsical perversity, and end in trouble. In "The Hitchhiking Game," for example, a young couple off for a vacation together decide on the way to their destination to play at being strangers, the girl pretending to be a hitchhiker and her boy friend just another man passing in his car. The ensuing confusion of identities, and the heightened eroticism this provokes in the lovers, with its scary sado-masochistic edge, is not so catastrophic to either of them as his joke turns out to be for Ludvík Jahn. Still, simply by fooling around and indulging their curiosity, the lovers find they have managed to deepen responsibility as well as passion—as if children playing doctor out in the garage were to look up from one another's privates to discover they were administering a national health program, or being summoned to perform surgery in the Mount Sinai operating room. What is so often laughable, in the stories of Kundera's Czechoslovakia, is how grimly serious just about everything turns out to be, jokes, games, and pleasure included; what's laughable is how terribly little there is to laugh at with any joy.

My own favorite story is "Edward and God." Like *The Joke,* it deals with a young Czech whose playfulness (with women, of course) and highly developed taste for cynicism and blasphemy expose him to the harsh judgments of a dogmatic society or, rather, expose him to those authorities who righteously promulgate and protect the dogmas, but do so stupidly and without even genuine conviction or understanding. What is particularly appealing here is that the young schoolteacher Edward, an erotic Machiavelli who feigns religious piety to seduce a pious knockout and so falls afoul of his atheistic school board, gets no more than he gives, and is more of a thoughtful Lucky Jim, really, than a Ludvík Jahn. His difficulties are not come by so innocently, nor are the consequences so brutal or humiliating as they are in *The Joke.* Indeed, the ugly school directress with a secret sexual need, who sets out to re-educate Edward the believer, winds up, in what is for Kundera a rare moment of thoroughgoing farce, naked and on her knees before him, reciting the Lord's Prayer at Edward's ministerial command, an "image of degradation" that, luckily (for his political future) and just in the nick of time, sets the machinery of tumescence in motion. "As the directress said, 'And lead us not into temptation,' he quickly threw off all his clothes. When she said 'Amen,' he violently lifted her off the floor and dragged her onto the couch." So, where there is something of an aggrieved tone and polemical intent in *The Joke*—a sense communicated, at least to a Westerner, that the novel is also a *statement* made in behalf of an abused nation, and in defiance of a heartless regime—"Edward and God" is more like a rumination, in anecdotal form, upon a social predicament that rouses the author to comic analysis and philosophical speculation, even to farce, rather than to angry exposé.

Not that one should minimize the cost to Edward (and probably to the author as well) of maintaining a detached, "amused" intellectual cunning in the midst of a social order rigidly devoted to simpleminded pieties having little to do with the realities of need and desire (other than the need and desire for pieties). "Yet even if [Edward] was inwardly laughing, and thus making an effort to mock them secretly (and so exonerate his accommodation), it didn't alter the case. For even malicious imitation remains imitation, and the shadow that mocks remains a shadow, subordinate, derivative, and wretched, and nothing more." Or, as Kundera comments wearily at the conclusion of Edward's story, "Ah, ladies and gentlemen, a man lives a sad life when he cannot take anything or anyone seriously." As the tone suggests, "Edward and God" does not derive from manifesto or protest literature, but connects in spirit as well as form to those humorous stories one hears by the hundreds in Prague these days, stories such as a powerless or oppressed people are often adept at telling about themselves, and in which they seem to take an aesthetic pleasure—what pleasure is there otherwise?—from the very absurdities and paradoxes that characterize their hardship and cause them pain.

3. Fredrica Wagman

(*Note to the French Reader:* I read *Playing House* first in manuscript, shortly after a mutual friend introduced me to Fredrica Wagman in Philadelphia, where she lived then in a large, rambling, suburban house with her husband and four children, and wrote novels in a room over her garage. The manuscript was one of several that she had already finished and consigned to a dresser drawer. I thought it was a remarkable thing to keep in a dresser drawer and I told the author as much. I also told my friend and editor, Aaron Asher, then at Holt, Rinehart and Winston, who subsequently read Wagman's novel and published it in 1973. As an expression of gratitude, and in recognition of the friendship that ensued, Fredrica Wagman graciously dedicated her first published book to me. Whether this dedication or our friendship should have constrained me from accepting her publisher's invitation to write a preface to the French edition of *Playing House* is a matter that I expect shall have to be taken up by the Guardians of Literary Standards when next they assemble at a cocktail party in Manhattan. In the meantime, until that court hands down its verdict, here is what I am pleased to say about Wagman's book.)

It would appear from *Playing House* that the prohibition forbidding sibling incest is designed primarily to protect impressionable chil-

---

Introduction to *Playing House, ou les jeux réprouvés* (Seghers, 1974), the French translation of Fredrica Wagman's first novel; it was a runner-up for the Prix Médicis Etranger.

dren against sex thrills so intense, and passionate unions so all-encompassing and exclusive, that life after the age of twelve can only be a frenzy of nostalgia for those who have known the bliss of such transgression. It is surely not the loss of childhood's famous *innocence* that unleashes this dazed outpouring from a young woman who was, as a girl, her sadistic, bullying brother's little mistress. Wagman's nameless heroine madly yearns to recapture her past, but not so she can dwell once more in the pure, untainted world of a Phoebe Caulfield, Holden's saintly kid sister in *The Catcher in the Rye*. Rather, some twenty years after Salinger's famous novel depicting adolescence as the fall from prepubescent grace, it is the lost *corruption* of childhood that is elegized and the passing of a little girl's erotic frenzy that is wretchedly mourned. Against the memory of that exquisite hellishness the heroine of *Playing House* measures the decency of the husband who would rescue her if only she were willing, and judges each impassioned lover who looks somewhat like, but alas is not, the blond and blue-eyed brother who turned her into his sexual slave. The grown woman asks, in one breath, "What was the boredom that made me border madness all the time?" only to answer herself in the next breath, and the next. After the masochistic splendors of girlhood enslavement and depravity, each and every lover who follows the brother is, in the end, "just another pair of shoes."

For her *everything* is "just" something else that will not satisfy. Schoolwork, painting, writing, marriage, children, religion, promiscuity, even madness—it is all as nothing to "the way it can be," which is to say, the way it once was and can never be again. In the clutch of her need—Need might as well be her name—the little growing mistress, as good as abandoned by the brother off in boarding school, even has a go at bestiality with the family dog; and the only degradation, from her standpoint, consists in ludicrously failing to accomplish the copulation, which might at least have been a kind of commemorative transgression honoring the incestuous union that has been torn asunder by school.

"In India," the molested child muses, while her seventh-grade teacher drones on, "the nine-year-old girls were married and having babies by now . . . if I lived in India I could have a husband and a child and it wouldn't all be so boring." The point of view is not Humbert Humbert's but Lolita's—only a Lolita with heart and nerves exposed, a little girl at once more ordinary and more loving, and, for that reason, more profoundly destroyed. This remarkably persuasive first novel about one who was a woman when she might better have been a girl—and as a consequence is still a little girl when she would herself prefer to be a woman—is as much of a love song to childhood incest as it is a perverse validation of that universal taboo . . . perverse because it says: "Little girl, thou shalt not know the bliss of being the ravished kid sister—otherwise the longings for the big bad brother will be a torment forevermore."

The nature of the grown sister's torment is expressed succinctly, perfectly, in the two words with which the book begins, and from which it takes its indirect course: "Can't concentrate." This is as short-winded as she will be. From there sentences unwind like ribbon off a spool of morbid desire and rapturous misery. *Can't concentrate.* The two words are spoken by the nameless heroine when? As she whiles away the time beneath her copulating husband, the "Turtle," who stolidly endures her. But the Turtle, like the Present, is an enormous distraction at the edge of her senses, there only to generate frenzied boredom. The Present is simply what bars her way back to those first thrills.

"Thrills." "Freaks." "Unreal." "Fucked-up." "Spooked." These catchwords of the late sixties, used to death finally by the underground press, by students, by adherents of rock, drugs, and "revolution," as well as by salesmen of bell-bottom jeans, turn up along the way in *Playing House*—somewhat surprisingly too, since the heroine seems to know nothing whatsoever of the turbulence out there beyond her incestuous preoccupation. This woman is no hippie and no "kid." True, after "dropping a tab," she screams, "It's a bummer," but when she is hospitalized her self-portrait emerges from something more private and painful than counterculture Morse code: "I'm standing in the middle of the room in a white hospital gown like a pillar that was once part of something more." And, though Wagman chooses to introduce a chapter with a quotation attributed to Bob Dylan about the "smoke rings of my mind"—and in straining to lay bare her heroine's misery sometimes twangs out a little pop-record poetry herself—"so you couldn't hear my song after all" . . . "a million dreams that broke my heart"—the fact is that her prose has more in common with Dylan Thomas's childhood recollections. It is there in the wide-eyed childishness of her cadences, in the breathy stringing together of the peculiar with the homely, in the characters who are named and seen as in a nursery rhyme. She can at her best be just as guileless and rhapsodic as the author of *Under Milk Wood,* and what's more, lacking his literary sophistication and his desire to charm, can pull it off without necessarily being *endearing* in the process. There is too much torment and depravity for the childishness, at age ten or thirty, to cloy. She may seem at one moment just a little too chummy with a swan she regularly talks to, but the swan is itself as unimpressed as the most rigid Freudian analyst. And life with her puppy dog is, for this little American girl, unambiguously unsentimental and unwholesome.

The traumatized child; the institutionalized wife; the haunting desire; the ghastly business of getting through the day—what is striking about Wagman's treatment of these contemporary motifs is the voice of longing in which the heroine unashamedly confesses to the incestuous need that is at once her undoing and her only hope. It is a voice that owes nothing, finally, to either of the Dylans, or to the demonic pop lingo of the last decade—or to post-Freudian currents in literature or psychology. To readers of Stekel or Virginia Woolf or hardcore pornography, it might appear that the writer is a student, in her fashion, of all three. But in fact, the sado-masochistic scenario, the fervent streamingness of the surface, and the graphic rendering of the sexually unsavory issue in one gush from the imagination of an authentic and unself-conscious middle-class primitive. Her moral outlook is so much a matter of personality that there is really no valid argument possible between her sense of things and anyone else's. I don't imagine that even at a later stage of development as a novelist she will ever come up against the kind of opposition, from without or within, that informs the novel of dramatic struggle. The only irony Fredrica Wagman's heroine is able to know is the irony of her own enslavement; she is beyond everyone's reach, poor woman, except the one who touched her first.

Imagining Jews

1. Portnoy's Fame—and Mine

Alas, it wasn't exactly what I'd had in mind. Particularly as I was one of those students of the fifties who came to books by way of a fairly good but rather priestly literary education, in which writing poems and novels was assumed to eclipse all else in what we called "moral seriousness." As it happened, our use of that word "moral"— in private conversations about our daily affairs as easily as in papers and classroom discussions—tended often to camouflage and dignify vast reaches of naïveté, and served frequently only to restore at a more prestigious cultural level the same respectability that one had imagined oneself in flight from in (of all places) the English department.

The emphasis upon literary activity as a form of ethical conduct, as perhaps even *the* way to the good life, certainly suited the times: the postwar onslaught of a mass electronically amplified philistine culture did look to some young literary people like myself to be the work of the Devil's legions, and High Art in turn the only refuge of the godly, a 1950's version of the pietistic colony established in Massachusetts Bay. Also, the idea that literature was the domain of the

---

Written in 1974.

truly virtuous would seem to have suited my character, which, though not exactly puritanical at heart, seemed that way in some key reflexes. So, inasmuch as I thought about Fame when I was starting out as a writer in my early twenties, I only naturally assumed that if and when it ever came my way, it would come as it had to Mann's Aschenbach, as Honor. *Death in Venice*, page 10: "But he had attained to honour, and honour, he used to say, is the natural goal towards which every considerable talent presses with whip and spur. Yes, one might put it that his whole career had been one conscious and overweening ascent to honour, which left in the rear all the misgivings or self-derogation which might have hampered him."

In the case of Aschenbach it was not his lustful fantasies (replete with mythological illusions but masturbatory at bottom) for which he is to be remembered by the "shocked and respectful world [that] received the news of his decease," but, altogether to the contrary, for powerful narratives like *"The Abject,* which taught a whole grateful generation that a man can still be capable of moral resolution even after he has plumbed the depths of knowledge. . . ." Now *that* is something like the sort of reputation I'd had in mind for myself. But, as it was to turn out, the narrative of mine that elicited a strong response from a part of a generation, at least, "taught" less about the capacity for moral resolve than about moral remission and its confusions—and about those masturbatory fantasies that generally don't come decked out in adolescence (and in Newark) in classical decor.

Instead of taking an honorific place in the public imagination à la Gustave von Aschenbach, with the publication of *Portnoy's Complaint*, in February 1969, I suddenly found myself famous from one end of the continent to the other for being everything that Aschenbach had suppressed and kept a shameful secret right down to his morally resolute end. Jacqueline Susann, discussing her colleagues with Johnny Carson, tickled ten million Americans by saying that she'd like to meet me but didn't want to shake my hand. Didn't want to shake my hand—she, of all people? And from time to time the columnist Leonard Lyons had a ten-word tidbit about my fiery romance with Barbra Streisand: "Barbra Streisand has no complaints about her dates with Philip Roth." Dot dot dot. True enough, in a manner of speaking, since, as it happened, the famous Jewish girl celebrity and the newly minted Jewish boy celebrity had and still have never met.

There was to be a considerable amount of this kind of media myth-making, sometimes benign and silly enough, and sometimes, for me at least, pretty unsettling. In order to be out of the direct line of fire, however, I had decided to leave my New York apartment just after publication day, and so while "Philip Roth" began boldly to put in public appearances where I myself had not yet dared to tread, or twist, I took up residence for four months at the Yaddo retreat for writers, composers, and artists in Saratoga Springs.

Mostly, news about my *Doppelgänger*'s activities, of which the foregoing is but a small sample, came to me through the mail: anecdotes in letters from friends, clippings from the columnists, communications (and gentle, amused admonitions) from my lawyer on inquiries from me about libel and defamation of character. One evening in the second month of my Yaddo stay, I received a phone call from an editor (and friend) in a New York publishing house. He apologized for intruding on me, but at work that afternoon he had heard that I had suffered a breakdown and been committed to a hospital; he was phoning just to be sure it wasn't so. In only a matter of weeks news of the breakdown and commitment had spread westward, across the Continental Divide, out to California, where they do things in a big way. There, preparatory to a discussion of my new novel at a temple book program, announcement of Philip Roth's misfortune was made to the audience from the platform; having thus placed the author in proper perspective, they apparently went on to an objective discussion of the book.

In May, finally, at about the time I was considering returning to New York, I telephoned down to Bloomingdale's one day to try to correct an error that had turned up in my charge account for several months in succession. At the other end, the woman in the charge department gasped and said, "Philip Roth? Is this *the* Philip Roth?" Tentatively: "Yes." "But *you're* supposed to be in an insane asylum!" "Oh, am I?" I replied lightheartedly, trying, as they say, to roll with the punch, but knowing full well that the charge department at Bloomingdale's wouldn't talk that way to Gustave von Aschenbach if he called to report an error in *his* charge account. Oh no, Tadzio-lover though he was, it would still be, "Yes, Herr von Aschenbach; oh, we're terribly sorry for any inconvenience, Herr von Aschenbach—oh, do forgive us, Maestro, please."

Which was, as I have said, more like what I'd had in mind upon starting out on my own conscious and overweening ascent to honor.

Why was *Portnoy's Complaint* at once such a hit and such a scandal? To begin, a novel in the guise of a confession was received and judged by any number of readers as a confession in the guise of a novel. That sort of reading, wherein a work is dwarfed in significance by the impulse or the personal circumstance which is imagined to have generated it, is nothing new; however, just such an interest in fiction was intensified in the late sixties by a passion for spontaneity and candor that colored even the drabbest lives and expressed itself in the pop rhetoric with phrases like "Tell it like it is," "Let it all hang out," etc. There were, of course, good solid reasons for this yearning for raw truth during the last years of the Vietnam War, but nonetheless its roots in individual consciousness were frequently pretty shallow, and had to do with little more than conforming to the psychological custom of the moment.

An example from the world of "bookchat" (as Gore Vidal has nicely named it): in what he charitably called his "thoughts" for the "end of the year," the *New York Times* book reviewer Christopher Lehmann-Haupt, who twice in 1969 had gone on record as an admirer of *Portnoy's Complaint*, announced himself to be a no-holds-barred kind of guy with this bold and challenging endorsement of first-person narration and the confessional approach: "I want the novelist," wrote Lehmann-Haupt, "to bare his soul, to stop playing games, to cease sublimating." Bold, challenging, and inevitably to be flatly contradicted by the *Times* daily reviewer when he caught hold of the pendulum of received opinion as it swung the other way in the ensuing years, toward disguise, artifice, fantasy, montage, and complicated irony. By 1974, Lehmann-Haupt could actually disapprove of Grace Paley's personal-*seeming* (and, in fact, highly stylized) short stories in *Enormous Changes at the Last Minute* for precisely the reasons he had given to praise such a book five years earlier—and without the slightest understanding that for a writer like Grace Paley (or Mark Twain or Henry Miller), as for an actor like Marlon Brando, creating the illusion of intimacy and spontaneity is not just a matter of letting your hair down and being yourself but of inventing a whole new idea of what "being yourself" sounds and looks like; "naturalness" happens not to grow on trees.

"You can see Mrs. Paley getting closer and closer to autobiography," Lehmann-Haupt writes about *Enormous Changes*, "leaning increasingly on a fictional self she calls Faith, and revealing more and more the sources of her imagination. In short, it now seems as if she no longer had the strength or the will to transmute life into art. . . . What has gone wrong, then? What has sapped the author of her will to turn experience into fiction—if that in fact is the trouble?" The trouble? Wrong? Well, mindlessness marches on. Still, by keeping track of the "thoughts" of a Lehmann-Haupt, one can over the years see just which hand-me-down, uncomprehended literary dogma is at work, in a given cultural moment, making fiction accessible and "important" to insensate readers like himself.

In the case of my own "confession," it did not diminish the

voyeuristic kick—to call it by its rightful name—to remember that the novelist who was assumed to be baring his soul and ceasing to sublimate had formerly drawn a rather long, serious, even solemn, face. Nor did it hurt that the subject which this supposed confession focused on at some length was known to one and all and publicly disowned by just about as many: masturbation. That this shameful, solitary addiction was described in graphic detail, and with gusto, must have done much to attract to the book an audience that previously had shown little interest in my writing. Till *Portnoy's Complaint*, no novel of mine had sold more than twenty-five thousand hardcover copies, and the hardcover edition of my first book of stories had sold only twelve thousand copies (and hadn't yet gained nationwide attention by way of the Ali McGraw movie, which was released some months after the publication of *Portnoy's Complaint*). For *Portnoy's Complaint*, however, 420,000 people—or seven times as many as had purchased my three previous books combined—stepped up to the bookstore cash register with $6.95, plus tax, in hand, and half of them within the first ten weeks the book was on sale.

It would seem then that masturbation was a dirtier little secret than even Alexander Portnoy had imagined. Indeed, I would think that the same highly charged preoccupation that prompted so many people who never buy a book to buy one that encouraged them to laugh at a "cunt crazy" masturbator of the respectable classes (and perhaps thereby to ease whatever concern might still attach to their own indulgences) also revealed itself in the coast-to-coast rumor assuring any in need of assurance that for his excesses the author himself had had to be carted off to that mythical lunatic asylum to which folklorists have been consigning unregenerate onanists since self-abuse began.

To be sure, the farcical treatment of masturbation does not explain entirely the avidity with which this particular bestseller was purchased and apparently even read. I think now that the moment when it was published—perhaps unlike any since the early days of World War II for sustained social disorientation—had much to do with their avidity and my own subsequent celebrity, and notoriety. Without the disasters and upheavals of the year 1968, coming as they did at the end of a decade that had been marked by blasphemous defiance of authority and loss of faith in the public order, I doubt that a book like mine would have achieved such renown in 1969. Even three or four years earlier, a realistic novel that treated family authority with comical impiety and depicted sex as the farcical side of a seemingly respectable citizen's life would probably have been a good deal less tolerable—and comprehensible—to the middle-class Americans who bought the book, and would have been treated much more marginally (and, I suspect, hostilely) by the media that publicized it. But by the final year of the sixties, the national education in the irrational and the extreme had been so brilliantly conducted by our Dr. Johnson, with help from both enemies and friends, that, for all its tasteless revelations about everyday sexual obsession and the unromantic side of the family romance, even something like *Portnoy's Complaint* was suddenly within the range of the tolerable. Finding that they *could* tolerate it may even have been a source of the book's appeal to a good number of its readers.

However: the impious and unseemly in *Portnoy's Complaint* would still not have been quite so alluring (and, to many, so offensive) if it weren't for the other key element which, I think, worked to make the wayward hero a somewhat more interesting case than he might otherwise have been at that moment for those Americans whose own psychic armor had been battered by the sixties: the man confessing to forbidden sexual acts and gross offenses against the family order and ordinary decency was a Jew. And that was true whether you read the novel as a novel or as a thinly veiled autobiography.

What gave those acts and offenses the special meaning they had for Portnoy, what made them so rich for him with danger, pleasure, and shame, and so comically inappropriate even in his estimation, is very like what I now believe made Portnoy himself as intriguing as apparently he was to the book's large audience of Jews and Gentiles alike. In brief: going wild in public is the last thing in the world that a Jew is expected to do—by himself, by his family, by his fellow Jews, and by the larger community of Christians whose tolerance for him is often tenuous to begin with, and whose code of respectability he flaunts or violates at his own psychological risk, and perhaps at the risk of his fellow Jews' physical and social well-being. Or so history and ingrained fears argue. He is not expected to make a spectacle of himself, either by shooting off his mouth or by shooting off his semen, and certainly not by shooting off his mouth about shooting off his semen. That pretty much takes the cake. And in fact it did.

"As the paradigmatic outsiders of Western society, Jews have, of course, been masters of social adaptation," writes David Singer, in an essay on the subject of "The Jewish Gangster" published in the winter 1974 issue of *Judaism*. It is no wonder then, says Singer, that "the American Jewish establishment—the defense agencies, the scholars, the historical societies" along with "American Jews [generally] have systematically denied any awareness of [this] important aspect of their history," whose major figures, according to Singer, constitute ". . . a veritable *Who's Who* in the annals of American crime, comparable to that contributed by any other ethnic group."

Of course an Arnold Rothstein, a Lepke Buchalter, a Bugsy Siegel, or a Meyer Lansky (to name only the supervillains on Singer's list) Portnoy is not. Yet *his* sense of himself as a Jewish criminal is a recurrent motif in his ambivalent seizures of self-excoriation; witness the book's last pages where, in concluding his manic aria, he imagines the cops out of a grade-B movie closing in on him, a grade-B racketeer named Mad Dog. It needs no Jewish "defense agencies" other than his own to impugn Portnoy for his conduct, and to make it seem to him that a preoccupation with the flesh is as compromising to the safety and well-being of a Jew in America as was Arnold Roth-stein's fixing—of all the stupid things for a Jewish boy to go and fix—a whole World Series.

That not even a Jew—perhaps society's most outstanding student of maneuvering and negotiation, whose most valued possession, envied even by his enemies, is his Kissingerian *sechel*—that not even a Jew could put up a successful fight any longer against non-negotiable demands of crude antisocial appetite and vulgar aggressive fan-tasy . . . this, it seems to me, may well have been precisely what engaged the attention of any number of middle-class readers whose own mastery of social adaptation had been seriously challenged by the more unsettling experiences of the decade. Surely to many it must have come as a kind of revelation to hear a Jew, of all people, and one whose public life had entirely to do with enforcing social jus-tice and legal controls, admit in italics and caps that, rather than shoring up his defenses and getting on with the business of being better (in all senses of the word), his secret desire was really to give way and be bad—or at the least, if he could manage it, worse. That in particular was something they may not have heard, or read much about recently in American novels written by Jews about Jews.

2. Heroes Jewish Writers Imagine

To see just how strongly the Jew in the post-holocaust decades has been identified in American fiction with righteousness and restraint, with the just and measured response rather than with those libidi-nous and aggressive activities that border on the socially acceptable and may even constitute criminal transgression, it might be well to begin with the novels of Saul Bellow, by now the grand old man of American-Jewish writers, and to my mind the country's most accomplished working novelist. And reading Bellow, what does one find? That almost invariably his heroes are Jewish in vivid and emphatic ways when they are actors in dramas of conscience where matters of principle or virtue are at issue, but are by comparison only faintly marked by their Jewishness, if they are Jews at all, when appetite and quasi- or outright libidinous adventure is at the heart of a novel.

Bellow's first Jewish (as distinguished from non-Jewish) Jew was Asa Leventhal in his second book, *The Victim*. Bellow himself now judges this excellent novel a "proper" book, by which I take him to mean, among other things, that it did not bear his particular stamp so much as convention's. To be Jewish in this novel is to be accessible, morbidly so, to claims made upon the conscience, and to take upon oneself, out of a kind of gruff human sympathy and a responsiveness bordering dangerously at times on paranoia, responsibility for another man's pain and misfortune. Being a Jew, to Asa Leventhal, is a burden at most, an irritation at least—and writing about such a Jew would appear after the fact to have been something of both to Bellow too, as though the enclosure of a victimized Jewish conscience happened also to constrain his inventiveness, and to exclude from imaginative consideration much that was pleasurable and exciting, involving appetite and the exuberant, rather than the ethical, life.

There is Bellow's own word "proper" to argue for this, and there is the next book, *The Adventures of Augie March*, where surely the least important ingredient in the lively and seductive hero's make-up is his sense of himself as a Jew. You could, in fact, take the Jew out of the adventurous Augie March without doing much harm to the whole of the book, whereas the same could not be said for taking Chicago out of the boy. (Whereas the same couldn't be said for taking the Jew out of the Levantine-looking Leventhal.) One can only speculate about how much writing *The Victim* may have served to settle the author's own conscience about touchy matters of survival and success (the bedeviling issue for Leventhal, right along with the issue of

Jewish self-defense) and to open the way for the unambiguous and loquacious delight in his own winning attractiveness that is Augie's charm. But what couldn't be clearer is that, while Bellow seems largely to locate in Leventhal's Jewishness the roots of his morbidity, gloom, uncertainty, touchiness, and moral responsiveness, he connects Augie's health, cheeriness, vigor, stamina, and appetite, as well as his enormous appeal to just about everyone in Cook County, if not in all creation, to his rootedness in a Chicago that is *American* to the core, a place where being Jewish makes of a boy nothing more special in the Virtue Department than any other immigrant mother's child. Though it might be argued that it is the sensibility and verbal energy that in some essential way encompass the book's "Jewishness," this is an argument that would probably be given shortest shrift by Augie himself: "Look at me," he cries triumphantly at the book's conclusion, "going everywhere!" Essentially the sensibility and the energy are those of an exuberant and greedy eclectic, a "Columbus of those near-at-hand," as he describes himself, perpetually outward-bound.

The movement away from the obsessively Jewish Jew Leventhal to the relatively non-Jewish Jew Augie, away from claustrophobic bondage to the Chosen People toward heady, delight-filled choosing, culminates in Bellow's next big novel, *Henderson the Rain King*, whose hoggish and greedy hero, hearty in an altogether different sense from Leventhal, is so much a creature possessed by strange ravenous hungers of the senses and the spirit that Bellow cannot see his way to making him even the most attenuated of Jews. To hang from his Jewishness by no more than a thread—that will do very nicely for Tommy (*né* Adler) Wilhelm, who wants more than anything his daddy. But it will not do at all for a hero who wants, in the way he wants it, what this hero wants.

Which is? To do good, to be just? No, that would be more like Leventhal's ambition, and one that seems to have less to do with "heart" than with a deal he has made to square it with the vengeful gods—playing ball with the superego. What then? To be adopted, abducted, and adored? No, that is more in brainy, handsome, egotistic Augie's line (Augie, who is, when you stop to think about it, everything that Tommy Wilhelm had in mind but hadn't the Chicago in him to pull off; his is the story of ego quashed). What then is Henderson after? "I want!" Exclamation point. "I want!" And that is it. It is the voice of the id—raw, untrammeled, uncompromising, insatiable, and unsocialized desire.

"I want." In a Bellow novel only a goy can talk like that and get away with it. As indeed Henderson does, for by the conclusion of the book he is said actually to have been regenerated by this quest he has been on for intensity and orgasmic release. Is there anyone happier in all of Bellow's books? No punishment or victimization for this unchosen person. To the contrary, what makes *Henderson the Rain King* a full-scale comedy is that what the clown wants he gets—"It's the richness of the mixture!" cries Henderson, swooning in Africa with *pleasure*. What he had not enough of, if he had any, he now gets more of than he knows what to do with. He is the king of rain, of gush, of geyser.

If the goy gets more than enough to burst his spirit's sleep, Bellow's next two heroes, very Jewish Jews indeed, get far less than they *deserve*. Desire or appetite has nothing to do with it. What is denied here are *ethical* hopes and expectations. Others should act otherwise, they don't, and the Jewish hero suffers. With Moses Herzog and Artur Sammler, Bellow moves from Henderson all the way back to the world of the victim—and, ineluctably, it would seem, back to the Jew, the man of acutely developed sensibilities and a great sense of personal dignity and inbred virtue, whose sanity in the one book, and whose human sympathies in the other, are continuously tried by the libidinous greed of the willful, the crazed, and the criminal.

Henderson's hoggish "I want!" is in fact something like the rallying cry of those others who make Herzog moan, "I fail to understand," and cause Sammler, who has seen and survived nearly everything, to admit at last in 1968 in New York City, "I am horrified." The pig-farmer goy as a noble Yahoo in black Africa—the morally elegant Jew as a maimed and grieving Houyhnhnm on a darkening Upper West Side. Augie, the Chicago adventurer, returns as a bleeding, punished Herzog, the irresistible egoist who has been bitten by what he had chewed off—the Moses-trainer Madeleine having had better luck with her bird in the Berkshires than the eagle-trainer Thea in Mexico—and Leventhal, he of the bilious temper and the brooding conscience, is reincarnated as the moral magistrate Sammler, whose New York is no longer simply "as hot as Bangkok" on some nights, but has *become* a barbarous Bangkok, even on the Broadway bus and in the Columbia University lecture hall. "Most outdoor telephones were smashed, crippled. They were urinals, also. New York was getting worse than Naples or Salonika. It was like an Asian or an African town. . . ."

How remote, how metaphorical—how "proper" indeed—Leventhal's suffering seems beside Mr. Sammler's. And what a mild, mild nuisance is Allbee, the insinuating down-and-out goy who ruins Leventhal's summer solitude, who sullies his marriage bed and embarrassingly strokes his Jewish hair—how mild he is compared to the lordly and ominous dude of a black pickpocket, whose uncircumcised member and "great oval testicles" are unveiled in all their iridescent grandeur for consideration by the superego's man in Manhattan. And yet, despite the difference in degree (and context and meaning) between the assault in the early book and in the later one, it is still the Jew who is aggressed *against*, the Jew who is on the receiving end when appetite and rage run wild: "the soul in its vehemence," as Sammler calls what horrifies him most, or, less delicately and more specifically, "sexual niggerhood." As opposed to what might similarly be described as "ethical Jewhood."

Now, there are obviously other ways to go about reading Saul Bellow: the intention here is not to diminish his achievement by reducing his novels to just this pile of bare bones but rather to trace the characteristic connection made in his work (and, in Bernard Malamud's work as well) between the Jew and conscience, and the Gentile and appetite—and thereby to point up how conditioned readers had become (one might say, how *persuaded*, given the imaginative authority of the writers in question) to associate the sympathetic Jewish hero with ethical Jewhood as it opposes sexual niggerhood, with victimization as opposed to vengeful aggression, with dignified survival rather than euphoric or gloating triumph, with sanity and renunciation as opposed to excessive desire—except the excessive desire to be good and to do good.

To the degree that Saul Bellow has been a source of pride or comfort (or at least has been little or no trouble, which can amount to the same thing) to what David Singer calls the "American Jewish establishment," I would suggest that it has had more to do with these bare bones I've laid out here than with the brimming novels themselves, which are too deliberately ambiguous, too self-challenging, too densely rendered and reflective to be vehicles of ethnic propaganda or comfort. The fact is that Bellow's deeply ironic humanism, coupled as it is with his wide-ranging sympathy for odd and dubious characters, for regular Chicago guys, for the self-mockery and self-love of the down-on-his-luck dauphin-type, has actually made him a figure of more importance to other Jewish writers than he is to the Jewish cultural audience—unlike, say, Elie Wiesel or Isaac Bashevis Singer, who, as they relate to the lost Jewish past, have a somewhat awesome spiritual meaning for the community-at-large that is not necessarily of pressing *literary* interest to their fellow writers. But Bellow, by closing the gap, as it were, between Damon Runyon and Thomas Mann—or to use loosely Philip Rahv's categories, between redskin and paleface—has, I think, inspired all sorts of explorations into immediate worlds of experience that American-born Jewish writers who have come after him might otherwise have overlooked or dumbly stared at for years without the ingenious example of *this* Columbus of those near-at-hand.

If Saul Bellow's longer works* tend generally to associate the Jewish Jew with the struggles of ethical Jewhood and the non-Jewish Jew and the Gentile with the release of appetite and aggression (Gersbach, the Buber-booster and wife-stealer in *Herzog*, is really no great exception, since he is a *spurious* Jewish Jew who can't even pronounce his Yiddish right; and Madeleine, that Magdalene, has of course worn a cross and worked at Fordham), in the work of Bernard

---

*I say "longer works" because the hard and ugly facts of life in a short story like "The Old System," published first in *Playboy* in 1967, are of the sort that have been known to set the phones ringing at the Anti-Defamation League. Baldly put (which is how these things tend to be put when the lines are drawn), it is a story of rich Jews and their money: first, how they make it big in the world with under-the-table payoffs (a hundred thousand delivered to an elegant old Wasp for lucrative countryclub acreage—and delivered by a Jew Bellow depicts as an orthodox religious man); and then it is about how Jews cheat and finagle one another out of the Almighty Dollar: a dying Jewish woman, with a dirty mouth no less, demands twenty thousand in cash from her businessman brother for the privilege of seeing her before she expires in her hospital bed. This scene of sibling hatred and financial cunning in a Jewish family is in fact the astonishing climax to which the story moves.

One wonders about the reception the defense agencies would have given to this story, especially appearing as it did in *Playboy* magazine, had it been the work of some unknown Schwartz or Levy instead of the author of *Herzog*. Indeed, in the aftermath of sixties' political radicalism and the traumatic shock upon Jews of the October 1973 war, one wonders what position the Jewish press and cultural journals would take if a first novel like *Dangling Man* were suddenly to be published, wherein the thoroughly deracinated and depressive hero seems to dislike no one quite so much as his Jewish brother's bourgeois family, or if out of the blue a book like *The Victim* were now to appear, in which the hero's Jewishness is at times made to resemble a species of psychopathology.

Malamud these tendencies are so sharply and schematically present as to give Malamud's novels the lineaments of moral allegory. For Malamud, generally speaking, the Jew is innocent, passive, virtuous, and this to the degree that he defines himself or is defined by others as a Jew; the Gentile, on the other hand, is characteristically corrupt, violent, and lustful, particularly when he enters a room or a store or a cell with a Jew in it.

Now, on the face of it, it would seem that a writer could not get very far with such evangelistic simplifications. And yet that is not at all the case with Malamud (as it isn't with Jerzy Kosinski in *The Painted Bird*), for so instinctively do the figures of a good Jew and a bad goy emerge from an imagination essentially folkloric and didactic that his fiction is actually most convincing the more strictly he adheres to these simplifications, and diminishes in moral conviction and narrative drive to the extent that he surrenders them, or tries, however slyly, to undo their hold on him.

His best book—containing as it does the classic Malamudian moral arrangement—is still *The Assistant*, which proposes that an entombed and impoverished grocer named Morris Bober shall by the example of his passive suffering and his goodness of heart transform a young thieving Italian drifter named Frank Alpine into another entombed, impoverished, and suffering Jewish grocer, and that this shall constitute an act of *assistance*, and set Alpine on the road to redemption—or so the stern morality of the book suggests.

Redemption from what? Crimes of violence and deceit against a good Jewish father, crimes of lust against the father's virginal daughter, whom the goy has spied upon naked and then raped. But oh how punitive is this redemption! We might almost take what happens to the bad goy when he falls into the hands of the good Jews as an act of enraged Old Testament retribution visited upon him by the wrathful Jewish author—if it weren't for the moral pathos and the gentle religious coloration with which Malamud invests the tale of conversion; and also the emphasis that is clear to the author throughout—that it is the good Jews who have fallen into the hands of the bad goy. It has occurred to me that a less hopeful Jewish writer than Malamud—Kosinski, say, whose novels don't put much stock in the capacity for redemption but concentrate rather determinedly on the persistence of brutality and malice—might not have understood Alpine's transformation into Jewish grocer and Jewish father (with all that those roles entail in this book) as a sign of moral improvement but as the cruel realization of Bober's revenge. "Now suffer, you goy bastard, the way I did."

To see how still another sort of Jewish writer, Norman Mailer, might have registered the implications of a story like *The Assistant*, we can look to his famous essay "The White Negro," published first in *Dissent* magazine in 1957, the very year Malamud's novel appeared. Imagining all of this independently of Malamud, Mailer nonetheless comes up with a scenario startlingly similar to the one with which *The Assistant* begins. In the Mailer version there are also two hoodlums who beat a defenseless shopkeeper over the head and take his money; however, quite characteristically for Mailer—and it is this that invariably distinguishes his concerns from Malamud's or Bellow's—he appraises the vicious act as it affects the well-being of the violator rather than the violated.

"It can of course be suggested," writers Mailer parenthetically, about "encourag[ing] the psychopath in oneself," "that it takes little courage for two strong eighteen-year-old hoodlums, let us say, to beat in the brains of a candy-store keeper, and indeed the act—even by the logic of the psychopath—is not likely to prove very therapeutic, for the victim is not an immediate equal. Still, courage of a sort is necessary, for one murders not only a weak fifty-year-old man but an institution as well, one violates private property, one enters into a new relation with the police and introduces a dangerous element into one's life. The hoodlum is therefore daring the unknown, and so no matter how brutal the act, it is not altogether cowardly."

These few lines on the positive value homicide has for the psychopath should make it clear why Jewish cultural audiences, which are generally pleased to hear Saul Bellow and Bernard Malamud identified by critics as Jewish writers, are perfectly content that by and large Norman Mailer, with all his considerable influence and stature, should go forth onto the lecture platform and the television talk shows as a writer, *period*. This is obviously okay too with the author of *The Deer Park* and *An American Dream*, to name just two of his books with heroes he chooses not to call Cohen. It is pointless to wonder what Jews (or Gentiles) would have made of those two books if the author had had other than an O'Shaugnessy as the libidinous voyager or a Rojack as the wife-murderer and spade-whipper in his American Gomorrah, for that an identifiably Jewish hero could perpetrate such spectacular transgressions with so much gusto and so little self-doubt or ethical disorientation turns out to be as inconceivable to Norman Mailer as it is to Bernard Malamud. And maybe for the same reason: it is just the Jew in one that says, "No, no, *restrain yourself*" to such grandiose lusts and drives. To which prohibition Malamud adds, "Amen," but to which Mailer replies, "Then I'll see ya' around."

I cannot imagine Mailer having much patience with the conclusion of the violent hoodlum–defenseless shopkeeper scenario as Malamud realizes it in *The Assistant*. Some other lines from "The White Negro" might in fact stand as Mailer's description of just what is happening to Frank Alpine, who dons Morris Bober's apron, installs himself for eighteen hours a day behind his cash register, and from the tomb of a dying grocery store takes responsibility for the college education (rather than the orgasmic, no-holds-barred, time-of-her-timish education) of Morris's Jewish daughter: ". . . new kinds of victories," Mailer writes, "increase one's power for new kinds of perception; and defeats, the wrong kind of defeats, attack the body and imprison one's energy until one is jailed in the prison air of other people's habits, other people's defeats, boredom, quiet desperation, and muted icy self-destroying rage. . . ."

It is precisely with an attack upon the body—upon the very organ with which Alpine had attacked Bober's daughter—that Malamud concludes *The Assistant*. Whether Malamud himself sees it as an attack, as something more like cruel and unusual punishment than poetic justice, is another matter; given the novel's own signposts, it would appear that the reader is expected to take the last paragraph in the book as describing the conclusive act of Frank's *redemption*, the final solution to his Gentile problem.

> One day in April Frank went to the hospital and had himself circumcised. For a couple of days he dragged himself around with a pain between his legs. The pain enraged and inspired him. After Passover he became a Jew.

So penance for the criminal penis has been done. No cautionary folktale on the dangers of self-abuse could be any more vivid or pointed than this, nor could those connections that I have tried to trace in Bellow's novels be more glaringly apparent than they are here: Renunciation is Jewish and renunciation is All. By comparison to the tyrannical Yahweh who rules over *The Assistant*, the Bellow of *Mr. Sammler's Planet* seems like a doting parent who asks only for contraceptive common sense and no hard drugs. *The Assistant* is a manifestation of ethical Jewhood with what one might legitimately call a vengeance. Beneath the austerity and the pathos, Malamud, as we shall see again, has a fury all his own.

The Fixer, page 69: "The fixer readily confessed he was a Jew. Otherwise he was innocent." Page 80: "I'm an innocent man. . . . I've had little in my life." Page 98: "I swear to you I am innocent of any serious crime. . . . It's not my nature." *What* isn't his nature? Ritual murder and sexual assault—vengeful aggression and brutal lust. So it is for the crimes of Frank Alpine and Ward Minogue, the two hoodlum goyim who prey upon the innocent, helpless Jewish family of *The Assistant*, that Yakov Bok, the helpless, innocent Russian-Jewish handyman of *The Fixer*, is arrested and imprisoned, and in something far worse even than a dungeon of a grocery store. In fact, I know of no serious authors whose novels have chronicled physical brutality and fleshly mortification in such detail and at such length, and who likewise have taken a single defenseless innocent and constructed almost an entire book out of the relentless violations suffered by that character at the hands of cruel and perverse captors, other than Malamud, the Marquis de Sade, and the pseudonymous author of *The Story of O. The Fixer*, the opening of Chapter V:

> The days were passing and the Russian officials were waiting impatiently for his menstrual period to begin. Grubeshov and the army general often consulted the calendar. If it didn't start soon they threatened to pump blood out of his penis with a machine they had for that purpose. The machine was a pump made of iron with a red indicator to show how much blood was being drained out. The danger of it was that it didn't always work right and sometimes sucked every drop of blood out of the body. It was used exclusively on Jews; only their penises fitted it.

The careful social and historical documentation of *The Fixer*—which Malamud's instinctive feel for folk material is generally able to transform from fiction researched into fiction imagined—envelops what is at its center a relentless work of violent pornography in which the pure and innocent Jew, whose queasiness at the sight of blood is at the outset almost maidenly, is ravished by the sadistic goyim, "men," a knowledgeable ghost informs him, "who [are] without morality."

To be sure, a few paragraphs from the end of the book, the defenseless Jew who has been falsely accused of murdering a twelve-year-old boy and drinking his blood, and has been unjustly brutalized for that crime for almost three hundred pages, has his revenge offered him suddenly on a silver platter—*and he takes it*. If it's murder they want, it's murder they'll get. With his revolver he shoots the Czar! "Yakov pressed the trigger. Nicholas"—the italics are mine—"*in the act of crossing himself*, overturned his chair, and fell, to his surprise, to the floor, the stain spreading on his breast." And there is no remorse or guilt in Yakov, not after what he has been through at the hands of Czar Nicholas's henchmen. "Better him than us," he thinks, dismissing with a commonplace idiom of four simple words the crime of crimes: regicide, the murder of the Goyische King.

Only it happens that all of this takes place in Yakov's imagination. It is a vengeful and heroic daydream that he is having on the way to the trial at which it would seem he is surely doomed. Which is as it must be in Malamud's world: for it is not in Yakov's nature, any more than it is in Morris Bober's (or Moses Herzog's), to press a real trigger and shed real blood. Remember Herzog with his pistol? "It's not everyone who gets the opportunity to kill with a clear conscience. They had," Herzog tells himself, "opened the way to justifiable murder." But at the bathroom window, peering in at his enemy Gersbach bathing his daughter Junie, he cannot pull the trigger. "Firing this pistol," writes Bellow in *Herzog* (though it could as well be Malamud at the conclusion of *The Fixer*), "was nothing but a thought." Vengeance then must come in other forms for these victimized Jewish men, if it comes at all. That vengeance *isn't* in his nature is a large part of what makes him heroic to the author himself.

In *Pictures of Fidelman* Malamud sets out to turn the tables on himself, and, gamely, to take a holiday from his own obsessive mythology: he imagines as a hero a Jewish man living without shame and even with a kind of virile, if shlemielish, forcefulness in a world of Italian gangsters, thieves, pimps, whores, and bohemians, a man who eventually finds love facedown with a Venetian glassblower who is the husband of his own mistress—and most of it has no more impact than the bullet that Yakov Bok fired in his imagination had on the real Czar of Russia. And largely, I think, because it has been conceived as a similar kind of compensatory daydream; in *Fidelman*, unfortunately, natural repugnance and constraints, and a genuine sense of what conversions cost, are dissolved in rhetorical flourishes rather than through the sort of human struggle that Malamud's own deeply held sense of things calls forth in *The Assistant* and *The Fixer*. It's no accident that this of all the longer works generates no internal narrative tension (a means whereby it might seek to test its own assumptions) and is without the continuous sequential development that comes to this kind of storyteller so naturally and acts in him as a necessary counterforce against runaway fantasy. This playful daydream of waywardness, criminality, transgression, lust, and sexual perversion simply could not have stood up against that kind of opposition.

There are of course winning and amusing pages along the way—there is a conversation between Fidelman and a talking light bulb in the section called "Pictures of the Artist" that is Malamud the folk comic at his best—but after the first section, "Last Mohican," the bulk of the book has an air of unchecked and somewhat unfocused indulgence, which is freewheeling about a libidinous and disordered life more or less to the extent that nothing much is at stake or seriously challenged. What distinguishes "Last Mohican" from all that comes after is that *its* Fidelman, so meticulous about himself, so very cautious and constrained, is not at all the same fellow who turns up later cleaning out toilets in a whorehouse, shacking up with prostitutes, and dealing one-on-one with a pimp; the author may have convinced himself that it was the experience with Susskind he undergoes in "Last Mohican" that, as it were, frees Fidelman for what follows, but, if so, that comes under the category, as a little too much does here, of magical thinking. Wherever the unconstraining processes, the struggles toward release, might appropriately be dramatized, there is a chapter break, and when the narrative resumes, the freedom is a *fait accompli*.

Of "Last Mohican's" Fidelman it is written: "He was, at odd hours in certain streets, several times solicited by prostitutes, some heart-breakingly pretty, one a slender, unhappy-looking girl with bags under her eyes whom he desired mightily, but Fidelman feared for his health." *This* Fidelman desires unhappy-looking girls bearing signs of wear and tear. *This* Fidelman fears for his health. And that isn't all he fears for. But then this Fidelman is not just a Jew in name only. "To be unmasked as a hidden Jew," which is what frightens Yakov Bok in the early stages of *The Fixer*, could in fact serve to describe just what happens to "Last Mohican's" Fidelman, with the assistance of his own Bober, the wily shnorring refugee Susskind. "Last Mohican" is a tale of conscience tried and human sympathy unclotted, arising out of very different interests from the fiction that comes after—and it abounds with references, humble, comic, and solemn, to Jewish history and life. But that is it, by and large, for the Jews: enter sex in Chapter 2, called "Still Life," and exit Susskind and Fidelman, the unmasked Jew. What is henceforth to be unmasked in Fidelman in this book—which would, if it could, be a kind of counter-*Assistant*—is the hidden goy, a man whose appetites are associated elsewhere with the lust-ridden "uncircumcised dog" Alpine.

And if there should be any doubt as to how fierce and reflexive is the identification in Malamud's imagination between renunciation and Jew, and appetite and goy, one need only compare the pathetic air of self-surrender that marks the ending of "Last Mohican"—

> "Susskind, come back," he shouted, half sobbing. "The suit is yours. All is forgiven."
>
> He came to a dead halt but the refugee ran on. When last seen he was still running.

to the comic and triumphant ending of "Still Life." The second chapter concludes with Fidelman's first successful penetration, which he is able, after much frustration, to accomplish upon a strong-minded Italian *pittrice* by inadvertently disguising himself in a priest's vest-

ments. There is both more and less to this scene than Malamud may
have intended:

> She grabbed his knees. "Help me, Father, for Christ's
> sake."
> Fidelman, after a short tormented time, said in a quaver-
> ing voice, "I forgive you, my child."
> "The penance," she wailed, "first the penance."
> After reflecting, he replied, "Say one hundred times
> each, Our Father and Hail Mary."
> "More," Annamaria wept. "More, more. Much more."
> Gripping his knees so hard they shook she burrowed her
> head into his black-buttoned lap. He felt the surprised
> beginnings of an erection.

But really it should not have come as such a surprise, this erection
that arrives while he is dressed in priest's clothing. What would have
been surprising is if Fidelman had disguised himself as a Susskind,
say, and found that working like an aphrodisiac, maybe even on a
Jewish girl like Helen Bober. Then would something have been at
stake, then would something have been challenged. But as it is written, with Fidelman copulating in a priest's biretta rather than a skull-
cap, the scene moves the novel nowhere, particularly as the final line
seems to me to get entirely backward the implications of the joke
that is being played here. "Pumping slowly," the chapter ends, "he
nailed her to her cross." But isn't it rather the Jew who is being
nailed, if not to his cross, to the structure of his inhibitions?

The trouble with lines like the last one in that chapter is that they
settle an issue with a crisp rhetorical flourish before it has even been
allowed to have much of a life. At the very moment that the writer
appears to be most forceful and candid, he is in fact shying away from
his own subject and suppressing whatever is psychologically rich or
morally troublesome with a clever, but essentially evasive, figure of

speech. Here, for instance, is Fidelman's detumescence described earlier. Premature ejaculation has just finished him off, much to the *pittrice*'s dismay, and though he hasn't as yet stumbled unwittingly upon the clerical disguise that will make him fully potent and desirable, we note that the figure for erotic revitalization is, as usual, Christian; also noteworthy is that, generally speaking in *Fidelman*, where the sex act is, there shall whimsical metaphor be. "Although he mightily willed resurrection, his wilted flower bit the dust." And here is the hero discovering himself to be a homosexual. "Fidelman had never in his life said 'I love you' without reservation to anyone. He said it to Beppo. If that's the way it works, that's the way it works." But that isn't the way it works at all. That is a dream of the way it works, and all of it neatly koshered with the superego and other defense agencies, with that reassuring word "love."

"Think of love," says Beppo, as he leaps on naked Fidelman from behind. "You've run from it all your life." And, magically, one might say, just by *thinking* of it, Fidelman instantaneously loves, so that between the homosexual act of anal intercourse—an act which society still generally considers a disgusting transgression indeed—and its transformation into ideal behavior, there is not even time for the reader to say ouch. Or for Fidelman to think whatever perplexing thoughts might well accompany entry into the world of the taboo by the tight-assed fellow who at the outset, in the marvelous "Last Mohican" chapter, would barely give the refugee Susskind the time of day.

One wonders why the taboo must be idealized quite so fast. Why must Fidelman dress up as a priest merely to get himself laid right, and not only think of love but *fall* in love, the very first time he gets buggered? Why not think of lust, of base and unseemly desire? And surrender himself to *that*? People, after all, have been known to run from it too all their lives, just as fast and as far. And when last seen were still running. "In America," the book concludes, "he worked as a craftsman in glass and loved men and women."

Recall the last lines of *The Assistant*. Frank Alpine should have it so easy with *his* appetites. But whereas in *The Assistant* the lusting goy's passionate and aggressive act of *genuinely* loving desire for the Jewish girl takes the form of rape, and requires penance (or retribution) of the harshest kind, in *Pictures of Fidelman*, the Jew's most wayward (albeit comfortingly passive) sexual act is, without anything faintly resembling Alpine's enormous personal struggle, converted on the spot into love. And if this is still insufficiently reassuring about a Jew and sexual appetite, the book manages by the end to have severed the bisexual Fidelman as thoroughly from things Jewish as *The Assistant*, by its conclusion, has marked the sexually constrained, if not desexed, Alpine as a Jew forevermore. Of all of Malamud's Jewish heroes, is there any who is by comparison so strikingly *un*-Jewish (after Chapter I is out of the way, that is), who insists upon it so little, and is so little reminded of it by the Gentile world? And is there any who, at the conclusion, is happier?

In short, Fidelman is Malamud's Henderson, Italy his Africa, and "love" is the name that Malamud, for reasons that by now should be apparent, gives in this book to getting finally what you want the way you want it. Suggesting precisely the disjunction between act and self-knowledge that accounts for the light-headed dreaminess of *Fidelman*, and that differentiates it so sharply from those wholly convincing novels, *The Assistant* and *The Fixer*, where no beclouding ambivalence stands between the author's imagination and the objects of his fury.

And now to return to *Portnoy's Complaint* and the hero imagined by this Jewish writer. Obviously the problem for Alexander Portnoy is that, unlike Arthur Fidelman, nothing *inflames* his Jewish self-consciousness so much as setting forth on a wayward libidinous adventure—that is, nothing makes it seem quite so wayward than that a Jewish man like himself should be wanting the things he wants. The hidden Jew is unmasked in *him* by the sight of his own erection. He cannot suppress the one in the interests of the other, nor can he imagine them living happily ever after in peaceful coexistence. Like the rest of us, he too has read Saul Bellow, Bernard Malamud, and Norman Mailer. His condition might be compared to Frank Alpine's, if, after his painful circumcision—with all that it means to him about virtuous renunciation—Alpine had all at once found his old disreputable self, the uncircumcised dog and Maileresque hoodlum of the forbidden lusts and desires, emerging from solitary confinement to engage his freshly circumcised and circumscribed self in hand-to-hand combat. In Portnoy the disapproving moralist who says "I am horrified" will not disappear when the libidinous slob shows up screaming "I want!" Nor will the coarse, antisocial Alpine in him be permanently subdued by whatever of Morris Bober, or of his own hard-working, well-intentioned Boberish father, there may be in his nature. This imaginary Jew also drags himself around with a pain between his legs, only it inspires him to acts of frenzied and embarrassing lust.

A lusting Jew. A Jew as sexual defiler. An odd type, as it turns out, in recent Jewish fiction, where it is usually the goy who does the sexual defiling; also, it has been alleged, one of the "crudest and most venerable stereotypes of anti-Semitic lore." I am quoting from a letter written by Marie Syrkin—a well-known American Zionist leader and daughter of one of Socialist Zionism's outstanding organizers and polemicists in the first quarter of the century—and published in *Commentary* in March 1973. The letter constituted her improvement on two separate attacks that had appeared several months earlier in *Commentary*, one by Irving Howe directed at my work (most specifically *Goodbye, Columbus* and *Portnoy's Complaint*), and the other by the magazine's editor, Norman Podhoretz, directed at what is assumed by him to be my cultural position and reputation. (*Commentary* associate editor Peter Shaw had already attacked *Portnoy's Complaint* for "fanaticism in the hatred of things Jewish" in the review he wrote when the novel first appeared and which somehow turned up in *Commentary* too.)

The historical references Syrkin employs to identify what is repugnant to her about *Portnoy's Complaint* suggest that to some I had gone beyond the odd or eccentric in this book, exceeded even the reductive "vulgarity" which Howe said "deeply marred" my fiction here as elsewhere, and had entered into the realm of the pathological. Here is Syrkin's characterization of Portnoy's lustful, even *vengefully* lustful, designs upon the Gentile world and its women—and particularly of the gratifications he seeks, and to some degree obtains, from a rich and pretty Wasp girl, a shiksa whom he would have perform fellatio upon him, if only she could master the skill without asphyxiating herself. It is of no interest to Syrkin that Portnoy goes about tutoring his "tender young countess" in techniques of breathing, rather more like a patient swimming instructor with a timid ten-year-old at a summer camp than in the manner of the Marquis de Sade or even Sergius O'Shaugnessy, nor does she give any indication that oral intercourse may not necessarily constitute the last word in human degradation, even for the participants themselves: "a classic description," writes Syrkin, "of what the Nazis called *rassenschande* (racial defilement)"; ". . . straight out of the Goebbels-Streicher script . . ."; "the anti-semitic indictment straight through Hitler is that the Jew is the defiler and destroyer of the Gentile world."

Hitler, Goebbels, Streicher. Had she not been constrained by limitations of space, Syrkin might eventually have had me in the dock with the entire roster of Nuremberg defendants. On the other hand, it does not occur to her that sexual entanglements between Jewish men and Gentile women might themselves be marked, in any number of instances, by the history of anti-Semitism that so obviously determines her own rhetoric and point of view, at least in this letter. Nor is she about to allow the most obvious point of all: that this Portnoy can no more enter into an erotic relationship unconscious of his Jewishness and his victim's or, if you will, his assistant's Gentileness than a Bober could enter into a relationship on terms less charged than these with Alpine, or Leventhal with Allbee. Rather, to Syrkin, for a Jew to have the kind of sexual desires Alexander Portnoy has (conflict-laden and self-defeating as they frequently are) is unimaginable to anyone but a Nazi.

Now, arguing as she does for what a Jew is not and could not be, other than to a pathological Nazi racist, Syrkin leaves little doubt that she herself has very strongly held ideas as to what a Jew in fact is, or certainly ought to be. As did Theodor Herzl; as did Weizmann, Jabotinsky, and Nahman Syrkin; as did Hitler, Goebbels, and Streicher; as do Jean-Paul Sartre, Moshe Dayan, Meir Kahane, Leonid Brezhnev, and the Union of American Hebrew Congregations . . . not to mention the lesser historical personages and institutions that were designated at the outset of the standard bar mitzvah speech of my childhood as "My dear grandparents, parents, assembled relatives, friends, and members of the congregation." In an era which had seen the avid and, as it were, brilliant Americanization of millions of uprooted Jewish immigrants and refugees, the annihilation as human trash of millions of Europeanized Jews, and the establishment and survival in the ancient holy land of a spirited, defiant modern Jewish state, it can safely be said that imagining what Jews are and ought to be has been anything but the marginal activity of a few American-Jewish novelists. The novelistic enterprise—particularly in books like *The Victim*, *The Assistant*, and *Portnoy's Complaint*—might itself be described as imagining Jews *being* imagined, by themselves and by others. Given all those projections, fantasies, illusions, programs, dreams, and solutions that the existence of the Jews has given rise to, it is no wonder that these three books, whatever may be their differences in literary merit and approach, are largely nightmares of bondage, each informed in its way by a mood of baffled, claustrophobic struggle.

As I see it, the task for the Jewish novelist has not been to go forth to forge in the smithy of his soul the *uncreated* conscience of his race, but to find inspiration in a conscience that has been created and undone a hundred times over in this century alone. Similarly, out of this myriad of prototypes, the solitary being to whom history or circumstance has assigned the appellation "Jew" has had, as it were, to imagine what *he* is and is not, must and must not do.

If he can, with conviction, assent to that appellation and imagine himself to be such a thing at all. And that is not always so easy to accomplish. For, as the most serious of American-Jewish novelists seem to indicate—in those choices of subject and emphasis that lead to the heart of what a writer thinks—there are passionate ways of living that not even imaginations as unfettered as theirs are able to attribute to a character forthrightly presented as a Jew.

"I Always Wanted You to Admire My Fasting";

or, Looking at Kafka

TO THE STUDENTS OF ENGLISH 275,
UNIVERSITY OF PENNSYLVANIA, FALL 1972

"I always wanted you to admire my fasting," said the hunger artist. "We do admire it," said the overseer, affably. "But you shouldn't admire it," said the hunger artist. "Well then we don't admire it," said the overseer, "but why shouldn't we admire it?" "Because I have to fast, I can't help it," said the hunger artist. "What a fellow you are," said the overseer, "and why can't you help it?" "Because," said the hunger artist, lifting his head a little and speaking, with his lips pursed, as if for a kiss, right into the overseer's ear, so that no syllable might be lost, "because I couldn't find the food I liked. If I had found it, believe me, I should have made no fuss and stuffed myself like you or anyone else." These were his last words, but in his dimming eyes remained the firm though no longer proud persuasion that he was still continuing to fast.

—Franz Kafka, *"A Hunger Artist"*

1

I am looking, as I write of Kafka, at the photograph taken of him at the age of forty (my age)—it is 1924, as sweet and hopeful a year as he may ever have known as a man, and the year of his death. His face

---

Written in 1973.

is sharp and skeletal, a borrower's face: pronounced cheekbones made even more conspicuous by the absence of sideburns; the ears shaped and angled on his head like angel wings; an intense, creaturely gaze of startled composure—enormous fears, enormous control; a black towel of Levantine hair pulled close around the skull the only sensuous feature; there is a familiar Jewish flare in the bridge of the nose, the nose itself is long and weighted slightly at the tip—the nose of half the Jewish boys who were my friends in high school. Skulls chiseled like this one were shoveled by the thousands from the ovens; had he lived, his would have been among them, along with the skulls of his three younger sisters.

Of course it is no more horrifying to think of Franz Kafka in Auschwitz than to think of anyone in Auschwitz—it is just horrifying in its own way. But he died too soon for the holocaust. Had he lived, perhaps he would have escaped with his good friend Max Brod, who found refuge in Palestine, a citizen of Israel until his death there in 1968. But *Kafka* escaping? It seems unlikely for one so fascinated by entrapment and careers that culminate in anguished death. Still, there is Karl Rossmann, his American greenhorn. Having imagined Karl's escape to America and his mixed luck here, could not Kafka have found a way to execute an escape for himself? The New School for Social Research in New York becoming *his* Great Nature Theatre of Oklahoma? Or perhaps, through the influence of Thomas Mann, a position in the German department at Princeton . . . But then, had Kafka lived, it is not at all certain that the books of his which Mann celebrated from *his* refuge in New Jersey would ever have been published; eventually Kafka might either have destroyed those manuscripts that he had once bid Max Brod to dispose of at his death or, at the least, continued to keep them his secret. The Jewish refugee arriving in America in 1938 would not then have been Mann's "religious humorist" but a frail and bookish fifty-five-year-old bachelor, formerly a lawyer for a government insurance firm in Prague, retired on a pension in Berlin at the time of

Hitler's rise to power—an author, yes, but of a few eccentric stories, mostly about animals, stories no one in America had ever heard of and only a handful in Europe had read; a homeless K., but without K.'s willfulness and purpose, a homeless Karl, but without Karl's youthful spirit and resilience; just a Jew lucky enough to have escaped with his life, in his possession a suitcase containing some clothes, some family photos, some Prague mementos, and the manuscripts, still unpublished and in pieces, of *Amerika, The Trial, The Castle*, and (stranger things happen) three more fragmented novels, no less remarkable than the bizarre masterworks that he keeps to himself out of oedipal timidity, perfectionist madness, and insatiable longings for solitude and spiritual purity.

July 1923: Eleven months before he will die in a Vienna sanatorium, Kafka somehow finds the resolve to leave Prague and his father's home for good. Never before has he even remotely succeeded in living apart, independent of his mother, his sisters, and his father, nor has he been a writer other than in those few hours when he is not working in the legal department of the Workers' Accident Insurance Office in Prague; since taking his law degree at the university, he has been by all reports the most dutiful and scrupulous of employees, though he finds the work tedious and enervating. But in June of 1923—having some months earlier been pensioned from his job because of his illness—he meets a young Jewish girl of nineteen at a seaside resort in Germany, Dora Dymant, an employee at the vacation camp of the Jewish People's Home of Berlin. Dora has left her Orthodox Polish family to make a life of her own (at half Kafka's age); she and Kafka—who has just turned forty—fall in love . . . Kafka has by now been engaged to two somewhat more conventional Jewish girls—twice to one of them—hectic, anguished engagements wrecked largely by his fears. "I am mentally incapable of marrying," he writes his father in the forty-five-page letter he gave to his mother to deliver. ". . . the moment I make up my mind to marry I can no longer sleep, my head burns day and night, life can no longer be called life." He explains why. "Marrying is barred to me," he tells his father, "because it is your domain. Sometimes I imagine the map of the world spread out and you stretched diagonally across it. And I feel as if I could consider living in only those regions that are not covered by you or are not within your reach. And in keeping with the conception I have of your magnitude, these are not many and not very comforting regions—and marriage is not among them." The letter explaining what is wrong between this father and this son is dated November 1919; the mother thought it best not even to deliver it, perhaps for lack of courage, probably, like the son, for lack of hope.

During the following two years, Kafka attempts to wage an affair with Milena Jesenká-Pollak, an intense young woman of twenty-four who has translated a few of his stories into Czech and is most unhappily married in Vienna; his affair with Milena, conducted feverishly, but by and large through the mails, is even more demoralizing to Kafka than the fearsome engagements to the nice Jewish girls. They aroused only the paterfamilias longings that he dared not indulge, longings inhibited by his exaggerated awe of his father— "spellbound," says Brod, "in the family circle"—and the hypnotic spell of his own solitude; but the Czech Milena, impetuous, frenetic, indifferent to conventional restraints, a woman of appetite and anger, arouses more elemental yearnings and more elemental fears. According to a Prague critic, Rio Preidner, Milena was "psychopathic"; according to Margaret Buber-Neumann, who lived two years beside her in the German concentration camp where Milena died following a kidney operation in 1944, she was powerfully sane, extraordinarily humane and courageous. Milena's obituary for Kafka was the only one of consequence to appear in the Prague press; the prose is strong, so are the claims she makes for Kafka's accomplishment. She is still only in her twenties, the dead man is hardly known as a writer

beyond his small circle of friends—yet Milena writes: "His knowledge of the world was exceptional and deep, and he was a deep and
exceptional world in himself. . . . [He had] a delicacy of feeling bordering on the miraculous and a mental clarity that was terrifyingly
uncompromising, and in turn he loaded on to his illness the whole
burden of his mental fear of life. . . . He wrote the most important
books in recent German literature." One can imagine this vibrant
young woman stretched diagonally across the bed, as awesome to
Kafka as his own father spread out across the map of the world. His
letters to her are disjointed, unlike anything else of his in print; the
word "fear" appears on page after page. "We are both married, you
in Vienna, I to my Fear in Prague." He yearns to lay his head upon
her breast; he calls her "Mother Milena"; during at least one of their
two brief rendezvous, he is hopelessly impotent. At last he has to tell
her to leave him be, an edict that Milena honors, though it leaves her
hollow with grief. "Do not write," Kafka tells her, "and let us not see
each other; I ask you only to quietly fulfill this request of mine; only
on those conditions is survival possible for me; everything else continues the process of destruction."

Then, in the early summer of 1923, during a visit to his sister, who
is vacationing with her children by the Baltic Sea, he finds young
Dora Dymant, and within a month Franz Kafka has gone off to live
with her in two rooms in a suburb of Berlin, out of reach at last of
the "claws" of Prague and home. How can it be? How can he, in his
illness, have accomplished so swiftly and decisively the leave-taking
that was beyond him in his healthiest days? The impassioned letter
writer who could equivocate interminably about which train to
catch to Vienna to meet with Milena (if he should meet with her for
the weekend at all); the bourgeois suitor in the high collar, who, during his drawn-out agony of an engagement with the proper Fräulein
Bauer, secretly draws up a memorandum for himself, countering the
arguments "for" marriage with the arguments "against"; the poet of
the ungraspable and the unresolved, whose belief in the immovable

barrier separating the wish from its realization is at the heart of his excruciating visions of defeat; the Kafka whose fiction refutes every easy, touching, humanish daydream of salvation and justice and fulfillment with densely imagined counterdreams that mock all solutions and escapes—this Kafka *escapes*. Overnight! K. penetrates the Castle walls—Joseph K. evades his indictment—"a breaking away from it altogether, a mode of living completely outside the jurisdiction of the Court." Yes, the possibility of which Joseph K. has just a glimmering in the Cathedral, but can neither fathom nor effectuate—"not . . . some influential manipulation of the case, but . . . a circumvention of it"—Kafka realizes in the last year of his life.

Was it Dora Dymant or was it death that pointed the new way? Perhaps it could not have been one without the other. We know that the "illusory emptiness" at which K. gazed, upon first entering the village and looking up through the mist and the darkness to the Castle, was no more vast and incomprehensible than the idea of himself as husband and father was to the young Kafka; but now, it seems, the prospect of a Dora forever, of a wife, home, and children everlasting, is no longer the terrifying, bewildering prospect it would once have been, for now "everlasting" is undoubtedly not much more than a matter of months. Yes, the dying Kafka is determined to marry, and writes to Dora's Orthodox father for his daughter's hand. But the imminent death that has resolved all contradictions and uncertainties in Kafka is the very obstacle placed in his path by the young girl's father. The request of the dying man Franz Kafka to bind to him in his invalidism the healthy young girl Dora Dymant is—denied!

If there is not one father standing in Kafka's way, there is another—and another behind him. Dora's father, writes Max Brod in his biography of Kafka, "set off with [Kafka's] letter to consult the man he honored most, whose authority counted more than anything else for him, the 'Gerer Rebbe.' The rabbi read the letter, put it to one side, and said nothing more than the single syllable, 'No.'" *No.* Klamm himself could have been no more abrupt—or any more removed from the petitioner. *No.* In its harsh finality, as telling and inescapable as the curselike threat delivered by his father to Georg Bendemann, that thwarted fiancé: "Just take your bride on your arm and try getting in my way. I'll sweep her from your very side, you don't know how!" *No.* Thou shalt not have, say the fathers, and Kafka agrees that he shall not. The habit of obedience and renunciation; also, his own distaste for the diseased and reverence for strength, appetite, and health. "'Well, clear this out now!' said the overseer, and they buried the hunger artist, straw and all. Into the cage they put a young panther. Even the most insensitive felt it refreshing to see this wild creature leaping around the cage that had so long been dreary. The panther was all right. The food he liked was brought him without hesitation by the attendants; he seemed not even to miss his freedom; his noble body, furnished almost to the bursting point with all that it needed, seemed to carry freedom around with it too; somewhere in his jaws it seemed to lurk; and the joy of life streamed with such ardent passion from his throat that for the onlookers it was not easy to stand the shock of it. But they braced themselves, crowded round the cage, and did not want ever to move away." So no is no; he knew as much himself. A healthy young girl of nineteen cannot, *should* not, be given in matrimony to a sickly man twice her age, who spits up blood ("I sentence you," cries Georg Bendemann's father, "to death by drowning!") and shakes in his bed with fevers and chills. What sort of un-Kafka-like dream had Kafka been dreaming?

And those nine months spent with Dora have still other "Kafka-esque" elements: a fierce winter in quarters inadequately heated; the inflation that makes a pittance of his own meager pension, and sends into the streets of Berlin the hungry and needy whose suffering, says Dora, turns Kafka "ash-gray"; and his tubercular lungs, flesh transformed and punished. Dora cares for the diseased writer as devotedly and tenderly as Gregor Samsa's sister does for her brother, the bug. Gregor's sister plays the violin so beautifully that Gregor "felt as if the way were opening before him to the unknown nourishment he craved"; he dreams, in his condition, of sending his gifted sister to the Conservatory! Dora's music is Hebrew, which she reads aloud to Kafka, and with such skill that, according to Brod, "Franz recognized her dramatic talent; on his advice and under his direction she later educated herself in the art . . ."

Only Kafka is hardly vermin to Dora Dymant, *or to himself.* Away from Prague and his father's home, Kafka, at forty, seems at last to have been delivered from the self-loathing, the self-doubt, and those guilt-ridden impulses to dependence and self-effacement that had nearly driven him mad throughout his twenties and thirties; all at once he seems to have shed the pervasive sense of hopeless despair that informs the great punitive fantasies of *The Trial*, "In the Penal Colony," and "The Metamorphosis." Years earlier, in Prague, he had directed Max Brod to destroy all his papers, including three unpublished novels, upon his death; now, in Berlin, when Brod introduces him to a German publisher interested in his work, Kafka consents to the publication of a volume of four stories, and consents, says Brod, "without much need of long arguments to persuade him." With Dora to help, he diligently resumes the study of Hebrew; despite his illness and the harsh winter, he travels to the Berlin Academy for Jewish Studies to attend a series of lectures on the Talmud—a very different Kafka from the estranged melancholic who once wrote in his diary, "What have I in common with the Jews? I have hardly anything in common with myself and should stand very quietly in a corner, content that I can breathe." And to further mark the change, there is ease and happiness with a woman: with this young and adoring companion, he is playful, he is pedagogical, and, one would guess, in light of his illness (*and* his happiness), he is chaste. If not a husband (such as he had striven to be to the conventional Fräulein Bauer), if not a lover (as he struggled hopelessly to be with Milena), he would seem to have become something no less miraculous in his scheme of things: a father, a kind of father to this sisterly, mothering daughter. *As Franz Kafka awoke one morning from uneasy dreams he found himself transformed in his bed into a father, a writer, and a Jew.*

"I have completed the construction of my burrow," begins the long, exquisite, and tedious story that he wrote that winter in Berlin, "and it seems to be successful. . . . Just the place where, according to my calculations, the Castle Keep should be, the soil was very loose and sandy and had literally to be hammered and pounded into a firm state to serve as a wall for the beautifully vaulted chamber. But for such tasks the only tool I possess is my forehead. So I had to run with my forehead thousands and thousands of times, for whole days and nights, against the ground, and I was glad when the blood came, for that was proof that the walls were beginning to harden; in that way, as everybody must admit, I richly paid for my Castle Keep."

"The Burrow" is the story of an animal with a keen sense of peril whose life is organized around the principle of defense, and whose deepest longings are for security and serenity; with teeth and claws—*and* forehead—the burrower constructs an elaborate and ingeniously intricate system of underground chambers and corridors that are designed to afford it some peace of mind; however, while this burrow does succeed in reducing the sense of danger from without, its maintenance and protection are equally fraught with anxiety: "these anxieties are different from ordinary ones, prouder, richer in content, often long repressed, but in their destructive effects they are perhaps much the same as the anxieties that existence in the outer world gives rise to." The story (whose ending is lost) terminates with the burrower fixated upon distant subterranean noises that cause it "to assume the existence of a great beast," itself burrowing in the direction of the Castle Keep.

Another grim tale of entrapment, and of obsession so absolute that no distinction is possible between character and predicament. Yet this fiction imagined in the last "happy" months of his life is touched by a spirit of personal reconciliation and sardonic self-acceptance, by a tolerance of one's own brand of madness, that is not apparent in "The Metamorphosis." The piercing masochistic irony of the earlier animal story—as of "The Judgment" and *The Trial*—has given way here to a critique of the self and its preoccupations that, though bordering on mockery, no longer seeks to resolve itself in images of the uttermost humiliation and defeat . . . Yet there is more here than a metaphor for the insanely defended ego, whose striving for invulnerability produces a defensive system that must in its turn become the object of perpetual concern—there is also a very unromantic and hardheaded fable about how and why art is made, a portrait of the artist in all his ingenuity, anxiety, isolation, dissatisfaction, relentlessness, obsessiveness, secretiveness, paranoia, and self-addiction, a portrait of the magical thinker at the end of his tether, Kafka's Prospero . . . It is an endlessly suggestive story, this story of life in a hole. For, finally, remember the proximity of Dora Dymant during the months that Kafka was at work on "The Burrow" in the two underheated rooms that were their illicit home. Certainly a dreamer like Kafka need never have entered the young girl's body for her tender presence to kindle in him a fantasy of a hidden orifice that promises "satisfied desire," "achieved ambition," and "profound slumber," but that, once penetrated and in one's possession, arouses the most terrifying and heartbreaking fears of retribution and loss. "For the rest I try to unriddle the beast's plans. Is it on its wanderings, or is it working on its own burrow? If it is on its wanderings then perhaps an understanding with it might be possible. If it should really break through to the burrow I shall give it some of my stores and it will go on its way again. It will go on its way again, a fine story! Lying in my heap of earth I can naturally dream of all sorts of things, even of an understanding with the beast, though I know well enough that no such thing can happen, and that at the instant when we see each other, more, at the moment when we merely guess at each other's presence, we shall blindly bare our claws and teeth . . ."

He died of tuberculosis of the lungs and larynx on June 3, 1924, a month before his forty-first birthday. Dora, inconsolable, whispers for days afterward, "My love, my love, my good one . . ."

2

1942. I am nine; my Hebrew-school teacher, Dr. Kafka, is fifty-nine. To the little boys who must attend his "four-to-five" class each afternoon, he is known—in part because of his remote and melancholy foreignness, but largely because we vent on him our resentment at having to learn an ancient calligraphy at the very hour we should be out screaming our heads off on the ball field—he is known as Dr. Kishka. Named, I confess, by me. His sour breath, spiced with intestinal juices by five in the afternoon, makes the Yiddish word for "insides" particularly telling, I think. Cruel, yes, but in truth I would have cut out my tongue had I ever imagined the name would become legend. A coddled child, I do not yet think of myself as persuasive, or, quite yet, as a literary force in the world. My jokes don't hurt, how could they, I'm so adorable. And if you don't believe me, just ask my family and the teachers in my school. Already at nine, one foot in college, the other in the Catskills. Little borscht-belt comic that I am outside the classroom, I amuse my friends Schlossman and Ratner on the dark walk home from Hebrew school with an imitation of Kishka, his precise and finicky professional manner, his German accent, his cough, his gloom. "Doctor *Kishka!*" cries Schlossman, and hurls himself savagely against the newsstand that belongs to the candy-store owner whom Schlossman drives just a little crazier each night. "Doctor Franz—Doctor Franz—Doctor Franz—*Kishka!*" screams Ratner, and my chubby little friend who lives upstairs from me on nothing but chocolate milk and Mallomars does not stop laughing until, as is his wont (his mother has asked me "to keep an eye on him" for just this reason), he wets his pants. Schlossman takes the occasion of Ratner's humiliation to pull the little boy's paper out of his notebook and wave it in the air—it is the assignment Dr. Kafka has just returned to us, graded; we were told to make up an alphabet of our own, out of straight lines and curved lines and dots. "That is all an alphabet is," he had explained. "That is all Hebrew is. That is all English is. Straight lines and curved lines and dots." Ratner's alphabet, for which he received a C, looks like twenty-six skulls strung in a row. I received my A for a curlicued alphabet, inspired largely (as Dr. Kafka seems to have surmised, given his comment at the top of the page) by the number eight. Schlossman received an F for forgetting even to do it—and a lot he seems to care. He is content—he is *overjoyed*—with things as they are. Just waving a piece of paper in the air and screaming, "Kishka! Kishka!" makes him deliriously happy. We should all be so lucky.

At home, alone in the glow of my goose-necked "desk" lamp (plugged after dinner into an outlet in the kitchen, my study), the vision of our refugee teacher, sticklike in a fraying three-piece blue suit, is no longer very funny—particularly after the entire beginners' Hebrew class, of which I am the most studious member, takes the name Kishka to its heart. My guilt awakens redemptive fantasies of heroism, I have them often about the "Jews in Europe." I must save him. If not me, who? The demonic Schlossman? The babyish Ratner? And if not now, when? For I have learned in the ensuing weeks that Dr. Kafka lives in a room in the house of an elderly Jewish lady on the shabby lower stretch of Avon Avenue, where the trolley still runs and the poorest of Newark's Negroes shuffle meekly up and down the street, for all they seem to know, still back in Mississippi. A *room.* And *there!* My family's apartment is no palace, but it is ours at least, so long as we pay the $38.50 a month in rent; and though our neighbors are not rich, they refuse to be poor and they refuse to be meek. Tears of shame and sorrow in my eyes, I rush into the living room to tell my parents what I have heard (though not that I heard it during a quick game of "aces up" played a minute before class against the synagogue's rear wall—worse, played directly beneath a stained-glass window embossed with the names of the dead): "My Hebrew teacher lives in a *room*."

My parents go much further than I could imagine anybody going in the real world. Invite him to dinner, my mother says. *Here?* Of course here—Friday night; I'm sure he can stand a home-cooked meal, she says, and a little pleasant company. Meanwhile, my father gets on the phone to call my Aunt Rhoda, who lives with my grandmother and tends her and her potted plants in the apartment house at the corner of our street. For nearly two decades my father has been introducing my mother's "baby" sister, now forty, to the Jewish bachelors and widowers of north Jersey. No luck so far. Aunt Rhoda, an "interior decorator" in the dry-goods department of the Big Bear, a mammoth merchandise and produce market in industrial Elizabeth, wears falsies (this information by way of my older brother) and sheer frilly blouses, and family lore has it that she spends hours in the bathroom every day applying powder and sweeping her stiffish hair up into a dramatic pile on her head; but despite all this dash and display, she is, in my father's words, "still afraid of the facts of life." He, however, is undaunted, and administers therapy regularly and gratis: "Let 'em squeeze ya, Rhoda—it *feels* good!" I am his flesh and blood, I can reconcile myself to such scandalous talk in our kitchen—*but what will Dr. Kafka think?* Oh, but it's too late to do anything now. The massive machinery of matchmaking has been set in motion by my undiscourageable father, and the smooth engines of my proud homemaking mother's hospitality are already purring away. To throw my body into the works in an attempt to bring it all to a halt—well, I might as well try to bring down the New Jersey Bell Telephone Company by leaving our receiver off the hook. Only Dr. Kafka can save me now. But to my muttered invitation, he replies, with a formal bow that turns me scarlet—who has ever seen a person do such a thing outside of a movie house?—he replies that he would be *honored* to be my family's dinner guest. "My aunt," I rush to tell him, "will be there too." It appears that I have just said something mildly humorous; odd to see Dr. Kafka smile. Sighing, he says, "I will be delighted to meet her." Meet her? He's supposed to *marry* her. How do I warn him? And how do I warn Aunt Rhoda (a very great admirer of me and my marks) about his sour breath, his roomer's pallor, his Old World ways, so at odds with her up-to-dateness? My face feels as if it will ignite of its own—and spark the fire that will engulf the synagogue, Torah and all—when I see Dr. Kafka scrawl our address in his notebook, and beneath it, some words *in German*. "Good night, Dr. Kafka!" "Good night, and thank you, thank you." I turn to run, I go, but not fast enough: out on the street I hear Schlossman—that fiend!—announcing to my classmates, who are punching one another under the lamplight down from the synagogue steps (where a card game is also in progress, organized by the bar mitzvah boys): "Roth invited Kishka to his *house!* To *eat!*"

Does my father do a job on Kafka! Does he make a sales pitch for familial bliss! What it means to a man to have two fine boys and a wonderful wife! Can Dr. Kafka imagine what it's like? The thrill? The satisfaction? The pride? He tells our visitor of the network of relatives on his mother's side that are joined in a "family association" of over two hundred people located in seven states, including the state of Washington! Yes, relatives even in the Far West: here are their photographs, Dr. Kafka; this is a beautiful book we published entirely on our own for five dollars a copy, pictures of every member of the family, including infants, and a family history by "Uncle" Lichtblau, the eighty-five-year-old patriarch of the clan. This is our family newsletter, which is published twice a year and distributed nationwide to all the relatives. This, in the frame, is the menu from the banquet of the family association, held last year in a ballroom of the "Y" in Newark, in honor of my father's mother on her seventy-fifth birthday. My mother, Dr. Kafka learns, has served *six consecutive years* as the secretary-treasurer of the family association. My father has served a two-year term as president, as have each of his three brothers. We now have fourteen boys in the family in uniform.

Philip writes a letter on V-mail stationery to five of his cousins in the army every single month. "Religiously," my mother puts in, smoothing my hair. "I firmly believe," says my father, "that the family is the cornerstone of everything."

Dr. Kafka, who has listened with close attention to my father's spiel, handling the various documents that have been passed to him with great delicacy and poring over them with a kind of rapt absorption that reminds me of myself over the watermarks of my stamps, now for the first time expresses himself on the subject of family; softly he says, "I agree," and inspects again the pages of our family book. "Alone," says my father, in conclusion, "alone, Dr. Kafka, is a stone." Dr. Kafka, setting the book gently down upon my mother's gleaming coffee table, allows with a nod that that is so. My mother's fingers are now turning in the curls behind my ears; not that I even know it at the time, or that she does. Being stroked is my life; stroking me, my father, and my brother is hers.

My brother goes off to a Boy Scout meeting, but only after my father has him stand in his neckerchief before Dr. Kafka and describe to him the skills he has mastered to earn each of his badges. I am invited to bring my stamp album into the living room and show Dr. Kafka my set of triangular stamps from Zanzibar. "Zanzibar!" says my father rapturously, as though I, not even ten, have already been there and back. My father accompanies Dr. Kafka and me into the "sun parlor," where my tropical fish swim in the aerated, heated, and hygienic paradise I have made for them with my weekly allowance and my Hanukkah *gelt*. I am encouraged to tell Dr. Kafka what I know about the temperament of the angelfish, the function of the catfish, and the family life of the black mollie. I know quite a bit. "All on his own he does that," my father says to Kafka. "He gives me a lecture on one of those fish, it's seventh heaven, Dr. Kafka." "I can imagine," Kafka replies.

Back in the living room my Aunt Rhoda suddenly launches into a rather recondite monologue on "Scotch plaids," intended, it would appear, for the edification of my mother alone. At least she looks fixedly at my mother while she delivers it. I have not yet seen her look directly at Dr. Kafka; she did not even turn his way at dinner when he asked how many employees there were at the Big Bear. "How would I know?" she had replied, and then continued right on conversing with my mother, about a butcher who would take care of her "under the counter" if she could find him nylons for his wife. It never occurs to me that she will not look at Dr. Kafka because she is shy—nobody that dolled up could, in my estimation, be shy. I can only think that she is outraged. *It's his breath. It's his accent. It's his age.*

I'm wrong—it turns out to be what Aunt Rhoda calls his "superiority complex." "Sitting there, sneering at us like that," says my aunt, somewhat superior now herself. "Sneering?" repeats my father, incredulous. "Sneering and laughing, yes!" says Aunt Rhoda. My mother shrugs. "*I* didn't think he was laughing." "Oh, don't worry, by himself there he was having a very good time—*at our expense.* I know the European-type man. Underneath they think they're all lords of the manor," Rhoda says. "You know something, Rhoda?" says my father, tilting his head and pointing a finger, "I think you fell in love." "With *him?* Are you *crazy?*" "He's too quiet for Rhoda," my mother says. "I think maybe he's a little bit of a wallflower. Rhoda is a very lively person, she needs lively people around her." "Wallflower? He's not a wallflower! He's a gentleman, that's all. And he's lonely," my father says assertively, glaring at my mother for going over his head like this *against* Kafka. My Aunt Rhoda is forty years old—it is not exactly a shipment of brand-new goods that he is trying to move. "He's a gentleman, he's an educated man, and I'll tell you something, he'd give his eyeteeth to have a nice home and a wife." "Well," says my Aunt Rhoda, "let him find one then, if he's so educated. Somebody who's his equal, who he doesn't have to look down his nose at with his big sad refugee eyes!" "Yep, she's in love," my father announces, squeezing Rhoda's knee in triumph. "With *him?*" she cries, jumping to her feet, taffeta crackling around her like a bonfire.

"With *Kafka?*" she snorts. "I wouldn't give an old man like him the time of day!"

Dr. Kafka calls and takes my Aunt Rhoda to a movie. I am astonished, both that he calls and that she goes; it seems there is more desperation in life than I have come across yet in my fish tank. Dr. Kafka takes my Aunt Rhoda to a play performed at the "Y." Dr. Kafka eats Sunday dinner with my grandmother and my Aunt Rhoda and, at the end of the afternoon, accepts with that formal bow of his the mason jar of barley soup that my grandmother presses him to carry back to his room with him on the No. 8 bus. Apparently he was very taken with my grandmother's jungle of potted plants—and she, as a result, with him. Together they spoke in Yiddish about gardening. One Wednesday morning, only an hour after the store has opened for the day, Dr. Kafka shows up at the dry-goods department of the Big Bear; he tells Aunt Rhoda that he just wants to see where she works. That night he writes in his diary: "With the customers she is forthright and cheery, and so managerial about 'taste' that when I hear her explain to a chubby young bride why green and blue do not 'go,' I am myself ready to believe that Nature is in error and R. is correct."

One night, at ten, Dr. Kafka and Aunt Rhoda come by unexpectedly, and a small impromptu party is held in the kitchen—coffee and cake, even a thimbleful of whiskey all around, to celebrate the resumption of Aunt Rhoda's career on the stage. I have only heard tell of my aunt's theatrical ambitions. My brother says that when I was small she used to come to entertain the two of us on Sundays with her puppets—she was at that time employed by the W.P.A. to travel around New Jersey and put on marionette shows in schools and even in churches; Aunt Rhoda did all the voices and, with the help of a female assistant, manipulated the manikins on their strings. Simultaneously she had been a member of the Newark Collective Theater, a troupe organized primarily to go around to strike groups to perform *Waiting for Lefty*. Everybody in Newark (as I understood it) had had high hopes that Rhoda Pilchik would go on to Broadway—everybody except my grandmother. To me this period of history is as difficult to believe in as the era of the lake dwellers, which I am studying in school; people say it was once so, so I believe them, but nonetheless it is hard to grant such stories the status of the real, given the life I see around me.

Yet my father, a very avid realist, is in the kitchen, schnapps glass in hand, toasting Aunt Rhoda's success. She has been awarded one of the starring roles in the Russian masterpiece *The Three Sisters*, to be performed six weeks hence by the amateur group at the Newark "Y." Everything, announces Aunt Rhoda, everything she owes to Franz and his encouragement. One conversation—"One!" she cries gaily—and Dr. Kafka had apparently talked my grandmother out of her lifelong belief that actors are not serious human beings. And what an actor *he* is, in his own right, says Aunt Rhoda. How he had opened her eyes to the meaning of things, by reading her the famous Chekhov play—yes, read it to her from the opening line to the final curtain, all the parts, and actually left her in tears. Here Aunt Rhoda says, "Listen, listen—this is the first line of the play—it's the key to everything. Listen—I just think about what it was like the night Pop passed away, how I wondered and wondered what would become of us, what would we all do—and, and, *listen*—"

"We're listening," laughs my father. So am *I* listening, from my bed.

Pause; she must have walked to the center of the kitchen linoleum. She says, sounding a little surprised, " 'It's just a year ago today that father died.' "

"Shhh," warns my mother, "you'll give the little one nightmares."

I am not alone in finding my aunt a "changed person" during the weeks of rehearsal. My mother says this is just what she was like as a little girl. "Red cheeks, always those hot, red cheeks—and everything exciting, even taking a bath." "She'll calm down, don't worry," says my father, "and then he'll pop the question." "Knock on wood," says my mother. "Come on," says my father, "he knows what side his bread is buttered on—he sets foot in this house, he sees what a family is all about, and believe me, he's licking his chops. Just look at him when he sits in that club chair. This is his dream come true." "Rhoda says that in Berlin, before Hitler, he had a young girl friend, years and years it went on, and then she left him. For somebody else. She got tired of waiting." "Don't worry," says my father, "when the time comes I'll give him a little nudge. He ain't going to live forever, either, and he knows it."

Then one weekend, as a respite from the "strain" of nightly rehearsals—which Dr. Kafka regularly visits, watching in his hat and coat at the back of the auditorium until it is time to accompany Aunt Rhoda home—they take a trip to Atlantic City. Ever since he arrived on these shores Dr. Kafka has wanted to see the famous boardwalk and the horse that dives from the high board. But in Atlantic City something happens that I am not allowed to know about; any discussion of the subject conducted in my presence is in Yiddish. Dr. Kafka sends Aunt Rhoda four letters in three days. She comes to us for dinner and sits till midnight crying in our kitchen. She calls the "Y" on our phone to tell them (weeping) that her mother is still ill and she cannot come to rehearsal again—she may even have to drop out of the play. No, she can't, she can't, her mother is too ill, she herself is too upset! goodbye! Then back to the kitchen table to cry. She wears no pink powder and no red lipstick, and her stiff brown hair, down, is thick and spiky as a new broom.

My brother and I listen from our bedroom, through the door that silently he has pushed ajar.

"Have you ever?" says Aunt Rhoda, weeping. "Have you *ever*?"

"Poor soul," says my mother.

"*Who*?" I whisper to my brother. "Aunt Rhoda or—"

"Shhhh!" he says. "Shut *up*!"

In the kitchen my father grunts. "Hmm. Hmm." I hear him getting up and walking around and sitting down again—and then grunting. I am listening so hard that I can hear the letters being folded and unfolded, stuck back into their envelopes, then removed to be puzzled over one more time.

"Well?" demands Aunt Rhoda. *"Well?"*

"Well what?" answers my father.

"Well, what do you want to say *now?"*

"He's *meshugeh*," admits my father. "Something is wrong with him all right."

"But," sobs Aunt Rhoda, "no one would believe me when *I* said it!"

"Rhody, Rhody," croons my mother in that voice I know from those times that I have had to have stitches taken, or when I have awakened in tears, somehow on the floor beside my bed. "Rhody, don't be hysterical, darling. It's over, kitten, it's all over."

I reach across to my brother's twin bed and tug on the blanket. I don't think I've ever been so confused in my life, not even by death. The speed of things! Everything good undone in a moment! By what? *"What?"* I whisper. *"What is it?"*

My brother, the Boy Scout, smiles leeringly and, with a fierce hiss that is no answer and enough answer, addresses my bewilderment: "Sex!"

Years later, a junior at college, I receive an envelope from home containing Dr. Kafka's obituary, clipped from *The Jewish News*, the tabloid of Jewish affairs that is mailed each week to the homes of the Jews of Essex County. It is summer, the semester is over, but I have stayed on at school, alone in my room in the town, trying to write short stories. I am fed by a young English professor and his wife in exchange for babysitting; I tell the sympathetic couple, who are also loaning me the money for my rent, why it is I can't go home. My tearful fights with my father are all I can talk about at their dinner table. "Keep him away from me!" I scream at my mother. "But, darling," she asks me, "what is going on? What is this all about?"—the very same question with which I used to plague my older brother, asked now of me and out of the same bewilderment and innocence. "He *loves* you," she explains.

But that, of all things, seems to me precisely what is blocking my way. Others are crushed by paternal criticism—I find myself oppressed by his high opinion of me! Can it possibly be true (and can I possibly admit) that I am coming to hate him for loving me so? praising me so? But that makes no sense—the ingratitude! the stupidity! the contrariness! Being loved is so obviously a blessing, *the* blessing, praise such a rare bequest. Only listen late at night to my closest friends on the literary magazine and in the drama society— they tell horror stories of family life to rival *The Way of All Flesh*, they return shell-shocked from vacations, drift back to school as though from the wars. What they would give to be in my golden slippers! "What's going on?" my mother begs me to tell her; but how can I, when I myself don't fully believe that this is happening to us, or that I am the one who is making it happen. That they, who together cleared all obstructions from my path, should seem now to be my final obstruction! No wonder my rage must filter through a child's tears of shame, confusion, and loss. All that we have constructed together over the course of two century-long decades, and look how I must bring it down—in the name of this tyrannical need that I call my "independence"! My mother, keeping the lines of communication open, sends a note to me at school: "We miss you"—and encloses the brief obituary notice. Across the margin at the bottom of the clipping, she has written (in the same hand with which she wrote notes to my teachers and signed my report cards, in that very same handwriting that once eased my way in the world), "Remember poor Kafka, Aunt Rhoda's beau?"

"Dr. Franz Kafka," the notice reads, "a Hebrew teacher at the Talmud Torah of the Schley Street Synagogue from 1939 to 1948, died on June 3 in the Deborah Heart and Lung Center in Brown Mills, New Jersey. Dr. Kafka had been a patient there since 1950. He was 70 years old. Dr. Kafka was born in Prague, Czechoslovakia, and was a refugee from the Nazis. He leaves no survivors."

He also leaves no books: no *Trial*, no *Castle*, no Diaries. The dead man's papers are claimed by no one, and disappear—all except those four *"meshugeneh"* letters that are, to this day, as far as I know, still somewhere in among the memorabilia accumulated by my spinster aunt, along with a collection of Broadway Playbills, sales citations from the Big Bear, and transatlantic steamship stickers.

Thus all trace of Dr. Kafka disappears. Destiny being destiny, how could it be otherwise? Does the Land Surveyor reach the Castle? Does K. escape the judgment of the Court, or Georg Bendemann the judgment of his father? "'Well, clear this out now!' said the overseer, and they buried the hunger artist, straw and all." No, it simply is not in the cards for Kafka ever to become *the* Kafka—why, that would be stranger even than a man turning into an insect. No one would believe it, Kafka least of all.